Japanese Vocabulary

WITHDRAWN

Shigeru Eguchi
Lecturer of Japanese Language
Department of East Asian Languages
Columbia University

Orie Yamada
Lecturer of Japanese Language
Department of East Asian Languages
Columbia University

Schaum's Outline Series

New York   Chicago   San Francisco   Lisbon   London   Madrid
Mexico City   Milan   New Delhi   San Juan   Seoul
Singapore   Sydney   Toronto

The **McGraw·Hill** Companies

SHIREGU EGUCHI graduated from Ibaraki University and earned his M.A. in Japanese Pedagogy at the University of Iowa in 1994. He is currently a lecturer of Japanese language at the Department of East Asian Languages and Cultures at Columbia University. He is also a coordinator of the summer language and culture program at Hokkaido International Foundation (H.I.F.), Hokkaido, Japan.

ORIE YAMADA is originally from Japan, where she taught Japanese language for students from all over the world at the ECC language school in Nagoya until 1995. She received her M.A. in Asian Studies from the University of Illinois in 1997. At present, she is a lecturer of Japanese language at Columbia University.

1 2 3 4 5 6 7 8 9 10   CUS/CUS   1 9 8 7 6 5 4 3 2 1

ISBN   978-0-07-176329-5
MHID   0-07-176329-5

McGraw-Hill books are available at special quantity discounts to use as premiums and sales promotions or for use in corporate training programs. To contact a representative, please e-mail us at bulksales@mcgraw-hill.com.

Contents

Preface

The purpose of this book is to provide the reader with the vocabulary needed to converse effectively in Japanese about everyday topics. Although the book contains a review of common, basic words that the reader has probably encountered in his or her early study of Japanese, the aim of *Japanese Vocabulary* is to enrich a student's knowledge of the language by providing words that seldom appear in typical textbooks but that are essential for communicating comfortably about a given situation.

The content of each chapter is focused on a real-life situation, such as making a telephone call, traveling by plane or train, staying at a hotel, or shopping for food. In order to enable readers to build and retain the new vocabulary, the book affords many opportunities to use the new words. Each chapter is divided into subtopics. The student acquires a few new words about a specific topic and is immediately directed to practice them in a multitude of exercises. Answers are provided so the student can make prompt self-correction.

In case the student should also wish to use this book as a reference tool, at the end of each chapter there is a Japanese to English reference list that contains the key words presented in that chapter. At the very end of the book there is a Japanese to English and English to Japanese glossary that contains all key words introduced in the book.

Japanese Vocabulary can be used as a review text or an enriching companion to any basic text.

Shigeru Eguchi
Orie Yamada

Chapter 1: At the airport
第1章：空港で
Kuukoo de

GETTING TO THE AIRPORT

空港には、**ターミナル**が二つあります。   terminal
Kuukoo ni wa, *taaminaru* ga futatsu arimasu.

第一ターミナルは、**国際線**ターミナルです。   international flight
Daiichi taaminaru wa, *kokusaisen* taaminaru desu.

第二ターミナルは、**国内線**ターミナルです。   domestic flight
Daini taaminaru wa, *kokunaisen* taaminaru desu.

空港まで、**車**や**タクシー**で行きます。   car, taxi
Kuukoo made, *kuruma* ya *takusii* de ikimasu.

タクシーより安い空港**行き**の**バス**や**電車**もあります。   bound for ~, bus, train
Takushii yori yasui kuukoo *iki* no *basu* ya *densha* mo arimasu.

バスは、**市内**の**バスターミナル**から出ます。   in the city, bus terminal
Basu wa, *shinai* no *basu taaminaru* kara demasu.

1. Complete.
私は空港まで、__1__で行きたくありません。__2__は高いからです。タクシーより__3__や__4__の
Watashi wa kuukoo made, __1__ de ikitaku arimasen. __2__ wa takai kara desu. Takushii yori __3__ ya __4__ no
方が安いです。バスは、__5__の__6__から出ます。一時間に二本か三本あって、便利です。
hoo ga yasui desu. Basu wa __5__ no __6__ kara demasu. Ichijikan ni nihon ka sanbon atte, benri desu.

2. Complete.
- どの__1__へ行きますか。

   Dono __1__ e ikimasu ka.

- 空港には、__2__がいくつあるんですか。

   Kuukoo ni wa, __2__ ga ikutsu aru n desu ka.

- 二つありますよ。第一ターミナルは__3__線で、第二ターミナルは__4__線です。

   Futatsu arimasu yo. Daiichi taaminaru wa __3__ sen de, daini taaminaru wa __4__ sen desu.

- 私はニューヨークへ行きます。だから、第一ターミナルですね。

   Watashi wa Nyuuyooku e kimasu. Dakara, daiichi taaminaru desu ne.

CHECKING IN

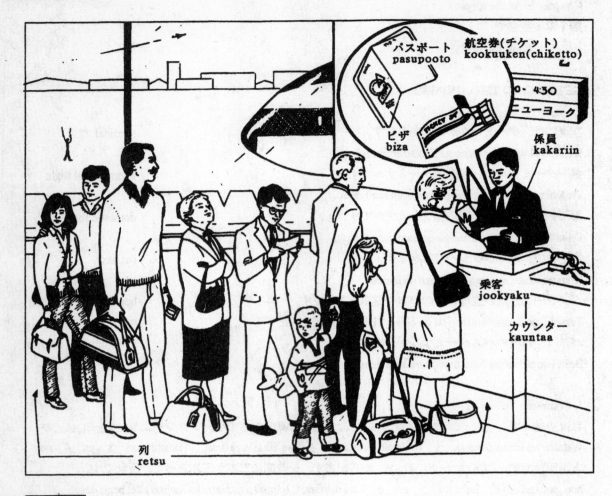

Fig. 1-1

搭乗口（ゲート）から飛行機に乗る前に、	boarding gate, airplane, get on
Toojooguchi (geeto) kara hikooki ni noru mae ni,	
航空会社のカウンターでチェックインをします。	airline company, counter
kookuu gaisha no kauntaa de chekkuin o shimasu	check in
カウンターにはたいてい長い列があって、人がたくさん	line
Kauntaa ni wa taitee nagai *retsu* ga atte, hito ga takusan	
並んでいます。	standing (in line)
narande imasu.	
カウンターで、係員に航空券（チケット）を見せます。	agent, ticket
Kauntaa de *kakariin* ni *kookuuken (chiketto)* o misemasu.	
国際線に乗る時には、パスポートも見せます。	passport
Kokusaisen ni noru toki ni wa, *pasupooto* mo misemasu.	

そして、大きい**荷物**を**預け**ます。　　　　　　　　　　　　　　　luggage, check in

Soshite, ookii *nimotsu* o *azukemasu*.

係員は、**乗客**に**搭乗券**を**渡し**ます。　　　　　　　　　passenger, boarding pass, give

Kakariin wa *jookyaku* ni *toojooken* o *watashimasu*.

3. Complete.

- すみませんが、搭乗口はどこですか。

　Sumimasen ga, toojooguchi wa doko desu ka.

- あちらです。でも、その前にそこの＿1＿の＿2＿でチェックインをしてください。

　Achira desu.　Demo, sono mae ni soko no ＿1＿ no ＿2＿ de chekkuin o shite kudasai.

- カウンターはどこですか。

　Kauntaa wa doko desu ka.

- あそこに長い＿3＿がありますね。あそこです。

　Asoko ni nagai ＿3＿ ga arimasu ne.　Asoko desu.

- あそこに並んで、＿4＿に＿5＿を見せてください。＿6＿も見せてくださいね。

　Asoko ni narande, ＿4＿ ni ＿5＿ o misete kudasai.　＿6＿ mo misete kudasai ne.

- はい。ありがとうございました。

　Hai.　Arigatoo gozaimashita.

SPEAKING WITH THE AGENT

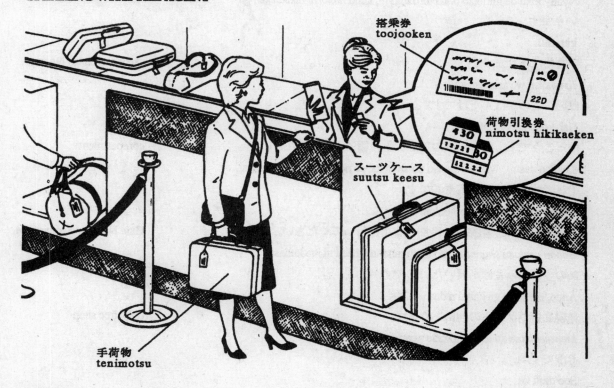

Fig. 1-2

- チケットをお願いします。　　　　　　　　　　　　　　　…, please.

   Chiketto o onegaishimasu.

- はい、どうぞ。　　　　　　　　　　　　　　　　　　　　Here you are.

   Hai, doozo.

- ニューヨーク行きですね。パスポートもお願いします。　　bound for ~

   Nyuuyooku *iki* desu ne.   Pasupooto mo onegai shimasu.

   窓側と通路側の座席がありますが、どちらの方が　　　　window side, aisle side, seat

   *Madogaw*a to *tsuurogaw*a no *zaseki* ga arimasu ga, dochira no hoo ga

   よろしいですか。

   yoroshii desu ka.

- 通路側を予約したんですが、窓側をお願いします。　　　　reserve

   Tsuurogawa o *yoyaku* shita n desu ga, madogawa o onegaishimasu.

- はい。それではこちら、座席番号、２２列のＡです。　　　seat number, row

   Hai.   Soredewa kochira, *zasekibangoo*, nijuuni *retsu* no ee desu.

   荷物はありますか。　　　　　　　　　　　　　　　　　luggage

   Nimotsu wa arimasu ka.

- はい。スーツケースが二つです。　　　　　　　　　　　　suitcase

   Hai.   *Suutsukeesu* ga futatsu desu.

- ニューヨークで荷物を受け取る時に、この荷物引換券が　　baggage claim stub

   Nyuuyooku de nimotsu o uketoru toki ni, kono *nimotsu hikikaeken* ga

   いります。

   irimasu.

- 手荷物はありますか。　　　　　　　　　　　　　　　　carry-on (hand) luggage

   Tenimotsu wa arimasu ka.

- はい、このかばんだけです。

   Hai, kono kaban dake desu.

- けっこうです。前の座席の下か、上の棚に入れてください。　compartment

   Kekkoo desu.   Mae no zaseki no shita ka, ue no *tana* ni irete kudasai.

- それでは、こちらが搭乗券です。

   Soredewa, kochira ga toojooken desu.

   五番ゲートに、出発の一時間前までに行ってください。　　Gate Number 5, departure

   Goban geeto ni *shuppatsu* no ichijikan mae made ni itte kudasai.

- あのう、おみやげが買いたいんですが。　　　　　　　　suvenior

   Anoo, *omiyage* ga kaitai n desu ga.

- 免税品店がゲートの前にあります。　　　　　　　　　　duty-free shop

   Menzeehinten ga geeto no mae ni arimasu.

- そうですか。

   Soo desu ka.

- それでは、どうぞお気をつけて。

   Soredewa, doozo oki o tsukete.

4. Complete.

1. スミスさんは、ニューヨーク＿＿＿の飛行機に乗ります。

   Sumisu san wa Nyuuyooku ___ no hikooki ni norimasu.

2. ニューヨーク＿＿＿は＿＿＿線だから、＿＿＿も見せます。

   Nyuuyooku ___ wa ___ sen dakara, ___ mo misemasu.

3. 座席は＿＿＿側と＿＿＿側がありますが、スミスさんは＿＿＿側の方がいいです。

   Zaseki wa ___ gawa to ___ gawa ga arimasu ga, Sumisu san wa ___ gawa no hoo ga iidesu.

4. スミスさんの＿＿＿は、２２＿＿＿のＡです。

   Sumisu san no ___ wa, nijuuni ___ no ee desu.

5. スミスさんはスーツケースが二つありますが、＿＿＿はかばんだけです。

   Sumisu san wa suutsukeesu ga futatsu arimasu ga, ___ wa kaban dake desu.

6. スミスさんは＿＿＿をもらって、＿＿＿の一時間前までに＿＿＿に行きます。

   Sumisu san wa ___ o moratte, ___ no ichijikan mae made ni ___ ni ikimasu.

7. スミスさんは＿＿＿が買いたいです。だから、＿＿＿で＿＿＿を買います。

   Sumisu san wa ___ ga kaitai desu.   Dakara, ___ de ___ o kaimasu.

Fig. 1-3

Fig. 1-4

5. Answer on the basis of Figs. 1-3 and 1-4.

1. この女の人は、どこにいますか。

   Kono onna no hito wa, doko ni imasu ka.

2. 誰と話していますか。

   Dare to hanashite imasu ka.

3. 係員に何を見せますか。

   Kakariin ni nani o misemasu ka.

4. この女の人は、スーツケースがいくつありますか。

   Kono onna no hito wa, suutsukeesu ga ikutsu arimasu ka.

5. 手荷物は、いくつありますか。

   Tenimotsu wa ikutsu arimasu ka.

6. 手荷物は、、どこに入れますか。

   Tenimotsu wa, doko ni iremasu ka.

7. 係員は、この女の人に何を渡しますか。

   Kakariin wa, kono onna no hito ni nani o watashimasu ka.

8. この女の人は、どこに行きますか。

   Kono onna no hito wa, doko ni ikimasu ka.

9. どの座席に座りますか。

   Dono zaseki ni suwarimasu ka.

10. その座席は窓側ですか、通路側ですか。

    Sono zaseki wa madogawa desu ka, tsuurogawa desu ka.

6. Choose the appropriate word.

1. ＿＿＿＿の飛行機に乗る時は、係員にパスポートを見せます。

    ＿＿＿ no hikooki ni noru toki wa kakariin ni pasupooto o misemasu.

    (a) 国際線 (b) 国内線 (c) 座席

    (a) kokusaisen (b) kokunaisen (c) zaseki

2. A 席は＿＿＿にあります。　　(a) 窓側 (b) 通路側 (c) 座席番号

    Ee seki wa ＿＿＿ ni arimasu.　　(a) madogawa (b) tsuurogawa (c) zasekibangoo

3. カウンターで預けた荷物をニューヨークで受け取る時に、＿＿＿がいります。

    Kauntaa de azuketa nimotsu o Nyuuyooku de uketoru toki ni, ＿＿＿ ga irimasu.

    (a) チケット (b) 搭乗券 (c) 荷物引換券

    (a) chiketto　(b) toojooken　(c) nimotsu hikikaeken

4. 搭乗口から飛行機に乗る時、＿＿＿がいります。

    Toojooguchi kara hikooki ni noru toki, ＿＿＿ ga irimasu.

    (a) チケット (b) 搭乗券 (c) 荷物引換券

    (a) chiketto　(b) toojooken　(c) nimotsu hikikaeken

5. 私の座席は22＿＿＿にあります。　　　　　(a) 列 (b) カウンター (c) 窓側

    Watashi no zaseki wa nijuuni ＿＿＿ ni arimasu.　　(a) retsu (b) kauntaa (c) madogawa

DEPARTURE AND ARRIVAL

搭乗口に行く前に、乗客は**セキュリティーチェック**を通ります。   security check
Toojooguchi ni iku mae ni, jookyaku wa *sekyuritii chekku* o toorimasu.

係員が富士航空 800 便の出発の**アナウンス**をします。   announcement
Kakariin ga Fuji kookuu happyaku bin no shuppatsu no *anaunsu* o shimasu.

この**便**の**目的地**はニューヨークです。   flight, destination
Kono *bin* no *mokutekichi* wa Nyuuyooku desu.

この便は、ニューヨーク**着**です   arriving at
Kono bin wa Nyuuyooku *chaku* desu.

乗客は、八番ゲートから飛行機に乗ります。
Jookyaku wa hachiban geeto kara hikooki ni norimasu.

新東京国際空港**発**の飛行機の**到着**は同じ日の午後四時です。   leaving from, arrival
Shin Tookyoo kokusai kuukoo *hatsu* no hikooki no *toochaku* wa onaji hi no gogo yoji desu.

飛行機は十番ゲートに**着きます**。そして乗客は飛行機を**降ります**。   arrive, deplane
Hikooki wa juuban geeto ni *tsukimasu*.　Soshite jookyaku wa hikooki o *orimasu*.

7. Complete.

1. ＿＿＿＿が出発の＿＿＿＿をします。

    ＿＿＿ ga shuppatsu no ＿＿＿o shimasu.

2. 飛行機の＿＿＿＿のアナウンスをします。

    Hikooki no ＿＿＿ no anaunsu o shimasu.

3. 新東京国際空港＿＿＿の 800＿＿＿の出発のアナウンスをします。

   Shin Tookyoo Kokusai Kuukoo ___ no happyaku ___ no shuppatsu no anaunsu o shimasu.

4. 乗客は＿＿＿を通らなければなりません。

   Jookyaku wa ___ o tooranakereba narimasen.

5. 乗客は八番＿＿＿から飛行機に＿＿＿。

   Jookyaku wa hachiban ___ kara hikooki ni ___.

6. この便の＿＿＿はニューヨークです。

   Kono bin no ___ wa Nyuuyooku desu.

7. この便の乗客はニューヨークで飛行機を＿＿＿。

   Kono bin no jookyaku wa Nyuuyooku de hikooki o ___.

8. Give the opposite of each of the following.

 1. 到着

     toochaku

 2. 〜発

     - hatsu

 3. 乗ります

     norimasu

CHANGING AN AIRLINE TICKET

スミスさんは、富士航空のニューヨーク行きの８００便に**乗り遅れました**。   missed

Sumisu san wa Fuji kookuu no Nyuuyooku iki no happyaku bin ni *noriokuremashita*.

道がこんでいて、空港行きのバスが遅く着いたからです。

Michi ga konde ite, kuukoo iki no basu ga osoku tsuita kara desu.

でも、ほかに東京航空の 13 時 20 分に出発する便があります。

Demo, hoka ni Tookyoo kookuu no juusan ji nijuppun ni shuppatsu suru bin ga arimasu.

その便は、**満席**じゃありません。**空席**があります。   full, vacant seat

Sono bin wa *manseki* ja arimsen. *Kuuseki* ga arimasu.

この便は、**直行便**じゃありません。シカゴ**経由**です。   nonstop flight, via

Kono bin wa *chokkoobin* ja arimasen.   Shikago *keeyu* desu.

でも、シカゴで飛行機を**乗り換える**必要はありません。   change planes

Demo, Shikago de hikooki o *norikaeru* hitsuyoo wa arimasen.

この二つの便の**料金**は、どちらも同じです。**値段**が同じだから、   fare, price

Kono futatsu no bin no *ryookin* wa dochiramo onaji desu.   *Nedan* ga onaji dakara,

追加料金を払わなくてもいいです。   additional fee

tsuikaryookin o harawanakute mo ii desu.

9. Complete.
- 道がこんでいて、バスが遅れました。800 便に＿1＿んですが、ニューヨーク行きの

Michi ga konde ite, basu ga okuremashita.   Happyaku bin ni __1__ n desu ga, Nyuuyooku iki no

ほかの便はありませんか。

hoka no bin wa arimasen ka.

- 東京航空の 13 時 20 分に __2__ する便があります。お一人ですか。

  Tookyoo kookuu no juusanji nijuppun ni __2__ suru bin ga arimasu.   Ohitori desu ka.

- はい、一人です。

  Hai, hitori desu.

- __3__ があるかどうか見てみましょう。 __4__ じゃありません。空席がありますよ。

  __3__ ga aru ka dooka mite mimashoo.   __4__ ja arimasen.   Kuuseki ga arimasu yo.

- そうですか。 どうもすみません。 __5__ は同じですか。

  Soo desu ka.   Doomo sumimasen.   __5__ wa onaji desu ka.

- はい、 どちらも __6__ は同じですから、 __7__ はいりません。

  Hai, dochira mo __6__ wa onaji desu kara, __7__ wa irimasen.

- じゃあ、お願いします。

  Jaa, onegaishimasu.

- この新しいチケットを持って、東京航空のカウンターに行ってください。

  Kono atarashii chiketto o motte, Tookyoo kookuu no kauntaa ni itte kudasai.

- その便は __8__ ですか。

  Sono bin wa __8__ desu ka.

- いいえ、シカゴ __9__ です。 でも、ニューヨークまで同じ飛行機ですよ。

  Iie, Shikago __9__ desu.   Demo, Nyuuyooku made onaji hikooki desu yo.

- そうですか。 それでお願いします。

  Soo desu ka.   Sore de onegaishimasu.

ジョンソンさんは空港へ着きました。この空港にはターミナルが二つあります。一つの

Jonson san wa kuukoo e tsukimashita.   Kono kuukoo ni wa taaminaru ga futatsu arimasu.   Hitotsu no

ターミナルは国際線で、もう一つは国内線です。ニューヨークへ行くので、国際線の

taaminaru wa kokusaisen de, moo hitotsu wa kokunaisen desu.   Nyuuyooku e iku node, kokusaisen no

ターミナルへ行きました。初めに航空会社のカウンターの前に並びました。そこでチェックイン

taaminaru e ikimashita.   Hajime ni kookuugaisha no kauntaa no mae ni narabimashita.   Soko de chekkuin

をしました。国際線の飛行機に乗るから、係員に航空券とパスポートを見せました。

o shimashita.   Kokusaisen no hikooki ni noru kara, kakariin ni kookuuken to pasupooto o misemashita.

それから荷物を預けました。スーツケースが二つありました。係員は二枚の荷物

Sorekara nimotsu o azukemashita.   Suutsukeesu ga futatsu arimashita.   Kakariin wa nimai no nimotsu

引換券をジョンソンさんの航空券につけて、「目的地のニューヨークで荷物が見つからない

hikikaeken o Jonson san no kookuuken ni tsukete, "Mokutekichi no Nyuuyooku de nimotsu ga mitsukaranai

時は、これを見せてください。」と言いました。係員は手荷物は前の座席の下か上の棚に

toki wa, kore o misete kudasai." to iimashita. Kakariin wa tenimotsu wa mae no zaseki no sita ka ue no tana ni

入れるように言いました。ジョンソンさんは通路側の座席を予約しましたが、窓側の座席に替えて

ireru yoo ni iimashita. Jonson san wa tsuurogawa no zaseki o yoyaku shimashita ga, madogawa no zaseki ni kaete

ほしいと頼みました。その便は満席じゃなかったし、窓側にも空席がたくさんあった
hoshii to tanomimashita.   Sono bin wa manseki ja nakatta shi, madogawa ni mo kuuseki ga takusan atta
から、係員は座席を替えてくれました。係員はジョンソンさんに搭乗券を渡しました。
kara, kakariin wa zaseki o kaete kuremashita.   Kakariin wa Jonson san ni toojooken o watashimashita.
彼女はその便が直行便かどうか聞きました。「この飛行機はサンフランシスコ経由です。
Kanojo wa sono bin ga chokkoobin ka dooka kikimashita.   "Kono hikooki wa Sanfuranshisuko keeyu desu.
サンフランシスコに止まりますが、同じ飛行機でニューヨークまで行きます。だから、
Sanfuranshisuko ni tomarimasu ga, onaji hikooki de Nyuuyooku made ikimasu. Dakara,
乗り換えなくてもいいですよ。」と係員は言いました。ジョンソンさんはチェックインが終わって、
norikaenakute mo ii desu yo." to kakariin wa iimashita.   Jonson san wa chekkuin ga owatte,
セキュリティーチェックを通って、ゲートに行きました。
sekyuritii chekku o tootte, geeto ni ikimashita.

10. Complete.

1. 空港には二つの＿＿＿＿があります。一つは＿＿＿＿線で、もう一つは＿＿＿＿線です。
    Kuukoo ni wa futatsu no ___ ga arimasu.   Hitotsu wa ___ sen de, moo hitotsu wa ___ sen desu.

2. ジョンソンさんは＿＿＿＿のターミナルを使いました。
    Jonson san wa ___ no taaminaru o tsukaimashita.

3. ジョンソンさんは＿＿＿＿の前の列に並んで、そこで＿＿＿＿をしました。
    Jonson san wa ___ no mae no retsu ni narande, soko de ___ o shimashita.

4. 乗客はそこで＿＿＿＿に＿＿＿＿を見せます。
    Jookyaku wa soko de ___ ni ___ o misemasu.
    ジョンソンさんは国際線に乗るから、＿＿＿＿も見せました。
    Jonson san wa kokusaisen ni noru kara, ___ mo misemashita.

5. ジョンソンさんは＿＿＿＿が二つありました。係員にその荷物を預けました。
    Jonson san wa ___ ga futatsu arimashita.   Kakariin ni sono nimotsu o azukemashita.

6. 係員は航空券に＿＿＿＿をつけました。＿＿＿＿が見つからない時に、これがいります。
    Kakariin wa kookuuken ni ___ o tsukemashita.   ___ ga mitsukaranai toki ni, kore ga irimasu.

7. 手荷物は前の＿＿＿＿に置かなくてはいけません。上の＿＿＿＿に入れてもいいです。
    Tenimotsu wa mae no ___ ni okanakutewa ikemasen.   Ue no ___ ni irete mo ii desu.

8. ジョンソンさんが＿＿＿＿したのは＿＿＿＿側の座席ですが、＿＿＿＿側に替えてもらいたかったです。
    Jonson san ga ___ shita no wa ___ gawa no zaseki desu ga, ___ gawa ni kaete moraitakatta desu.

9. その便は＿＿＿＿側にも＿＿＿＿がたくさんあるから、ジョンソンさんは＿＿＿＿側に座れました。
    Sono bin wa ___ gawa ni mo ___ ga takusan aru kara, Jonson san wa ___ gawa ni suwaremashita.

10. その便は＿＿＿＿便じゃありません。ニューヨークに着く前に、サンフランシスコに＿＿＿＿。
    Sono bin wa ___ bin ja arimasen.   Nyuuyooku ni tsuku mae ni, Sanfuranshisuko ni ___.

11. ジョンソンさんは＿＿＿＿を通って、＿＿＿＿に行きました。
    Jonson san wa ___ o tootte, ___ ni ikimashita.

Key Words

agent	係員	*kakariin*	gate number ~	〜番ゲート	*~ ban geeto*
airline company	航空会社	*kookuugaisha*	get on	乗る	*noru*
			give	渡す	*watasu*
airplane	飛行機	*hikooki*	Here you are.	はい、どうぞ	*Hai, doozo.*
aisle side	通路側	*tsuurogawa*	in the city	市内	*shinai*
announcement	アナウンス	*anaunsu*	international flight	国際線	*kokusaisen*
arrival	到着	*toochaku*			
arrive	着く	*tsuku*	leaving from ~	〜発	*~ hatsu*
arriving at ~	〜着	*~ chaku*	line, row	列	*retsu*
baggage claim stub	荷物引換券	*nimotsu hikikaeken*	luggage	荷物	*nimotsu*
			miss	乗り遅れる	*noriokureru*
boarding gate	搭乗口（ゲート）	*toojooguchi (geeto)*	nonstop flight	直行便	*chokkoobin*
			passenger	乗客	*jookyaku*
boarding pass	搭乗券	*toojooken*	passport	パスポート	*pasupooto*
bound for ~	〜行き	*~ iki*	~, please.	〜をお願いします	*~ o onegai shimasu.*
bus	バス	*basu*			
bus terminal	バスターミナル	*basu taaminaru*	price	値段	*nedan*
car	車	*kuruma*	reserve	予約する	*yoyaku suru*
carry-on (hand) luggage	手荷物	*tenimotsu*	seat	座席	*zaseki*
			seat number	座席番号	*zaseki bangoo*
change planes	乗り換える	*norikaeru*	security check	セキュリティーチェック	*sekyuritiichekku*
check in	預ける	*azukeru*			
check in	チェックイン	*chekkuin*	souvenir	おみやげ	*omiyage*
compartment	棚	*tana*	stand (in line)	並ぶ	*narabu*
counter	カウンター	*kauntaa*	suitcase	スーツケース	*suutsukeesu*
departure	出発	*shuppatsu*	taxi	タクシー	*takushii*
deplane	降りる	*oriru*	terminal	ターミナル	*taaminaru*
destination	目的地	*mokutekichi*	ticket	航空券（チケット）	*Kookuuken (chiketto)*
domestic flight	国内線	*kokunaisen*			
duty-free shop	免税品店	*menzeehinten*	train	電車	*densha*
fare	料金	*ryookin*	vacant seat	空席	*kuuseki*
flight	便	*bin*	~ via	〜経由	*~ keeyu*
full	満席	*manseki*	window side	窓側	*madogawa*

Chapter 2: On the airplane
第2章：飛行機の中（機内）で
Hikooki no naka (Kinai) de

WELCOME ON BOARD

前方キャビン
zenpoo kyabin

後方キャビン
koohoo kyabin

客室乗務員
kyakushitsu joomuin

操縦室（コックピット）
soojuushitsu(kokkupitto)

操縦士（パイロット）
soojuushi(pairotto)

EXIT

Fig. 2-1

飛行機の中には乗務員がいます。

Hikooki no naka ni wa *joomuin* ga imasu.

操縦士（パイロット）と客室乗務員が働いています。

Soojuushi (pairotto) to *kyakushitsu joomuin* ga hataraite imasu.

機内では客室乗務員が乗客を迎えます。

Kinai de wa kyakushitsu joomuin ga *jookyaku* o *mukaemasu*.

前方キャビンはファーストクラスです。

Zenpoo kyabin wa *faasuto kurasu* desu.

airplane, crew

pilots, flight attendants

inside the airplane, passengers,

welcome

forward cabin, first class

後方キャビンはエコノミークラスです。   rear cabin. economy class

Koohoo kyabin wa *ekonomii kurasu* desu.

乗客は**操縦室（コックピット）**に入ってはいけません。   cockpit

Jookyaku wa *soojuushitsu (kokkupitto)* ni haitte wa ikemasen.

この飛行機はニューヨーク・ケネディ空港を**離陸して、**   take off

Kono hikooki wa Nyuuyooku Kenedii kuukoo o *ririkushite,*

新東京国際空港に**着陸**します。   land

ShinTookyoo kokusai kuukoo ni *chakuriku shimasu.*

1. Complete.

1. 飛行機の中で働いているのは、＿＿＿です。

   Hikooki no naka de hataraite iru no wa, ＿＿ desu.

2. ＿＿＿は操縦室にいます。

   ＿＿ wa soojuushitsu ni imasu.

3. ＿＿＿は乗客を迎えて、機内でいろいろな世話をします。

   ＿＿ wa jookyaku o mukaete, kinai de iroirona sewa o shimasu.

4. ＿＿＿の乗客は後方キャビンに座ります。

   ＿＿ no jookyaku wa koohoo kyabin ni suwarimasu.

5. 乗客は＿＿＿に入ることはできません。

   Jookyaku wa ＿＿ ni hairu koto wa dekimasen.

6. 出発する時、飛行機は＿＿＿します。

   Shuppatsu suru toki, hikooki wa ＿＿ shimasu.

7. 到着する時、飛行機は＿＿＿します。

   Toochaku suru toki, hikooki wa ＿＿ shimasu.

ANNOUNCEMENTS ON BOARD

この飛行機の**飛行時間**は13時間30分です。**高度**10,000メートル   flying time, altitude, meters

Kono hikooki no *hikoojikan* wa juusanjikan sanjuppun desu. *Koodo* ichiman *meetoru*

を**時速**800キロメートルのスピードで**飛行**します。   speed an hour, kilometers, fly

o *jisoku* happyaku *kiromeetoru* no supiido de *hikoo shimasu.*

2. Complete.

本日はご搭乗いただき、ありがとうございます。乗務員一同、皆様の東京行きのご搭乗を

Honjitsu wa gotoojoo itadaki, arigatoo gozaimsu. Joomuin ichidoo, minasama no Tookyoo iki no gotoojoo o

心より歓迎いたします。この飛行機はあと五分で＿1＿します。本日のニューヨークから

kokoroyori kangee itashimasu. Kono hikooki wa ato gofun de ＿1＿ shimasu. Honjitsu no Nyuuyooku kara

東京までの＿2＿は１４時間を予定しています。＿3＿10,000メートルを＿4＿800キロメートルで

Tookyoo made no ＿2＿ wa juuyojikan o yotee shite imasu. ＿3＿ ichiman meetoru o ＿4＿ happyaku kiromeetoru de

＿5＿します。

＿5＿ shimasu.

SAFETY ON BOARD

非常口
hijooguchi

酸素マスク
sanso masuku

救命胴衣
kyuumee dooi

Fig. 2-2

救命胴衣は座席の下にあります。

Kyuumeedooi wa *zaseki* no shita ni arimasu.

life jackets, seat

機内の気圧が変わると、酸素マスクが自動的におりてきます。

Kinai no *kiatsu* ga kawaru to, *sansomasuku* ga *jidooteki ni* orite kimasu.

air pressure, oxygen mask, automatically

非常口は前方キャビンに二つと後方キャビンに二つあります。

Hijooguchi wa zenpoo kyabin ni futatsu to koohoo kyabin ni futatsu arimasu.

emergency exits

主翼の近くにも非常口が四つあります。

Shuyoku no chikaku ni mo hijooguchi ga yottsu arimasu.

wings (lit. main wings)

緊急の場合は、乗客は座席で乗務員の指示を

Kinkyuu no baai wa jookyaku wa zaseki de joomuin no *shiji* o

in case of emergency, instruction

待たなくてはいけません。

matanakute wa ikemasen.

離陸と着陸の時には、通路を歩いてはいけません。

Ririku to chakuriku no toki ni wa, *tsuuro* o aruite wa ikemasen.

aisles

座席ベルト（シートベルト）をしめなくてはいけません。

Zaseki beruto (shiito beruto) o shimenakute wa ikemasen.

seat belt, must fasten

安全のために、座席ベルトは**飛行中**もしめていた方がいいです。   safety, during the flight

Anzen no tame ni, zaseki beruto wa *hikoochuu* mo shimete ita hoo ga ii desu.

3. Answer.

1. 救命胴衣はどこにありますか。

   Kyuumeedooi wa doko ni arimasu ka.

2. 機内の気圧が変わると、何が自動的におりてきますか。

   Kinai no kiatsu ga kawaru to, nani ga jidooteki ni orite kimasu ka.

3. 緊急の場合は、乗客は何を待たなくてはいけませんか。

   Kinkyuu no baai wa, jookyaku wa nani o matanakute wa ikemasen ka.

4. Complete.

離陸と着陸の時、乗客は座っていなくてはなりません。__1__ を歩いてはいけません。それに__2__ をしめ

Ririku to chakuriku no toki, jookyaku wa suwatte inakute wa narimasen. __1__ o aruite wa ikemasen. Soreni __2__ o

なくてはいけません。離陸した後も__3__ のために__4__ はずっとしめていた方がいいです。

shimenakute wa ikemasen. Ririku shita ato mo __3__ no tame ni __4__ wa zutto shimete ita hoo ga ii desu.

機内はいつも**禁煙**です。   no-smoking

Kinai wa itsumo *kin-en* desu.

飛行機の中では、**たばこを吸う**ことはできません。   smoke

Hikooki no naka de wa, *tabako o suu* koto wa dekimasen.

お手洗いの中でも、吸ってはいけません。   toilets

Otearai no naka de mo, sutte wa ikemasen.

たばこは着陸した後で、空港の**喫煙所**で吸ってください。   smoking areas

Tabako wa chakuriku shita ato de, kuukoo no *kitsuenjo* de sutte kudasai.

5. Complete.

1. 飛行機の中は、いつも__1__ だから、__2__ を吸うことはできません。

   Hikooki no naka wa, itsumo __1__ da kara, __2__ o suu koto wa dekimasen.

2. たばこは__3__ の中でも吸ってはいけません。

   Tabako wa __3__ no naka de mo sutte wa ikemasen.

3. たばこが吸いたければ、空港に着いて__4__ に行くまで待たなければなりません。

   Tabako ga suitakereba, kuukoo ni tsuite __4__ ni iku made matanakereba narimasen.

手荷物を通路に置くことはできません。   carry-on luggage

Tenimotsu o tsuuro ni oku koto wa dekimasen.

手荷物は前の**座席の下**に入れます。   under the seats

Tenimotsu wa mae no *zaseki no shita* ni iremasu.

座席の下に入らなければ、**上の棚**の中に入れます。   overhead compartments

Zaseki no shita ni hairanakereba, *ue no tana* ni iremasu.

離陸と着陸の時には、座席の**背もたれ**を**倒して**はいけません。   seat back, recline

Ririku to chakuriku no toki ni wa, zaseki no *semotae* o *taoshite* wa ikemasen.

座席の前の**テーブル**も、**元の位置**に**戻して**ください。   tray table, original position,

Zaseki no mae no *teeburu* mo, *moto no ichi* ni *modoshite* kudasai.   put back

上の棚
ue no tana

背もたれ
semotare

座席の下
zaseki no shita

Fig. 2-3

6. Complete.

乗客は＿1＿を通路に置いてはいけません。＿2＿は前の座席の下か＿3＿に入れてください。

Jookyaku wa ＿1＿ o tsuuro ni oite wa ikemasen. ＿2＿ wa mae no zaseki no shita ka ＿3＿ ni irete kudasai.

離陸と着陸の時には、倒した＿4＿を元の位置に戻してください。＿5＿も元の位置に

Ririku to chakuriku no toki ni wa, taoshita ＿4＿ o moto no ichi ni modoshite kudasai. ＿5＿ mo moto no ichi ni

戻してください。

modoshite kudasai.

SERVICES ON BOARD

機内では、**食事**の**サービス**があります。   meal, service

Kinai de wa, *shokuji* no *saabisu* ga arimasu.

日本語と英語の**新聞**や**雑誌**も置いてあります。   newspapers, magazines

Nihongo to eego no *shinbun* ya *zasshi* mo oite arimasu.

音楽や**ニュース**の**チャンネル**があって、**ヘッドホン**で楽しむ   music, channels, headsets

Ongaku ya *nyuusu* no *chan-neru* ga atte, *heddohon* de tanoshimu

ことができます。

koto ga dekimasu.

日本語と英語で**映画が上映されます。**   movies will be shown

Nihongo to eego de *eega ga jooee saremasu.*

毛布と**枕**もあります。   blankets, pillows

Moofu to *makura* mo arimasu.

座席の前の**ポケット**には、気分が悪い時のための**紙袋**も   seat pocket, paper bags

Zaseki no mae no *poketto* ni wa, kibun ga warui toki no tame no *kamibukuro* mo

入っています。

haitte imasu.

毛布
moofu

枕
makura

ヘッドホン
heddohon

Fig. 2-4

7. Complete.

飛行機の中では、客室乗務員が__1__を運んでくれます。日本語と英語の__2__や__3__も

Hikooki no naka de wa, kyakushitsu joomuin ga __1__ o hakonde kuremasu. Nihongo to eego no __2__ ya __3__ mo

あるので、読むことができます。機内では __4__ を使って、いろいろな __5__ やニュースを聞くことが
aru node, yomu koto ga dekimasu. Kinai de wa __4__ o tsukatte, iroiro na __5__ ya nyuusu o kiku koto ga
できます。そのほかに、映画を見ることもできます。日本語と英語で映画が __6__ ので、好きな方で
dekimasu. Sono hoka ni, eega o miru koto mo dekimasu. Nihongo to eego de eega ga __6__ node, sukina hoo de
楽しめます。ゆっくり寝たければ、 __7__ と __8__ を使ってください。
tanoshimemasu. Yukkuri netakereba, __7__ to __8__ o tsukatte kudasai.

8. Complete.

今、とても疲れています。何も食べたくないので、 __1__ はいりません。少し休みたいから、 __2__ と __3__ を
Ima, totemo tsukarete imasu. Nani mo tabetakunai node, __1__ wa irimasen. Sukoshi yasumitai kara, __2__ to __3__ o
持って来てください。気分が悪くなったら、座席の前の __4__ に __5__ があるので、それを使います。
mottekite kudasai. Kibun ga waruku nattara, zaseki no mae no __4__ ni __5__ ga aru node, sore o tsukaimasu.

　毎日、世界中をたくさんの飛行機が飛んでいます。飛行機の中で乗務員が乗客を迎えます。
　Mainichi, sekaijuu o takusan no hikooki ga tonde imasu. Hikooki no naka de joomuin ga jookyaku o mukaemasu.
客室乗務員に聞けば、座席を教えてくれます。たいていの飛行機では、後方キャビンが
Kyakushitsu joomuin ni kikeba, zaseki o oshiete kuremasu. Taitee no hikooki de wa, koohoo kyabin ga
エコノミークラスで、前方キャビンがファーストクラスになっています。
ekonomii kurasu de, zenpoo kyabin ga faasuto kurasu ni natte imasu.
　機内ではいろいろなアナウンスがあります。離陸の前に客室乗務員が酸素マスクや救命胴衣
　Kinai de wa iroiro na anaunsu ga arimasu. Ririku no mae ni kyakushitsu joomuin ga sansomasuku ya kyuumeedooi
について説明します。手荷物は前の座席の下か上の棚に入れなくてはいけません。機内は
ni tsuite setsumee shimasu. Tenimotsu wa mae no zaseki no shita ka ue no tana ni irenakute wa ikemasen. Kinai wa
禁煙なので、たばこは吸ってはいけません。また、離陸と着陸の時には、背もたれや前のテーブルを
kin-en nanode, tabako wa sutte wa ikemasen. Mata, ririku to chakuriku no toki ni wa, semotare ya mae no teeburu o
元の位置に戻して、シートベルトをしめなくてはいけません。飛行中はシートベルトをいつも
moto no ichi ni modoshite, shiitoberuto o shimenakute wa ikemasen. Hikoochuu wa shiitoberuto o itsumo
しめておいた方がいいでしょう。
shimete oita hoo ga ii deshoo.
　機内では、客室乗務員が食事や飲み物を運んでくれます。休みたい乗客のため
　Kinai de wa, kyakushitsu joomuin ga shokuji ya nomimono o hakonde kuremasu. Yasumitai jookyaku no tame
には毛布や枕も持って来てくれます。そのほかにも、音楽やニュースや映画のサービスがあって、
ni wa moofu ya makura mo mottekite kuremasu. Sono hoka ni mo, ongaku ya nyuusu ya eega no saabisu ga atte,
ヘッドホンで楽しむことができます。
heddohon de tanoshimu koto ga dekimasu.
　乗客は操縦士がいるコックピットに入ることはできません。操縦士は飛行中に、乗客に
　Jookyaku wa soojuushi ga iru kokkupitto ni hairu koto wa dekimasen. Soojuushi wa hikoochuu ni, jookyaku ni
飛行時間、到着時間、高度などを伝えます。
hikoo jikan, toochaku jikan, koodo nado o tsutaemasu.

9. Complete.

1. たいてい飛行機には＿＿＿が二つあります。ファーストクラスの乗客は＿＿＿に、エコノミークラスの

   Taitee hikooki ni wa ＿＿ ga futatsu arimasu. Faasuto kurasu no jookyaku wa ＿＿ ni, ekonomii kurasu no

   乗客は後ろの＿＿＿に座ります。

   jookyaku wa ushiro no ＿＿ ni suwarimasu.

2. ＿＿＿や＿＿＿については、客室乗務員が離陸の前に乗客に説明します。

   ＿＿ ya ＿＿ ni tsuite wa, kyakushitsu joomuin ga ririku no mae ni jookyaku ni setsumee shimasu.

3. ＿＿＿を入れるところは、前の座席の下か、＿＿＿です。

   ＿＿ o ireru tokoro wa, mae no zaseki no shita ka, ＿＿ desu.

4. 飛行機の中は＿＿＿です。たばこは吸うことができません。

   Hikooki no naka wa ＿＿ desu. Tabako wa suu koto ga dekimasen.

5. ＿＿＿をたおして座っている乗客は、離陸と着陸の時に＿＿＿に戻します。

   ＿＿ o taoshite suwatte iru jookyaku wa, ririku to chakuriku no toki ni ＿＿ ni modoshimasu.

6. 機内では＿＿＿を使って、音楽やニュースや映画を楽しめます。

   Kinai de wa ＿＿ o tsukatte, ongaku ya nyuusu ya eega o tanoshimemasu.

7. 寝たい時には、乗務員に頼んで＿＿＿や＿＿＿を持って来てもらいます。

   Netai toki ni wa, joomuin ni tanonde ＿＿ ya ＿＿ o mottekite moraimasu.

10. Match.

1. 操縦士がいるところ	(a) ヘッドホン
soojuushi ga iru tokoro	heddohon
2. 機内で乗客の世話をしてくれる人	(b) 操縦席
kinai de jookyaku no sewa o shite kureru hito	soojuuseki
3. 機内の気圧が変わると、自動的におりてくる物	(c) シートベルト
kinai no kiatsu ga kawaru to, jidooteki ni oritekuru mono	shiitoberuto
4. 手荷物を入れておくところ	(d) 高度
tenimotsu o irete oku tokoro	koodo
5. 離陸と着陸の時に元の位置に戻す物	(e) 上の棚
ririku to chakuriku no toki ni moto no ichi ni modosu mono	ue no tana
6. 離陸と着陸の時に乗客がしめる物	(f) 後方キャビン
ririku to chakuriku no toki ni jooyaku ga shimeru mono	koohoo kyabin
7. 緊急の場合に、乗客が飛行機の外に出るところ	(g) 客室乗務員
kinkyuu no baai ni, jookyaku ga hikooki no soto ni deru tokoro	kyakushitsu joomuin
8. 飛行機が飛んでいる時の高さ	(h) 非常口
hikooki ga tonde iru toki no takasa	hijooguchi
9. たいていエコノミークラスがあるところ	(i) 背もたれ
taitee ekonomii kurasu ga aru tokoro	semotare
10. 音楽やニュースを聞くために使う物	(j) 酸素マスク
ongaku ya nyuusu o kiku tame ni tsukau mono	sansomasuku

11. Answer.

1. たいてい飛行機にはキャビンがいくつありますか。

   Taitee hikooki ni wa kyabin ga ikutsu arimasu ka.

2. 離陸と着陸の時、乗客は何をしてはいけませんか。

   Ririku to chakuriku no toki, jookyaku wa nani o shite wa ikemasen ka.

3. 乗務員は離陸する前に、乗客に何について説明しますか。

   Joomuin wa ririku suru mae ni, jookyaku ni nani ni tsuite setsumee shimasu ka.

4. たばこが吸いたい人は、空港のどこで吸えますか。

   Tabako ga suitai hito wa, kuukoo no doko de suemasu ka.

5. ゆっくり休みたい時は、乗務員に何を持って来てもらえますか。

   Yukkuri yasumitai toki wa, joomuin ni nani o mottekite moraemasu ka.

6. 機内では音楽やニュースが聞けるほかに、何を見ることができますか。

   Kinai de wa ongaku ya nyuusu ga kikeru hoka ni, nani o miru koto ga dekimasu ka.

Key Words

air pressure	気圧	kiatsu
airplane	飛行機	hikooki
aisles	通路	tsuuro
altitude	高度	koodo
automatically	自動的に	jidooteki ni
be shown	上映される	jooee sareru
blanket	毛布	moofu
carry-on luggage	手荷物	tenimotsu
channels	チャンネル	channeru
cigarettes,	たばこ	tabako
cockpit	操縦室（コックピット）	soojuushitsu (kokkupitto)
crew	乗務員	joomuin
during the flight	飛行中	hikoochuu
emergency exit	非常口	hijooguchi
fasten	しめる	shimeru
first class	ファーストクラス	faasuto kurasu
flight attendants	客室乗務員	kyakushitsu joomuin
fly	飛行する	hikoo suru
flying time	飛行時間	hikoo jikan
forward cabin	前方キャビン	zenpoo kyabin
headsets	ヘッドホン	heddohon
in case of emergency	緊急の場合	kinkyuu no baai
inside the airplane	機内	kinai
instruction	指示	shiji
kilometers	キロメートル	kiromeetoru
land	着陸する	chakuriku suru
life jackets	救命胴衣	kyuumeedooi
magazines	雑誌	zasshi
meal	食事	shokuji
meters	メートル	meetoru
movies	映画	eega
music	音楽	ongaku
newspapers	新聞	shinbun
no-smoking	禁煙	kin-en
original position	元の位置	moto no ichi
overhead compartments	上の棚	ue no tana
oxygen mask	酸素マスク	sansomasuku
paper bags	紙袋	kamibukuro
passengers	乗客	jookyaku
pillows	枕	makura
pilot	操縦士（パイロット）	soojuushi (pairotto)
put back	戻す	modosu
rear cabin	後方キャビン	koohoo kyabin
recline	倒す	taosu
safety	安全	anzen

seat pocket	座席の前のポケット	*zaseki no mae no poketto*	under the seats	座席の下	*zaseki no shita*
service	サービス	*saabisu*	seat	座席	*zaseki*
smoke	吸う	*suu*	seat back	背もたれ	*semotare*
smoking areas	喫煙所	*kitsuenjo*	seat belt	座席ベルト（シートベルト）	*zasekiberuto (shiitoberuto)*
speed an hour	時速	*jisoku*			
take off	離陸する	*ririku suru*	welcome (meet)	迎える	*mukaeru*
toilets	お手洗い	*otearai*			
tray table	座席の前のテーブル	*zaseki no mae no teeburu*	wings (lit. main wings)	主翼	*shuyoku*

Chapter 3: Passport control and customs
第3章：入国審査と税関
Nyuukoku shinsa to zeekan

PASSPORT CONTROL AND IMMIGRATION

これが私の**パスポート（旅券）**です。   passport

Kore ga watashi no *pasupooto (ryoken)* desu.

          ビザ（査証）   visa

          biza (sashoo)

          外国人入国記録   disembarkation card for

          gaikokujin nyuukoku kiroku   foreigner

日本にどのぐらい**滞在する予定**ですか。   plan to stay

Nihon ni donogurai *taizai suru yotee* desu ka.

商用（ビジネス）ですか。   on business

Shooyoo (bijinesu) desu ka.

観光ですか。   for pleasure (lit. sightseeing)

Kankoo desu ka.

どこにお**泊まります**か。   stay over

Doko ni *tomarimasu* ka.

1. Complete.

＿1＿ を見せてください。

＿1＿ o misete kudasai.

はい、どうぞ。

Hai, doozo.

どのぐらい ＿2＿ する予定ですか。

Donogurai ＿2＿ suru yotee desu ka.

二週間です。

Nishuukan desu.

どこに ＿3＿ か。

Doko ni ＿3＿ ka.

東京ホテルに ＿4＿ 。

Tookyoo hoteru ni ＿4＿ .

＿5＿ ですか、 ＿6＿ ですか。

＿5＿ desu ka, ＿6＿ desu ka.

＿7＿ です。今、夏休みなんです。

＿7＿ desu. Ima, natsuyasumi nandesu.

AT CUSTOMS

税関申告書を出してください。　customs declaration
Zeekan shinkokusho o dashite kudasai.

申告する物はありますか。　something to declare
Shinkoku suru mono wa arimasu ka.

申告する物がなければ、緑の矢印の方へ行ってください。　follow the green arrow
Shinkoku suru mono ga nakereba, *midori no yajirushi no hoo e itte* kudasai.

申告する物があれば、赤い矢印の方へ行ってください。　follow the red arrow
Shinkoku suru mono ga areba, *akai yajirushi no hoo e itte* kudasai.

税関の係員が質問します。　customs agent
Zeekan no kakariin ga shitsumon shimasu.

たばこを持っていますか。　cigarettes
Tabako o motte imasu ka.

お酒を持っていますか。　alcohol
Osake o motte imasu ka.

くだものを持っていますか。　fruit
Kudamono o motte imasu ka.

自分の荷物だけです。　my own belongings
Jibun no nimotsu dake desu.

ウィスキーを三本、申告します。　three bottles of whisky
Wisukii o sannbon, shinkoku shimasu.

スーツケースを開けてください。　suitcase
Suutsukeesu o akete kudasai.

このかばんも開けてください。　bag
Kono *kaban* mo akete kudasai.

ウィスキーを三本以上持ち込む時は、税金を払わなくてはいけません。　three or more bottles, bring in
Wisukii o *sanbon ijoo mochikomu* toki wa, *zeekin* o harawanakute wa ikemasen.　tax

2. Complete.

1. この空港ではすべての____を検査する(check)わけではありません。____する物がない人は
   Kono kuukoo de wa subete no ___ o kensa suru (check) wake de wa arimasen. ___ suru mono ga nai hito wa
   緑の矢印の方へ行きます。____する物がある人は赤い矢印の方へ行きます。
   midori no yajirushi no hoo e ikimasu. ___ suru mono ga aru hito wa akai yajirushi no hoo e ikimasu.

2. 日本には、ウィスキーを持ち込むことができますが、____以上持っている時は申告をして____を
   Nihon ni wa, wisukii o mochikomu koto ga dekimasu ga, ___ ijoo motte iru toki wa shinkoku o shite ___ o
   払わなくてはいけません。
   harawanakute wa ikemasen.

3. 税関の係員は____を見ます。
   Zeekan no kakariin wa ___ o mimasu.

4. 自分の＿＿＿しかないので、申告する物はありません。

   Jibun no ___ shika nai node, shinkoku suru mono wa arimasen.

Key Words

alcohol	お酒	*osake*	on business	商用（ビジネス）	*shooyoo (bijinesu)*
bag	かばん	*kaban*			
belongings	荷物	*nimotsu*	one's own ~	自分の～	*~ jibun no*
bring in	持ち込む	*mochikomu*	~ or more (over; more than)	～以上	*~ ijoo*
cigarettes	たばこ	*tabako*			
customs	税関	*zeekan*			
customs agent	税関の係員	*zeekan no kakariin*	passport	パスポート（旅券）	*pasupooto (ryoken)*
customs declaration	税関申告書	*zeekan shinkokusho*	passport control	入国審査	*nyuukoku shinsa*
			plan	予定	*yotee*
declare	申告する	*shinkoku suru*	red arrow	赤い矢印	*akai yajirushi*
disembarkation card for foreigner	外国人入国記録	*gaikokujin nyuukoku kiroku*	stay	滞在する	*taizai suru*
			stay over	泊まる	*tomaru*
for pleasure (lit. sightseeing)	観光	*kankoo*	suitcase	スーツケース	*suutsukeesu*
			tax	税金	*zeekin*
fruit	くだもの	*kudamono*	visa	ビザ（査証）	*biza (sashoo)*
green arrow	緑の矢印	*midori no yajirushi*	whisky	ウィスキー	*wisukii*

GETTING A TICKET

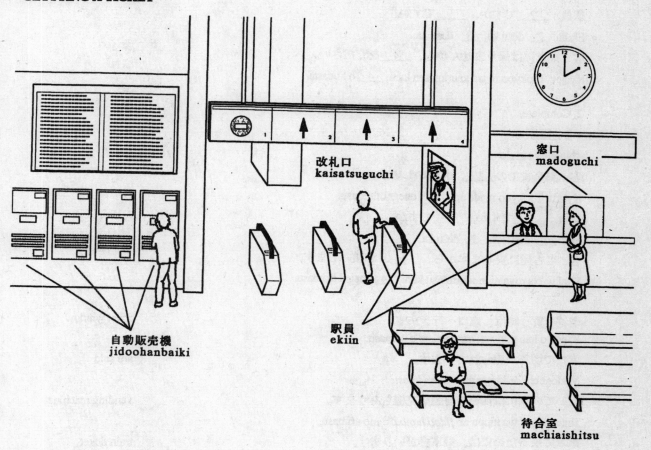

改札口
kaisatsuguchi

窓口
madoguchi

自動販売機
jidoohanbaiki

駅員
ekiin

待合室
machiaishitsu

Fig. 4-1

駅で電車の切符を買います。	station, train, tickets
Eki de *densha* no *kippu* o kaimasu.	
東京から大阪まで行きます。そして、また東京に戻ります。	return
Tookyoo kara Oosaka made ikimasu. Soshite, mata Tookyoo ni *modorimasu*.	
東京から大阪までの往復切符を買います。	round trip ticket
Tookyoo kara Oosaka made no *oofuku kippu* o kaimasu.	
東京から名古屋まで行きます。東京には戻りません。	
Tookyoo kara Nagoya made ikimasu. Tookyoo ni wa modorimasen.	
東京から名古屋までの片道切符を買います。	one-way ticket
Tookyoo kara Nagoya made no *katamichi kippu* o kaimsu.	

1. Complete.

<東京駅で>

<Tookyoo eki de>

客：大阪までの＿1＿、お願いします。

Kyaku: Oosaka made no ＿1＿, onegai shimasu.

駅員：＿2＿ですか、＿3＿ですか。

Ekiin: ＿2＿ desu ka, ＿3＿ desu ka.

客：東京には帰りませんから、＿4＿をください。

Kyaku: Tookyoo ni wa kaerimasen kara, ＿4＿ o kudasai.

2. Complete.

<名古屋駅で>

<Nagoya eki de>

客：東京までの＿1＿、お願いします。

Kyaku: Tookyoo made no ＿1＿, onegai shimasu.

駅員：＿2＿ですか、＿3＿ですか。

Eki: ＿2＿ desu ka, ＿3＿ desu ka.

客：名古屋に戻りますから、＿4＿、お願いします。

Kyaku: Nagoya ni modorimasu kara, ＿4＿, onegai shimasu.

切符を買う時は、**窓口**へ行きます。 Kippu o kau toki wa, *madoguchi* e ikimasu.	ticket window
窓口で切符が**売られています**。 Madoguchi de kippu ga *urarete imasu*.	are sold
たいてい駅には切符の**自動販売機**もあります。 Taitee eki ni wa kippu no *jidoo hanbaiki* mo arimasu.	vending machine
電車に乗るためには、**乗車券**がいります。 Densha ni noru tame ni wa, *jooshaken* ga irimasu.	train ticket
特急電車は**普通電車**より高いです。 *Tokkyuu densha* wa *futsuu densha* yori takai desu.	express train, local train
特急に乗る時には、特急**料金**を払って**特急券**を買わなくては Tokkyuu ni noru toki ni wa, tokkyuu *ryookin* o haratte *tokkyuuken* o kawanakute wa いけません。 ikemasen.	fare, ticket for express
東京から大阪に行くのには、**新幹線**が速くて便利です。 Tookyoo kara Oosaka ni iku no ni wa, *shinkansen* ga hayakute benri desu.	Shinkansen (bullet train)
新幹線に乗るときには、新幹線の切符を買います。 Shinkansen ni noru toki ni wa, shinkansen no kippu o kaimasu.	
電車の**出発**までの時間に駅の近くの**デパート**で買い物が Densha no *shuppatsu* made no jikan ni eki no chikaku no *depaato* de kaimono ga	departure, department store

したければ、荷物を**コインロッカー**に**預け**ます。   leave in a coin-operated locker

shitakereba, nimotsu o *koin rokkaa ni azukemasu.*

3. Complete

客：すみません。＿1＿が買いたいんですが。

Kyaku: Sumimasen. _1_ ga kaitai ndesu ga.

駅員：あちらの＿2＿へ行ってください。ああ、そちらに切符の＿3＿もありますが。

Ekiin: Achira no _2_ e itte kudasai. Aa, sochira ni kippu no _3_ mo arimasu ga.

客：そうですか。じゃあ、窓口へ行ってみます。どうも。

Kyaku: Soo desu ka. Jaa, madoguchi e itte mimasu. Doomo.

客：あのう、すみません。甲府まで行きたいんですが。

Kyaku: Anoo, sumimasen. Koofu made ikitai ndesu ga.

駅員：特急ですか。＿4＿券と＿5＿券で、4,980円になります。

Ekiin: Tokkyuu desu ka. _4_ ken to _5_ ken de, yonsen kyuuhyaku hachijuu en ni narimasu.

客：電車の＿6＿まで時間があるので、荷物をどこかに預けたいんですが。

Kyaku: Densha no _6_ made jikan ga aru node, nimotsu o dokoka ni azuketai ndesu ga.

駅員：じゃあ、あちらに＿7＿がありますよ。

Ekiin: Jaa, achira ni _7_ ga arimasu yo.

WAITING FOR THE TRAIN

駅には**時刻表**があります。   train schedule

Eki ni wa *jikokuhyoo* ga arimasu.

時刻表には出発時間が書いてあります。

Jikokuhyoo ni wa shuppatsu jikan ga kaite arimasu.

松本**行き**の電車は14時20分に**出発する**ことになっています。   bound for ~, leave

Matsumoto *iki* no densha wa juuyoji nijuppun ni *shuppatsu suru* koto ni natte imasu.

その電車は**時間通りに**は出発しません。   on time

Sono densa wa *jikan doori ni* wa shuppatsu shimasen.

事故があったので、**遅れて**出発します。   accident, late

Jiko ga atta node, *okurete* shuppatsu shimasu.

一時間ぐらい遅れるそうです。

Ichijikan gurai okureru soo desu.

到着も遅れるでしょう。   arrival

Toochaku mo okureru deshoo.

駅の**キオスグ**で買った新聞を読みながら**待合室**で待ちます。   kiosk (newsstand),

Eki no *kiosuku* de katta shinbun o yominagara *machiaishitsu* de machimasu.   waiting room

4. Answer.

1. 駅で出発時間を何で見ますか。

   Eki de shuppatsu jikan o nan de mimasu ka.

2. 松本行きの電車は何時に出発するはずでしたか。

   Matsumoto iki no densha wa nanji ni shuppatsu suru hazu deshita ka.

3. その電車は時間通りに出ますか。

   Sono densha wa jikan doori ni demasu ka.

4. どうしてですか。

   Dooshite desu ka.

5. 何時ごろ出るでしょうか。

   Nanji goro deru deshoo ka.

6. 乗客は電車をどこで待ちますか。

   Jookyaku wa densha o doko de machimasu ka.

7. 新聞はどこで買えますか。

   Shinbun wa doko de kaemasu ka.

5. Complete

事故があって、電車は___1___に出ません。電車は 14 時 20 分ではなくて、一時間ぐらい___2___

Jiko ga atte, densha wa ___1___ ni demasen. Densha wa juuyoji nijuppun de wa nakute, ichijikan gurai ___2___

出発します。

shuppatsu shimasu.

乗客は___3___で電車を待ちます。

Jookyaku wa ___3___ de densha o machimasu.

GETTING ON THE TRAIN

切符を買ったら、**改札口**を通って**ホーム**へ行きます。　　　　　　ticket gate, platform (track)

Kippu o kattara, *kaisatsuguchi* o tootte *hoomu* e ikimasu.

大きな駅には**自動改札機**もあります。　　　　　　an automatic ticket gate

Ookina eki ni wa *jidoo kaisatsuki* mo arimasu.

松本行きの電車はあと五分で出ます。

Matsumoto iki no densha wa ato gofun de demasu.

6 番ホームから出発します。　　　　　　track number 6

Rokuban hoomu kara shuppatsu shimasu.

その電車には**指定席**と**自由席**があります。　　　　　　reserved seat, unreserved seat

Sono densha ni wa *shiteeseki* to *jiyuuseki* ga arimasu.

私は指定席の切符を買いました。

Watashi wa shiteeseki no kippu o kaimashita.

その電車は **8 両の電車**です。　　　　　　a 8-car train

Sono densha wa *hachiryoo no densha* desu.

私の席は**四号車**の **20-C** です。　　　　　　　　　　　car number 4, seat number 20-C

Watashi no seki wa *yongoosha* no *nijuu no shii* desu.

私の席は**禁煙席**です。**喫煙席**じゃありません。　　　　non-smoking seat, smoking seat

Watashi no seki wa *kin-enseki* desu. *Kitsuenseki* ja arimasen.

6. Complete.

1. 電車に乗る前に＿＿＿を買って、＿＿＿を通ります。

　　Densha ni noru mae ni ___ o katte, ___ o toorimasu.

2. 松本＿＿＿の電車は6番＿＿＿から出ます。

　　Matsumoto ___ no densha wa rokuban ___ kara demasu.

3. 私の席は自由席じゃありません。＿＿＿です。

　　Watashi no seki wa jiyuuseki ja arimasen. ___ desu.

4. その電車は8＿＿＿の電車でした。

　　Sono densha wa hachi ___ no densha deshita.

5. 私の席は4＿＿＿の 20-C でした。

　　Watashi no seki ha yon ___ no nijuu no shii deshita.

ON THE TRAIN

電車の中に**車掌**がいます。　　　　　　　　　　　conductor

Densha no naka ni *shashoo* ga imasu.

車掌は乗客の切符を**見ます**。　　　　　　　　　　check (lit. see)

Shashoo wa jookyaku no kippu o *mimasu*.

寝台車がある電車もあります。　　　　　　　　　sleeping car

Shindaisha ga aru densha mo arimasu.

乗客は**食堂車**で食事をします。　　　　　　　　　dining car

Jookyaku wa *shokudoosha* de shokuji o shimasu.

特急電車の中にはジュースやお茶の自動販売機もあります。

Tokkyuu densha no naka ni wa juusu ya ocha no jidoo hanbaiki mo arimasu.

公衆電話がある電車からは、電話をかけることもできます。　public telephone

Kooshuu denwa ga aru densha kara wa, denwa o kakeru koto mo dekimasu.

7. Complete.

1. 電車の中で乗客の切符を見る人は＿＿＿です。

　　Densha no naka de jookyaku no kippu o miru hito wa ___ desu.

2. 乗客は＿＿＿車で寝ます。

　　Jookyaku wa ___ sha de nemasu.

3. おなかがすいたら、＿＿＿車で食事をすることができます。

　　Onaka ga suitara, ___ sha de shokuji o suru koto ga dekimasu.

4. のどがかわいたら、＿＿＿で飲み物も買えます。

　　　Nodo ga kawaitara, ___ de nomimono mo kaemasu.

5. 電話がかけたければ、電車の中の＿＿＿が使えます。

　　　Denwa ga kaketakereba, densha no naka no ___ ga tsukaemasu.

　　ブラウンさんは電車で旅行をします。一時半ごろ駅の前でタクシーを降りました。ブラウンさんが
　　Buraun san wa densha de ryokoo o shimasu. Ichiji han goro eki no mae de takushii o orimashita. Buraun san ga
乗りたい新幹線は4時10分に出るので、時間はまだたくさんあります。ブラウンさんは大きい荷物を
noritai shinkansen wa yoji juppun ni deru node, jikan wa mada takusan arimasu. Buraun san wa ookii nimotsu o
持っていたので、その荷物をコインロッカーに預けることにしました。ロッカーに荷物を入れた後で、
motte ita node, sono nimotsu o koin rokkaa ni azukeru koto ni shmashita. Rokkaa ni nimotsu o ireta ato de,
切符を買いに窓口へ行きました。そこで仙台行きの新幹線の切符を買いました。指定席に
kippu o kai ni madoguchi e ikimashita. Soko de Sendai iki no shinkansen no kippu o kaimashita. Shiteeseki ni
しました。それから駅の前のデパートで買い物をしました。駅に戻って、待合室で
shimashita. Sorekara eki no mae no depaato de kaimono o shimashita. Eki ni modotte, machiaishitsu de
椅子に座って出発まで待ちました。四時少し前にブラウンさんは荷物をコインロッカーから
isu ni suwatte shuppatsu made machimashita. Yoji sukoshi mae ni Buraun san wa nimotsu o koin rokkaa kara
出しました。改札口を通って10番ホームに行きました。ホームにはもう電車が来ていました。
dashimashita. Kaisatsuguchi o tootte juuban hoomu ni ikimashita. Hoomu ni wa moo densha ga kite imashita.
人がたくさんいましたが、ブラウンさんは指定席なので座れました。この電車は5号車が
Hito ga takusan imashita ga, Buraun san wa shiteeseki nanode suwaremashita. Kono densha wa gogoosha ga
指定席で、ブラウンさんの席は21-Aでした。電車が出発すると、車掌が来てブラウンさん
shiteeseki de Buraun san no seki wa nijuuichi no ee deshita. Densha ga shuppatsu suru to shashoo ga kite Buraun san
の切符を見ました。ブラウンさんは何か飲みたかったので、車掌に自動販売機があるかどうか
no kippu o mimashita. Buraun san wa nanika nomitakatta node, shashoo ni jidoo hanbaiki ga aru ka dooka
聞きました。車掌は自動販売機は2号車だと言いました。
kikimashita. Shashoo wa jidoo hanbaiki wa nigoosha da to iimashita.

8. Based on the story, write true or false.

1. ブラウンさんは新幹線で旅行をしました。

　　　Buraun san wa shinkansen de ryokoo o shimashita.

2. バスで駅まで行きました。

　　　Basu de eki made ikimashita.

3. 駅に着いてからコインロッカーに荷物を預けました。

　　　Eki ni tsuite kara koin rokkaa ni nimotsu o azukemahista.

4. 自動販売機で切符を買いました。

　　　Jidoo hanbaiki de kippu o kaimashita.

5. ブラウンさんは席に座れませんでした。

　　　Buraun san wa seki ni suwaremasen deshita.

9. Answer.

1. ブラウンさんは駅まで何で行きましたか。

   Buraun san wa eki made nan de ikimashita ka.

2. どこに荷物を預けましたか。

   Doko ni nimotsu o azukemashita ka.

3. どこで切符を買いましたか。

   Doko de kippu o kaimashita ka.

4. どんな電車で旅行しましたか。

   Don-na densha de ryokoo shimashita ka.

5. 自由席と指定席とどちらの切符を買いましたか。

   Jiyuuseki to shiteeseki to dochira no kippu o kaimashita ka.

6. 何号車に乗りましたか。

   Nan goosha ni norimashita ka.

7. 席はどこでしたか。

   Seki wa doko deshita ka.

8. 車掌に何を聞きましたか。

   Shashoo ni nani o kikimashita ka.

10. Match.

1. 荷物
   nimotsu

2. ホーム
   hoomu

3. 窓口
   madoguchi

4. 車掌
   shashoo

5. コインロッカー
   koin rokkaa

6. 改札口
   kaisatsuguchi

(a) 乗客が荷物を預けるところ
    jookyaku ga nimotsu o azukeru tokoro

(b) 乗客が持って行くスーツケースや他の物
    jookyaku ga motteiku suutsukeesu ya hoka no mono

(c) 電車に乗る前に切符を見せて通るところ
    densha ni noru mae ni kippu o misete tooru tokoro

(d) 電車が出発するところ
    densha ga shuppatsu suru tokoro

(e) 乗客が切符を買うところ
    jookyaku ga kippu o kau tokoro

(f) 乗客の切符を見る人
    jookyaku no kippu o miru hito

Key Words

accident	事故	*jiko*	~ car train	〜両の電車	*~ ryoo no densha*
an automatic ticket gate	自動改札機	*jidookaisatsuki*	check (lit. see)	見る	*miru*
arrival	到着	*toochaku*	coin-operated locker	コインロッカー	*koin rokkaa*
be sold	売られる	*urareru*	conductor	車掌	*shashoo*
bound for ~	〜行き	*~ iki*	department store	デパート	*depaato*
car number ~	〜号車	*~ goosha*			

departure	出発	*shuppatsu*	(bullet train)		
dining car	食堂車	*shokudoosha*	sleeping car	寝台車	*shindai sha*
express train	特急電車	*tokkyuu densha*	smoking seat	喫煙席	*kitsuen seki*
fare	料金	*ryookin*	station	駅	*eki*
kiosk (newsstand)	キオスク	*kiosuku*	station employee	駅員	*ekiin*
late	遅れる	*okureru*	ticket	切符	*kippu*
leave	預ける	*azukeru*	ticket for express	特急券	*tokkyuu ken*
local train	普通電車	*futsuu densha*			
non-smoking seat	禁煙席	*kin-enseki*	ticket gate	改札口	*kaisatsuguchi*
			ticket window	窓口	*madoguchi*
on time	時間通りに	*jikan doori ni*	track number ~	~番ホーム	*~ ban hoomu*
one-way ticket	片道切符	*katamichi kippu*	train	電車	*densha*
platform (track)	ホーム	*hoomu*	train schedule	時刻表	*jikokuhyoo*
public telephone	公衆電話	*kooshuu denwa*	train ticket	乗車券	*joosha ken*
			unreserved seat	自由席	*jiyuu seki*
reserved seat	指定席	*shitee seki*	vending machine	自動販売機	*jidoo hanbaiki*
return	戻る	*modoru*	waiting room	待合室	*machiaishitsu*
round trip ticket	往復切符	*oofuku kippu*			
Shinkansen	新幹線	*shinkansen*			

Chapter 5: The automobile
第5章：自動車
　　　Jidoosha

RENTING A CAR

車が借りたいんですが。
Kuruma ga karitai ndesu-ga.

want to rent a car

レンタカー
Renta kaa

rent-a-car

いくらかかりますか。
Ikura kakarimasu ka.

How much does it cost?

一日でいくらですか。
Ichinichi de ikura desu ka.

How much is it by the day?

一週間で
Isshuukan de

by the week

料金は走行距離によって違いますか。
Ryookin wa sookookyori ni yotte chigaimasu ka.

Do you charge by mileage?

(lit. Does the charge depend on mileage?)

200キロを越えると、1キロにつきいくらですか。
Nihya k*kiro o koeru* to, *ichi kiro ni tsuki* ikura desu ka.

kilometer, exceed, per one kilometer

ガソリンは含まれていますか。
Gasorin wa *fukumarete imasu* ka.

gas, is included

オートマチック車はありますか。
Ootomachikkusha wa arimasu ka.

automatic car

マニュアル車
Manyuarusha

manual car

保証金がいりますか。
Hoshookin ga irimasu ka.

deposit

保険はいくらですか。
Hoken wa ikura desu ka.

insurance

これが私の運転免許証です。
Kore ga watashi no *unten menkyoshoo* desu.

driver's license

クレジットカードで払うことができますか。
Kurejitto kaado de *harau* koto ga dekimasu ka.

credit card, pay

1. Complete.

1. 電車で旅行したくありません。車を＿＿＿方がいいです。

　　Densha de ryokoo shitakuarimasen. Kuruma o ＿＿ hoo ga ii desu.

2.料金は＿＿によって違います。

     Ryookin wa ___ ni yotte chigaimasu.

3. ある(certain)走行距離を＿＿と、１キロ＿＿いくらか払わなくてはいけません。

     Aru (certain) sookoo kyori o ___ to, ichikiro ___ ikuraka harawanakute wa ikemasen.

4. 車を借りるのに＿＿がいります。

     Kuruma o kariru no ni ___ ga irimasu.

5.マニュアル車じゃなくて＿＿車がいいです。

     Manyuarusha ja nakute ___ sha ga ii desu.

2. Complete.

- ＿1＿が借りたいんですが。

- _1_ ga karitai ndesu ga.

- どんなのがいいですか。

- Donna no ga ii desu ka.

- ワゴン(station wagon)をお願いします。一日で＿2＿ですか。

- Wagon (station wagon) o onegai shimasu. Ichinichi de _2_ desu ka.

- ＿3＿が200キロまでで二万五千円です。ガソリンは＿4＿います。

- _3_ ga nihyakkiro made de niman gosen en desu. Gasorin wa _4_ imasu.

- そうですか。じゃあ、この車を一日借ります。

- Soo desu ka. Jaa, kono kuruma o ichinichi karimasu.

- ＿5＿を見せていただけますか。

- _5_ o misete itadakemasu ka.

- はい、これです。＿6＿で払いますが、＿7＿金がいります..。

- Hai, kore desu. _6_ de haraimasu ga, _7_ kin ga irimasu ka.

- いいえ、いりませんよ。

- Iie, irimasen yo.

CHECKING OUT THE CAR

Fig 5-1

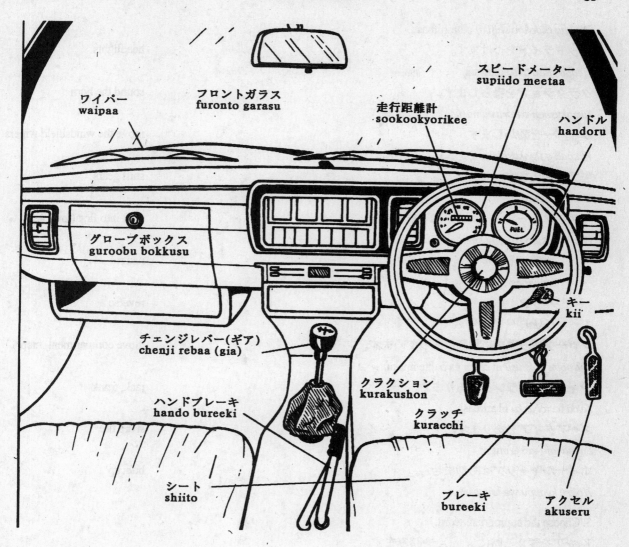

ワイパー
waipaa

フロントガラス
furonto garasu

走行距離計
sookookyorikee

スピードメーター
supiido meetaa

ハンドル
handoru

グローブボックス
guroobu bokkusu

キー
kii

チェンジレバー(ギア)
chenji rebaa (gia)

クラクション
kurakushon

ハンドブレーキ
hando bureeki

クラッチ
kuracchi

シート
shiito

ブレーキ
bureeki

アクセル
akuseru

Fig. 5-2

ブレーキを踏みます。	brake (lit. step on the brake)
Bureeki o fumimasu.	
クラッチ	clutch
Kuracchi	
アクセル	step on the accelerator
Akuseru	
エンジンをかけます。	start the engine
Enjin o kakemasu.	
止めます	stop the engine
tomemasu	
ウィンカー（方向指示器）を出します。	blinkers

Winkaa (hookoo shijiki) o dashimasu.

ヘッドライトをつけます。   headlights

Heddo raito o tsukemasu.

クラクションを鳴らします。   sound the horn

Kurakushon o narashimasu.

ワイパーを動かします。   move the windshield wipers

Waipaa o ugokashimasu.

ギアを変えます。   shift gears

Gia o kaemasu.

ギアをファースト（ロー）にします。   shift into first (low) gear

Gia o faasuto (roo) ni shimasu.

　　　ニュートラル   neutral

　　　nyuutoraru

　　　バック   reverse

　　　bakku

グローブボックスに地図が入っています。   glove compartment, map

Guroobu bokkusu ni *chizu* ga haitte imasu.

ジャッキはトランクにあります。   jack, trunk

Jakki ha *toranku* ni arimasu.

スペアタイアもあります。   spare tire

Supea taia mo arimasu.

ホイールキャップはありません。   hubcap

Hoiiru kyappu wa arimasen.

3. Choose the appropriate word.

1. ギアを変える時に、＿＿＿を踏みます。

　　Gia o kaeru toki ni, ＿＿ o fumimasu.

(a) ブレーキ　(b) クラッチ　(c) アクセル

(a) bureeki　　(b) kuracchi　(c) akuseru

2. 車を止めるためには、＿＿＿を踏みます。

　　Kuruma o tomeru tame ni ha ＿＿ o fumimasu.

(a) ブレーキ　(b)　クラッチ　(c) アクセル

(a) bureeki　　　(b) kuracchi　　(c) akuseru

3. 曲がる(make a turn)時に、＿＿＿をつけます。

　　Magaru (make a turn) toki ni, ＿＿ o tsukemasu.

(a) クラクション　(b)　ウィンカー　(c) ギア

(a) kurakushon　　　(b) winkaa　　　(c) gia

4. 夜、＿＿＿をつけます。

　　Yoru, ＿＿ o tsukemasu.

(a) ヘッドライト　(b) ワイパー　(c) ウィンカー

(a) heddo raito　　　(b) waipaa　　　(c) winkaa

5. 車の前に人がいてあぶないです。＿＿＿を鳴らします。

　　Kuruma no mae ni hito ga ite abunai desu. ＿＿ o narashimasu.

(a) スピードメーター　(b) ブレーキ　(c) クラクション

(a) supiido meetaa　　　　(b) bureeki　　(c) kurakushon

6. ＿＿＿＿がきたなくて前がよくみえません。

　　＿＿ ga kitanakute mae ga yoku miemasen

(a) クラクション　(b) バンパー　(c) フロントガラス

(a) kurakushon　　　　(b) banpaa　　　(c) furonto garasu

7. ＿＿＿＿はトランクの中にあります。

　　＿＿ ha toranku no naka ni arimasu.

(a) ハンドル　(b) スピードメーター　(c) ジャッキ

(a) handoru　　(b) supiido meetaa　　(c) jakki

4. Complete.

1. ＿＿＿＿をかける時、＿＿＿＿をニュートラルにします。

　　＿＿ o kakeru toki, ＿＿ o nyuutoraru ni shimasu.

2. この町は初めてでよく分からないので、グローブボックスに＿＿＿＿が入れてあります。

　　Kono machi wa hajimete de yoku wakaranai node, guroobu bokkusu ni ＿＿ ga irete arimasu.

3. スペアタイヤは＿＿＿＿の中に入っています。

　　Supea taiya wa ＿＿ no naka ni haitte imasu.

4. 雨が降っている時は、＿＿＿＿を動かします。

　　Ame ga futte iru toki wa, ＿＿ o ugokashimasu.

5. Put the following actions in starting a car in the proper order.　Omit any item that does not belong.

(a) ブレーキを踏む

　　bureeki o fumu

(b) アクセルを踏む

　　akuseru o fumu

(c) クラッチを踏む

　　kuracchi o fumu

(d) クラクションを鳴らす

　　kurakushon o narasu

(e) エンジンをかける

　　enjin o kakeru

(f) ギアをファーストにする

　　gia o faasuto ni suru

AT THE GAS STATION

ガソリンを入れなくてはいけません。

Gasorin o irenakute wa ikemasen.

gas

ガソリンタンクはほとんど空です。	gas tank, empty
Gasorin tanku wa hotondo *kara* desu.	
ガソリンスタンドに行きます。	gas station
Gasorin sutando ni ikimasu.	
ガソリンを **2,000** 円分入れてください。	2,000 yen worth
Gasorin o *nisen en bun* irete kudasai.	
20 リットル	20 liters
nijuu rittoru	
無鉛ガソリンを 20 リットル入れてください。	unleaded
Muen gasorin o nijuu rittoru irete kudasai.	
ハイオクガソリン	high-octane
Haioku gasorin	
満タンにしてください。	fill it up
Mantan ni shite kudasai.	
ラジエーターの水をチェックしてください。	water in the radiator, check
Rajieetaa no mizu o *chekku shite* kudasai.	
バッテリー	battery
Batterii	
ブレーキオイル	brake fluid
Bureeki oiru	
オイル	oil
Oiru	
スパークプラグ	spark plugs
Supaaku puragu	
タイヤとタイヤの空気圧	tire, tire pressure
Taiya to *taiya no kuukiatsu*	
タイヤを交換してください。	tire, change
Taiya o *kookan shite* kudasai.	
フロントガラスをふいてくれませんか。	windshield, wipe
Furonto garasu o *fuite* kuremasen ka.	

6. Complete.

1. ガソリンを入れなければなりません。＿＿＿がほとんど空です。＿＿＿に行かなくてはいけません。

   Gasorin o irenakereba narimasen. ___ ga hotondo kara desu. ___ ni ikanekute wa ikemasen.

2. ＿＿＿にしたくありません。20＿＿＿だけ入れたいです。

   ___ ni shitaku arimasen. 20 ___ dake iretai desu.

3. ＿＿＿の水をチェックしてください。

   ___ no mizu o chekku shite kudasai.

4. ＿＿＿の空気圧をチェックしてください。

   ___ no kuukiatsu o chekku shite kudasai.

5. ＿＿＿をふかなければなりません。とても汚くてよく見えません。

   ＿＿ o fukanakereba narimasen. Totemo kitanakute yoku miemasen.

6. 1,000 キロ走るたびに、＿＿＿と＿＿＿をチェックした方がいいです。

   Ichiman kiro hashiru tabi ni, ＿＿ to ＿＿ o chekku shita hoo ga ii desu.

SOME MINOR PROBLEMS

車が**故障**しました。 — broke down
Kurumia ga *koshoo shimashita.*

車が**エンスト**しました。 — engine failure (stalling of an engine)
Kuruma ga *ensuto* shimahsita.

エンジンが**かかり**ません。 — engine, not start
Enjin ga *kakarimasen.*

オーバーヒートしました。 — overheat
oobaa hiito shimashita.

変な音がします。 — knocking (lit. making a strange sound)
Hen na oto ga shimasu.

オイルが**漏れて**います。 — leaking
Oiru ga *morete imasu.*

タイヤが**パンク**しました。 — got punctured
Taiya ga *panku shimashita.*

けん引車を**呼んで**もらえませんか。 — tow truck, call
Ken-in sha o *yonde* moraemasen ka.

車を**けん引して**もらわなくてはいけません。 — tow
Kuruma o *ken-in shite* morawanakute wa ikemasen.

修理することができますか。 — repair
Shuuri suru koto ga dekimasu ka.

部品がありますか。 — parts
Buhin ga arimasu ka.

7. Complete.

1. 車がエンストすると、＿＿＿がかかりません。

   Kuruma ga ensuto suru to, ＿＿ ga kakarimasén.

2. ラジエーターから水がたくさん＿＿＿います。エンジンが＿＿＿したんでしょう。

   Rajieetaa kara mizur ga takusan ＿＿ imasu. Enjin ga ＿＿ shita ndeshoo.

3. 車が動かない(won't start)時は、＿＿＿を呼んだ方がいいでしょう。

   Kuruma ga ugokanai (won't start) toki wa, ＿＿ o yonda hoo ga ii deshoo.

4. 修理の人が、＿＿＿があれば車を修理できると言いました。

   Shuuri no hito ga, ＿＿ ga areba kuruma o shuuri dekiru to iimashita.

5. タイヤが＿＿＿しました。スペアタイヤを使います。

   Taiya ga ＿＿ shimashita. Supea taiya o tsukaimasu.

ROAD SIGNS AND TRAFFIC REGULATIONS

通行止め
tsuukoodome

No thoroughfare

車両通行止め
sharyoo tsuukoodome

No thoroughfare for vehicles

進入禁止
shin-nyuu kinshi

Do not enter

駐停車禁止
chuuteesha kinshi

No stopping (5 min)/No parking

駐車禁止
chuusha kinshi

No parking

Uターン禁止
yuutaan kinshi

No U turn

追い越し禁止
oikoshi kinshi

No passing

最高速度
saikoo sokudo

Speed limit (50 km/h)

一時停止
ichiji teeshi

Stop

徐行
jokoo

Go slow

一方通行
ippoo tsuukoo

One way

駐車可
chuusha ka

Parking

横断歩道
oodanhodoo
Crosswalks

国道番号
kokudoo bangoo
National road number

信号機あり
shingooki ari
Traffic light

道路工事中
dooro koojichuu
Under construction

踏切あり
fumikiri ari
Railroad crossing

すべりやすい
suberiyasui
Slippery

Key Words

accelerator	アクセル	*akuseru*	glove compartment	グローブボックス	*guroobu bokkusu*
automatic car	オートマチック車	*ootomachikkusha*	Go slow	徐行	*jokoo*
automobile	自動車	*jidoosha*	hand brake	ハンドブレーキ	*hando bureeki*
battery	バッテリー	*batterii*	headlight	ヘッドライト	*heddoraito*
blinkers	ウィンカー（方向指示器）	*winkaa (hookoo shijiki)*	high-octane	ハイオクガソリン	*haioku gasorin*
brake	ブレーキ	*bureeki*	hood	ボンネット	*bon-netto*
brake fluid	ブレーキオイル	*bureeki oiru*	how much	いくら	*ikura*
break down	故障する	*koshoo suru*	hubcap	ホイールキャップ	*hoiiru kyappu*
bumper	バンパー	*banpaa*	insurance	保険	*hoken*
by the day	一日で	*ichinichi de*	is included	含まれている	*fukumarete iru*
by the week	一週間で	*isshuukan de*	jack	ジャッキ	*jakki*
car	車	*kuruma*	key	キー（かぎ）	*kii*
change	交換する	*kookan suru*	kilometer	キロ	*kiro*
charge	料金	*ryookin*	knocking (lit. making a strange sound)	変な音がする	*hen na oto ga suru*
check	チェックする	*chekku suru*			
clutch	クラッチ	*kuracchi*			
cost	かかる	*kakaru*	liters	リットル	*rittoru*
credit card	クレジットカード	*kurejitto kaado*	manual car	マニュアル車	*manyuarusha*
			map	地図	*chizu*
Crosswalks	横断歩道	*oodan hodoo*	mileage	走行距離	*sookoo kyori*
depend on ~	～によって違う	*~ ni yotte chigau*	move	動かす	*ugokasu*
			national road number	国道番号	*kokudoo bangoo*
deposit	保証金	*hoshookin*	neutral	ニュートラル	*nyuutoraru*
Do not enter	進入禁止	*shinnyuu kinshi*	No parking	駐車禁止	*chuusha kinshi*
driver's license	運転免許証	*unten menkyoshoo*	No passing	追い越し禁止	*oikoshi kinshi*
empty	空	*kara*	No stopping /No parking	駐停車禁止	*chuuteesha kinshi*
engine	エンジン	*enjin*			
engine failure (stalling of an engine)	エンスト	*ensuto*	No thoroughfare	通行止め	*tsuukoo dome*
engine starts	エンジンがかかる	*enjin ga kakaru*	No thoroughfare for vehicles	車両通行止め	*sharyoo tsuukoo dome*
exceed	越える	*koeru*	No U turn	Uターン禁止	*yuutaan kinshi*
fill it up	満タンにする	*mantan ni suru*	odometer	走行距離計	*sookoo kyorikee*
first (low) gear	ファースト（ロー）	*faasuto (roo)*	oil	オイル	*oiru*
			One way	一方通行	*ippoo tsuukoo*
gas	ガソリン	*gasorin*	overheat	オーバーヒート	*oobaahiito*
gas station	ガソリンスタンド	*gasorin sutando*	Parking	駐車可	*chuusha ka*
gas tank	ガソリンタンク	*gasorin tanku*	parts	部品	*buhin*
			pay	払う	*harau*
gear	ギア	*gia*	per ~	～につき	*~ ni tsuki*
get punctured	パンクする	*panku suru*	radiator	ラジエーター	*rajieetaa*

Railroad crossing	踏切あり	*fumikiri ari*	step on	踏む	*fumu*
registration plate	ナンバープレート	*nanbaa pureeto*	Stop	一時停止	*ichiji teeshi*
rent	借りる	*kariru*	stop the engine	エンジンを止める	*enjin o tomeru*
rent-a-car	レンタカー	*rentakaa*	the horn	クラクション	*kurakushon*
repair	修理する	*shuuri suru*	tire	タイヤ	*taiya*
reverse	バック	*bakku*	tire pressure	タイヤの空気圧	*taiya no kuukiatsu*
seat	シート	*shiito*	tow	けん引	*ken-in*
shift gears	ギアを変える	*gia o kaeru*	Traffic light	信号機あり	*shingooki ari*
slippery	すべりやすい	*suberiyasui*	trunk	トランク	*toranku*
sound	鳴らす	*narasu*	Under construction	道路工事中	*dooro koojichuu*
spare tire	スペアタイア	*supea taiya*	unleaded	無鉛ガソリン	*muen gasorin*
spark plugs	スパークプラグ	*supaaku puragu*	windshield	フロントガラス	*furonto garasu*
Speed limit	最高速度	*saikoo sokudo*			
speedometer	スピードメーター	*supiido meetaa*	windshield wipers	ワイパー	*waipaa*
start the engine	エンジンをかける	*enjin o kakeru*	wipe	ふく	*fuku*
steering wheel	ハンドル	*handoru*	worth	分	*bun*

Chapter 6: Asking for directions
第6章：道を聞く
Michi o kiku

ASKING FOR DIRECTIONS WHILE ON FOOT

町の地図を持っていません。   city map
Machi no chizu o motte imasen.

すみませんが、道に迷ってしまいました。   I'm lost
Sumimasen ga, *michi ni mayotte shimai mashita.*

駅前通りはどこですか。   street (avenue)
Ekimae *doori* wa doko desu ka.

遠いですか、近いですか。   far, near
Tooi desu ka, *chikai* desu ka.

歩いていけますか。   on foot
Aruite ikemasu ka.

戻らなくてはいけません。   must return
Modoranakute wa ikemasen.

右に曲がってください。   turn to the right
Migi ni *magatte* kudasai.

左に   left
Hidari ni

まっすぐ行ってください。   straight ahead
Massugu itte kudasai.

反対方向にあります。   opposite direction
Hantai hookoo ni arimasu.

二つ目の角です。   second corner
Futatsu me no kado desu.

ここから三本目の道です。   three blocks (lit. the third street)
Koko kara *sanbon me no michi* desu.   street

1. Complete.

- すみませんが、ここがどこか分かりません。道に＿1＿しまいました。

  Sumimasen ga, koko ga doko ka wakarimasen. Michi ni ＿1＿ shimai mashita.

- そうですか。どこに行きたいんですか。

  Soo desu ka. Doko ni ikitai ndesu ka?

- 桜通りです。

  Sakura doori desu.

- 桜通りのどこですか。

  Sakura doori no doko desu ka?

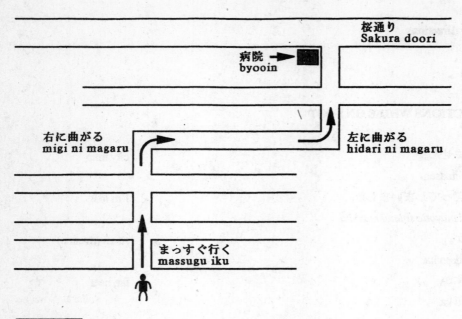

Fig. 6-1

- 桜通りにある病院(hospital)に行きたいんです。

    Sakura doori ni aru byooin ni ikitai ndesu.

- ああ、そうですか。

    Aa, soo desu ka.

- ここから遠いですか。

    Koko kara tooi desu ka?

- いいえ、遠くありません。とても＿2＿ですよ。

    Iie, tooku arimasen. Totemo ＿2＿ desu yo.

- 歩いていけますが、＿3＿ですから、戻らなくてはいけません。

    Aruite ikemasu ga, ＿3＿ desu kara, modoranakute wa ikemasen.

    この道を＿4＿行って、三本目の道を右に曲がります。

    Kono michi o ＿4＿ itte, sanbon me no michi o migi ni magarimasu.

    そして一つ目の＿5＿を左に＿6＿。病院は＿7＿の角にありますよ。

    Soshite hitotsu me no ＿5＿ o hidari ni ＿6＿. Byooin wa ＿7＿ no kado ni arimasu yo.

すみませんが、大学通りはどこですか。

Sumimasen ga, daigaku doori wa doko desu ka.

とても遠いですよ。**バス**で行った方がいいですよ。   bus

Totemo tooi desu yo. *Basu* de itta hoo ga ii desu yo.

バス停が次の角にあります。   bus stop

Basu tee ga tsugi no kado ni arumasu.

10番のバスに**乗って**、**六つ目**のバス停で**降ります**。   get on, the sixth, get off

Juu ban no basu ni *notte*, *muttsu me* no basutee de *orimasu*.

そこが大学通りです。

Soko ga daigaku doori desu.

分かりました。どうも。

Wakarimashita. Doomo.

2. Complete.

- すみません。大学通りはどこですか。

    Sumimasen. Daigaku doori wa doko desu ka.

- ここからはとても__1__ですよ。バスに__2__ください。

    Koko kara wa totemo __1__ desu yo. Basu ni __2__ kudasai.

- どこでそのバスに乗ればいいですか。

    Doko de sono basu ni noreba ii desu ka.

- 次の角に__3__があります。10番のに乗ってください。六つ目のバス停で__4__ください。そこが

    Tsugi no kado ni __3__ ga arimasu. Juu ban no ni notte kudasai. Muttsu me no basutee de __4__ kudasai. Soko ga

    大学通りです。

    daigaku doori desu.

- ありがとうございました。

    Arigatoo gozaimashita.

- どういたしまして。

    Doo itashimashite.

ASKING FOR DIRECTIONS WHILE IN A CAR

ここから長野までどうやって行けばいいですか。	How does one get to -?
Koko kara Nagano *made dooyatte ikeba ii desu ka.*	
国道で長野に行けます。	national highway
Kokudoo de Nagano ni ikemasu.	
国道19号線です。	National highway 19
Kokudoo juukyuu goosen desu.	
国道の代わりに高速道路でも行けます。	instead of, express way
Kokudoo *no kawari ni koosoku dooro* demo ikemasu.	
どこから高速道路に入れますか。	
Doko kara koosoku dooro ni hairemasu ka?	
二つ目の信号まで行きます。	traffic signal
Futatsu me no *shingoo* made ikimasu.	
二つ目の信号で左へ曲がって、まっすぐ行きます。	
Futatsu me no shingoo de hidari e magatte, massugu ikimasu.	
その道は一方通行です。	one-way street
Sono michi wa *ippoo tsuukoo* desu.	

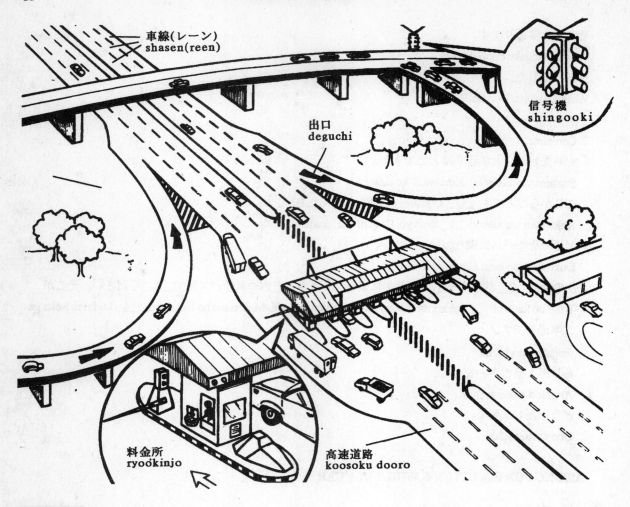

車線(レーン)
shasen(reen)

出口
deguchi

信号機
shingooki

料金所
ryookinjo

高速道路
koosoku dooro

Fig. 6-2

料金所で通行料金を払ってください。   tollbooth, pay a toll

Ryookinjo de *tsuukoo ryookin* o haratte kudasai.

道が混んでいるかもしれません。   crowded

Michi ga *konde iru* kamo shiremasen.

ラッシュアワーには渋滞があります。   rush hour, traffic jam

Rasshu awaa ni wa *juutai* ga arimasu.

3. Complete.

1. 長野に行くには＿＿＿行けばいいですか。

   Nagano ni iku ni wa ＿＿ ikeba ii desu ka.

2. 今日は車がとても多いです。とても＿＿＿います。

   Kyoo wa kuruma ga totemo ooi desu. Totemo ＿＿ imasu.

3. 朝はたいていみんな同じ時間に仕事に行くから、＿＿＿です。

   Asa wa taitee min-na onaji jikan ni shigoto ni iku kara, ＿＿ desu.

4. 国道より、＿＿＿を使った方が速いでしょう。

Kokudoo yori, ___ o tsukatta hoo ga hayai deshoo.

5. 高速道路を使うためには、＿＿＿を払わなくてはいけません。

Koosoku dooro o tsukau tame ni wa, ___ o harawanakutewa ikemasen.

6. ＿＿＿で高速料金を払います。

___ de koosoku ryookin o haraimasu.

7. 次の＿＿＿で降りるので、左側の＿＿＿に移ります (change)。

Tsugi no ___ de oriru no de, hidari gawa no ___ ni utsurimasu.

8. この道は反対方向には行けません。＿＿＿です。

Kono michi wa hantai hookoo ni wa ikemasen. ___ desu.

9. ＿＿＿をよく見てください。赤(red)ですよ。

___ o yoku mite kudasai. Aka desu yo.

10. ラッシュアワーの時は、たいてい＿＿＿があります。

Rasshu awaa no toki wa, taitee ___ ga arimasu.

4. Identify each item in Fig. 6-3.

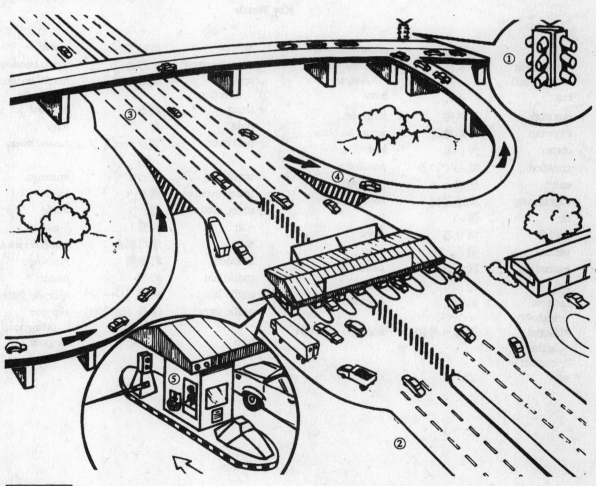

Fig. 6-3

4. Match.

1. 高速道路を使うために払うお金
   koosoku dooro o tsukau tamé ni harau okane

2. 高速道路を降りるところ
   koosoku dooro o oriru tokoro

3. 同じ方向にしか行けない道
   onaji hookoo ni shika ikenai michi

4. 二本の道が交差する(cross)ところ
   nihon no michi ga koosa suru tokoro

5. 高速道路のお金を払うところ
   koosoku dooro no okane o harau tokoro

6. 車が多い時間
   kuruma ga ooi jikan

7. 右にも左にも曲がらない
   migi ni mo hidari ni mo magaranai

(a) まっすぐ行く
    massugu iku

(b) 高速料金
    koosoku ryookin

(c) 角
    kado

(d) 出口
    deguchi

(e) ラッシュアワー
    rasshu awaa

(f) 料金所
    ryookinjo

(g) 一方通行
    ippoo tsuukoo

Key Words

be lost	道に迷う	*michi ni mayou*	on foot	歩いて	*aruite*
~ blocks (lit. ~th street)	~本目	*~ bonme(~ponme, ~honme)*	one-way street	一方通行	*ippoo tsuukoo*
			opposite direction	反対方向	*hantai hookoo*
bus	バス	*basu*			
bus stop	バス停	*basu tee*	return	戻る	*modoru*
city map	町の地図	*machi no chizu*	right	右	*migi*
corner	角	*kado*	rush hour	ラッシュアワー	*rasshu awaa*
crowded	混んでいる	*konde iru*			
exit	出口	*deguchi*	straight	まっすぐ	*massugu*
express way	高速道路	*koosoku dooro*	street (avenue)	通り	*toori*
far	遠い	*tooi*	street, road	道	*michi*
get off	降りる	*oriru*	~th	~目	*~ me*
get on	乗る	*noru*	toll	通行料金	*tsuukoo ryookin*
instead of	代わりに	*kawari ni*	tollbooth	料金所	*ryookinjo*
left	左	*hidari*	traffic jam	渋滞	*juutai*
national highway	国道	*kokudoo*	traffic lane	車線（レーン）	*sharyoo (reen)*
			traffic signal	信号（信号機）	*shingoo (shingooki)*
National highway number ~	国道~号線	*kokudoo ~ goosen*	turn	曲がる	*magaru*
near	近い	*chikai*			

CHECKING IN

ボーイ
booi

ルームキー
ruumu kii

宿泊カード
shukuhaku kaado

客（宿泊客）
kyaku
(shukuhaku kyaku)

クレジットカード
kurejitto kaado

Fig. 7-1

この**客**は**フロント**にいます。	guest, front desk
Kono *kyaku* wa *furonto* ni imasu.	
フロント係と話しています。	receptionist
Furonto gakari to hanashite imasu.	
シングルの部屋をお願いします。	single room
Shinguru no heya o onegaishimasu.	
ダブルの部屋	double
Daburu no heya	
ツインの部屋	twin
Tsuin no heya	
海側の部屋がいいです。	the side of the ocean
Umi gawa no heya ga ii desu.	

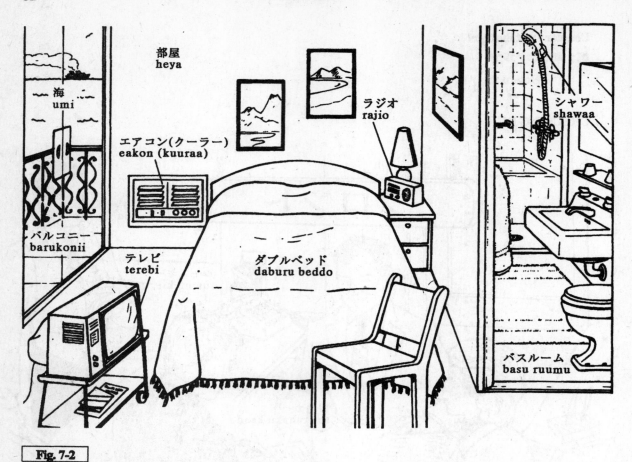

部屋
heya

海
umi

エアコン（クーラー）
eakon (kuuraa)

ラジオ
rajio

シャワー
shawaa

バルコニー
barukonii

テレビ
terebi

ダブルベッド
daburu beddo

バスルーム
basu ruumu

Fig. 7-2

庭側 *Niwa gawa*	courtyard
道路側 *Dooro gawa*	street
プール側 *Puuru gawa*	swimming pool
山側 *Yama gawa*	mountains
エアコン（クーラー）付きの部屋はありますか。 *Eakon (Kuuraaa) tsuki no heya wa arimasu ka.*	with air-conditioner
ヒーター（暖房） *Hiitaa (Danboo)*	heater
バルコニー *Barukonii*	balcony
テレビ *Terebi*	television set

バストイレ

Basu toire

bathroom (lit. bath and toilet)

シャワー

Shawaa

shower

食事付きですか。朝食付きですか。

Shokuji tsuki desu ka. *Chooshoku tsuki* desu ka.

with meal, with breakfast

宿泊料はいくらですか。

Shukuhakuryoo wa ikura desu ka.

hotel bill

サービス料込みですか。

Saabisuryoo komi desu ka.

service charges, included

税込みですか。

Zee komi desu ka.

tax

一泊でお願いします。

Ippaku de onegaishimashita.

one night stay

予約した田中です。

Yoyaku shita Tanaka desu.

reserved

満室ではありません。

Manshitsu dewa arimasen.

no vacancies (full)

部屋が空いています。空室があります。

Heya ga *aite imasu. Kuushitsu* ga arimasu.

vacant, vacant room

この宿泊カードにお名前とご住所をお願いします。

Kono *shukuhaku kaado* ni onamae to gojuusho o onegaishimasu.

hotel registeration card

お支払いはクレジットカードですか。

Oshiharai wa *kurejitto kaado* desu ka.

payment, credit card

ボーイが荷物を運びます。

Booi ga nimotsu o *hakobimasu.*

porter, carry

出かける時は、ルームキーをフロントにお預けください。

Dekakeru toki wa, *ruumukii* o furonto ni oazuke kudasai.

room key

1. Complete.

1. ＿＿＿の部屋は一人用(for one person)です。

   ___ no heya wa hitori yoo desu.

2. 二人用の部屋は、＿＿＿の部屋です。

   Futari yoo no heya wa, ___ no heya desu.

3. 二人の時は、＿＿＿の部屋と＿＿＿の部屋があります。

   Futari no toki wa, ___ no heya to ___ no heya ga arimasu.

4. 車が多いので、＿＿＿側の部屋はうるさいです。

   Kuruma ga ooi node, ___ gawa no heya wa urusai desu.

5. 海が見たいから、＿＿＿の部屋の方がいいです。

   Umi ga mitai kara, ___ no heya no hoo ga ii desu.

6. 今晩は外で食べます。＿＿＿はいりません。

   Konban wa soto de tabemasu. ___ wa irimasen.

7. 宿泊料はたいてい＿＿＿料込みですが、税込みじゃありません。

   Shukuhakuryoo wa taitee ___ ryoo komi desu ga, zee komi ja arimasen.

8. ＿＿＿で宿泊料を払う人が多いです。

   ___ de shukuhakuryoo o harau hito ga ooi desu.

9. 夏は暑いので＿＿＿を、冬は寒いので＿＿＿をつけます。

   Natsu wa atusi node ___ o, fuyu wa samui no de ___ o tsukemasu.

10. 少し高いでしょうが、バス＿＿＿付きの部屋がいいです。

    Sukoshi takai deshoo ga, basu ___ tsuki no heya ga ii desu.

11. 先週、電話でダブルの部屋を＿＿＿んですが。

    Senshuu, denwa de daburu no heya o ___ n desu ga.

12. フロントでは＿＿＿が働いています。

    Furonto de wa ___ ga hataraite imasu.

13. ホテルが＿＿＿の時は、部屋は空いていません。

    Hoteru ga ___ no toki wa, heya wa aite imasen.

14. ＿＿＿が荷物を部屋まで運んでくれます。

    ___ ga nimotsu o heya made hakonde kuremasu.

2. Complete.

＜ホテルのフロントで＞

＜Hoteru no furonto de＞

- いらっしゃいませ。

  Irasshaimase.

- 二人なんですが、＿1＿がありますか。

  Futari nan desu ga, _1_ ga arimasu ka.

- ご予約はありますか。

  Goyoyaku wa arimasu ka.

- いいえ、ありません。

  Iie, arimasen.

- 今日はほとんど＿2＿ですが、二人用のお部屋は二つあります。＿3＿のお部屋と＿4＿のお部屋と

  Kyoo wa hotondo _2_ desu ga, futari yoo no oheya wa futatsu arimasu. _3_ no oheya to _4_ no oheya to

  どちらの方がよろしいですか。

  dochira no hoo ga yoroshii desu ka.

- ダブルの方をお願いします。その部屋は海＿5＿ですか。

  Daburu no hoo o onegai shimasu. Sono heya wa umi _5_ desu ka.

- 申し訳ありません。空いているダブルのお部屋はすべて道路＿6＿です。

  Mooshiwake arimasen. Aite iru daburu no oheya wa subete dooro _6_ desu.

- そうですか。その部屋はいくらですか。

  Soo desu ka. Sono heya wa ikura desu ka.

- 一 _7_ 二万八千円です。

  I _7_ niman hassen en desu.

- _8_ 込みですか。

  _8_ komi desu ka.

- いいえ、税金(tax)は込みじゃありません。

  Iie, zeekin wa komi ja arimasen.

- そうですか。じゃあ、その部屋をお願いします。

  Soo desu ka. Jaa, sono heya o onegaishimasu.

- 何_9_ですか。

  Nan _9_ desu ka?

- 一_10_です。明日までです。

  I _10_ desu. Ashita made desu.

- では、この_11_にお名前とご住所をお願いします。

  Dewa, kono _11_ ni onamae to gojuusho o onegaishimasu.

ROOM SERVICE

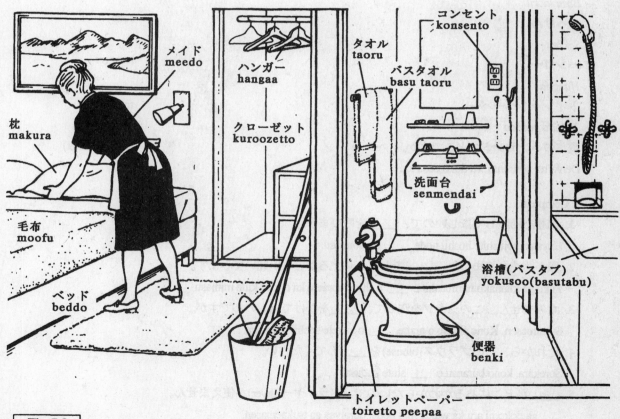

Fig. 7-3

洗濯をお願いできますか。   cleaning (laundry service)

Sentaku o onegai dekimasu ka.

これを**洗って**、**アイロンをかけて**ください。   wash, iron

Kore o *aratte, airon o kakete* kudsai.

ドライクリーニングをお願いします。   dry-cleaning

Dorai kuriiningu o onegai shimasu.

いつまでに**できます**か。   be ready

Itsu made ni *dekimasu* ka.

部屋を**掃除して**ください。   clean

Heya o *sooji* shite kudasai.

枕をもう一つください。   pillow

Makura o moo hitotsu kudasai.

毛布   blanket

Moofu

タオル   towel

Taoru

バスタオル   bath towel

Basu taoru

せっけん   soap

Sekken

ハンガー   hangers

Hangaa

トイレットペーパー   toilet paper

Toiretto peepaa

電気の**コンセント**はどこですか。   socket (outlet)

Denki no *konsento* wa doko desu ka.

3. Complete.

1. 部屋を掃除してほしいので、＿＿＿を呼びます。

   Heya o sooji shite hoshii node, ＿＿＿ o yobimasu.

2. 服が汚くなりました。＿＿＿をしてもらえるかどうか聞いてみます。

   Fuku ga kitanaku narimashita. ＿＿＿ o shite moraeru ka dooka kiite mimasu.

3. すみません。このシャツを洗って、＿＿＿をかけてほしいんですが。

   Sumimasen. Kono shatsu o aratte, ＿＿＿ o kakete hoshii ndesu ga.

4. それから、このブラウス(blouse)を＿＿＿してください。

   Sorekara, kono burausu o ＿＿＿ shite kudasai.

5. ＿＿＿がどこにあるかわからないので、ドライヤー(dryer)が使えません。

   ＿＿＿ ga doko ni aru ka wakaranai node, doraiyaa ga tsukaemasen.

6. 夕べはとても寒かったです。＿＿＿がもう一枚ほしいです。

   Yuube wa totemo samukatta desu. ＿＿＿ ga moo ichimai hoshii desu.

7. シャワーを使いたいんですが、小さいタオルはあるけれど＿＿＿がありません。

   Shawaa o tsukaitai ndesu ga, chiisai taoru wa aru keredo ＿＿＿ ga arimasen.

8. 手が洗いたいんですが、＿＿＿がありません。

   Te ga araitai ndesu ga, ＿＿ ga arimasen.

9. ＿＿＿の中にハンガーがあります。

   ＿＿ no naka ni hangaa ga arimasu.

10. トイレには予備(extra)の＿＿＿があります。

   Toire ni wa yobi no ＿＿ ga arimasu.

4.　Identify each item in Fig. 7-4.

Fig. 7-4

SOME PROBLEMS YOU MAY HAVE

洗面台がつまっています。

Senmendai ga tsumatte imasu.   washbasin, clogged

蛇口がこわれています。

Jaguchi ga kowarete imasu.   faucet, broken

ライト（電気）がつきません。

Raito (Denki) ga tsukimasen.   light, doesn't work

電球が切れています。

Denkyuu ga kirete imasu.   light bulb, burned out

スイッチがこわれています。   switch

Suicchi ga kowarete imasu.

トイレの水が流れません。   toilet, doesn't flush

Toire no mizu ga nagaremasen.

お湯が出ません。   hot water, doesn't come out

Oyu ga *demasen.*

5. Complete.

1. 電気をつけましたが、つきません。＿＿＿が切れているか、＿＿＿がこわれているのでしょう。

    Denki o tsukemashita ga, tsukimasen. ___ ga kirete iru ka, ___ ga kowarete iru no deshoo.

2. ＿＿＿がこわれているようです。全然、水が出ません。

    ___ ga kowarete iru yoo desu. Zenzen, mizu ga demasen.

3. ＿＿＿がつまっていて、手が洗えません。

    ___ ga tsumatte ite, te ga araemasen.

4. ＿＿＿が出ないから、シャワーが使えません。

    ___ ga denai kara, shawaa ga tsukaemasen.

CHECKING OUT

＜フロントの会計＞   cashier

＜Furonto no *kaikee*＞

何時までにチェックアウトしなければなりませんか。   check out

Nanji made ni chekku auto shinakereba narimasen ka.

811 号室ですが、請求書をお願いします。   bill

Happyaku juuichi gooshitsu desu ga, *seekyuusho* o onegai shimasu.

このルームサービスの請求は私のではありません。   room service, charge

Kono *ruumu saabisu* no *seekyuu* wa watashi no dewa arimasen.

クレジットカードが使えますか。   credit card

Kurejitto kaado ga tsukaemasu ka.

お電話をおかけになりましたか。   telephone

O*denwa* o okake ni narimashita ka.

合計で三万二千円になります。   in total

Gookoo de sanman nisen en ni narimasu.

6. Complete.

- 811 号室の＿1＿書をお願いします。

    Happyaku juuichi gooshitsu no ＿1＿ sho o onegaishimasu.

- お名前は。

    Onamae wa.

- ブラウンです。

    Buraun desu.

- 今朝、お＿2＿をおかけになりましたか。

  Kesa, o ＿2＿ o okake ni narimashita ka.

- いいえ。

  Iie.

- では、＿3＿二万八千円になります。

  Dewa, ＿3＿ niman hassen en ni narimasu.

- あのう。すみませんが、この＿4＿の請求は私のではありません。私は部屋で何も

  Anoo. Sumimasen ga, kono ＿4＿ no seekyuu wa watashi no dewa arimasen. Watashi wa heya de nani mo

  頼んでいませんから。

  tanonde imasen kara.

- あ、これは911号室のでした。申し訳ありません。

  A, kore wa kyuuhyaku juuichi gooshitsu no deshita. Mooshiwake arimasen.

- ＿5＿が使えますか。

  ＿5＿ ga tsukaemasu ka.

- はい、どちらのカードをお使いになりますか。

  Hai, dochira no kaado o otsukai ni narimasu ka.

7. Complete.

1. ホテルに着いたら、まず＿＿＿へ行って＿＿＿と話します。

    Hoteru ni tsuitara, mazu ＿＿ e itte ＿＿ to hanashimasu.

2. たいてい、客は＿＿＿に住所と名前を書かなければなりません。

    Taitee, kyaku wa ＿＿ ni juusho to namae o kakanakereba narimasen.

3. 一人の時は、＿＿＿の部屋に泊まります。二人の時は、ベッドが二つある＿＿＿の部屋か、大きい

    Hitori no toki wa, ＿＿ no heya ni tomarimasu. Futari no toki wa, beddo ga futatsu aru ＿＿ no heya ka, ookii

    ベッドが ある＿＿＿の部屋に泊まります。

    beddo ga aru ＿＿ no heya ni tomarimasu.

4. たいていのホテルでは＿＿＿料込みです。

    Taihee no hoteru de wa ＿＿ ryoo komi desu.

5. ＿＿＿側の部屋は車の音(sound)がするのであまり静かじゃありません。

    ＿＿ gawa no heya wa kuruma no oto ga suru node amari shizuka ja arimasen.

6. ホテルに泊まる時、＿＿＿をしてから行った方がいいでしょう。

    Hoteru ni tomaru toki, ＿＿ o site kara itta hoo ga ii deshoo.

7. ホテルの部屋が空いていない時、そのホテルは＿＿＿です。

    Hoteru no heya ga aite inai toki, sono hoteru wa ＿＿ desu.

8. ボーイは客が＿＿＿を運ぶのを手伝います。

    Booi wa kyaku ga ＿＿ o hakobu no o tetsudaimasu.

9. ＿＿＿は部屋の掃除をします。

    ＿＿ wa heya no sooji o shimasu.

10. 暑い時のために、部屋には＿＿＿があります。

    Atsui toki no tame ni, heya ni wa ＿＿ ga arimasu.

11. 寝る時、寒ければ＿＿をもう一枚もらいます。

   Neru toki, samukereba ___ o moo ichimai moraimasu.

12. 服をかける(hang)ために＿＿の中にハンガーがあります。

   Fuku o kakeru tame ni ___ no naka ni hangaa ga arimasu.

13. ホテルでは洗濯がしてもらえます。服を＿＿、それからアイロンをかけてくれます。

   Hoteru de wa sentaku ga shite moraemasu. Fuku o ___, sorekara airon o kakete kuremasu.

14. ＿＿の時間が決まっています。客はホテルを出る日の昼ごろまでに部屋を出なければなりません。

   ___ no jikan ga kimatte imasu. Kyaku wa hoteru o deru hi no hiru goro made ni heya o denakereba narimasen.

15. チェックアウトする時はフロントの＿＿でします。

   Chekku auto suru toki wa, furonto no ___ de shimasu.

16. ＿＿料をクレジットカードで払う客が多いです。

   ___ ryoo o kurejitto kaado de harau kyaku ga ooi desu.

Fig. 7-5

8. Answer on the basis of Fig. 7-5.

1. この部屋は道路側ですか。

   Kono heya wa dooro gawa desu ka.

2. バルコニーがありますか。

   Barukonii ga arimasu ka.

3. どんなベッドがありますか。

   Don-na beddo ga arimasu ka.

4. この部屋はどんな部屋ですか。

   Kono heya wa don-na heya desu ka.

5. バスルームがありますか。

   Basu ruumu ga arimasu ka.

9. Look at Fig. 7-6 and correct each false statement.

Fig. 7-6

1. この人たちはホテルの部屋にいます。

   Kono hitotachi wa hoteru no heya ni imasu.

2. この人たちはホテルを出ます。

   Kono hitotachi wa hoteru o demasu.

3. この人たちはボーイと話しています。

   Kono hitotachi wa booi to hanashite imasu.

4. この男の人は請求書に住所と名前を書いています。

   Kono otoko no hito wa seekyuusho ni juusho to namae o kaite imasu.

5. フロント係はルームキーを持っています。

Furonto gakari wa ruumukii o motte imasu.

Fig. 7-7

10. Answer on the basis of Fig. 7-7.

1. この部屋はどんな部屋ですか。

Kono heya wa don-na heya desu ka.

2. ベッドはありますか。

Beddo wa arimasu ka.

3. 誰が部屋で働いていますか。

Dare ga heya de hataraite imasu ka.

4. この人は何をしていますか。

Kono hito wa nani o shite imasu ka.

5. クローゼットには何がありますか。

Kuroozetto ni wa nani ga arimasu ka.

6. 洗面台は部屋にありますか、バスルームにありますか。

Senmendai wa heya ni arimasu ka, basu ruumu ni arimasu ka.

7. バスルームにシャワーがありますか。

Basu ruumu ni shawaa ga arimasu ka.

Key Words

air-conditioner	エアコン（クーラー）	eakon (kuuraa)	iron	アイロンをかける	airon o kakeru
balcony	バルコニー	barukonii	light	ライト（電気）	raito (denki)
bathtab	浴槽（バスタブ）	yokusoo (basu tabu)	light bulb	電球	denkyuu
bath towel	バスタオル	basu taoru	maid	メイド	meido
bathroom	バスルーム	basu ruumu	mountains	山	yama
bathroom (lit. bath and toilet)	バストイレ	basu toire	no vacancies (full)	満室	manshitsu
			ocean	海	umi
be ready	できる	dekiru	one night stay	一泊	ippaku
bed	ベッド	beddo	payment	支払い	shiharai
bill	請求書	seekyuusho	pillow	枕	makura
blanket	毛布	moofu	porter	ボーイ	booi
broken	こわれている	kowarete iru	radio	ラジオ	rajio
burned out	切れている	kirete iru	receptionist	フロント係	furonto gakari
carry	運ぶ	hakobu	reserve	予約する	yoyaku
charge	請求	seekyuu	room	部屋	heya
check out	チェックアウト	chekku auto	room key	ルームキー（かぎ）	ruumukii (kagi)
clean	掃除する	sooji suru	room service	ルームサービス	ruumu saabisu
cleaning (laundry service)	洗濯	sentaku	service charges	サービス料	saabisuryoo
			shower	シャワー	shawaa
clogged	つまっている	tsumatte iru	single room	シングルの部屋	shinguru no heya
closet	クローゼット	kuroozetto			
come out	出る	deru	soap	せっけん	sekken
courtyard	庭	niwa	socket (outlet)	コンセント	konsento
credit card	クレジットカード	kurejitto kaado	street	道路	dooro
			swimming pool	プール	puuru
double	ダブルの部屋	daburu no heya	switch	スイッチ	suicchi
double bed	ダブルベッド	daburu beddo	tax	税	zee
dry-cleaning	ドライクリーニング	dorai kuriiningu	telephone	電話	denwa
			television set	テレビ	terebi
			the side of ~	～側	~ gawa
faucet	蛇口	jaguchi	toilet	トイレ	toire
flush	流れる	nagareru	toilet	便器	benki
front desk	フロント	furonto	toilet paper	トイレットペーパー	toiretto peepaa
guests	客	kyaku			
hanger	ハンガー	hangaa	towel	タオル	taoru
heater	ヒーター（暖房）	hiitaa (danboo)	turn on, work	つく	tsuku
			twin	ツインの部屋	tsuin no heya
hot water	お湯	oyu	vacant	空いている	aite iru
hotel bill	宿泊料	shukuhakuryoo	vacant room	空室	kuushitsu
hotel registration card	宿泊カード	shukuhaku kaado	wash	洗う	arau
			washbasin	洗面台	senmendai
in total	合計で	gookee de	with breakfast	朝食付き	chooshoku tsuki
included	込み	komi	with meal	食事付き	shokuji tsuki

Chapter 8: At the bank
第8章：銀行で
Ginkoo de

EXCHANGING MONEY

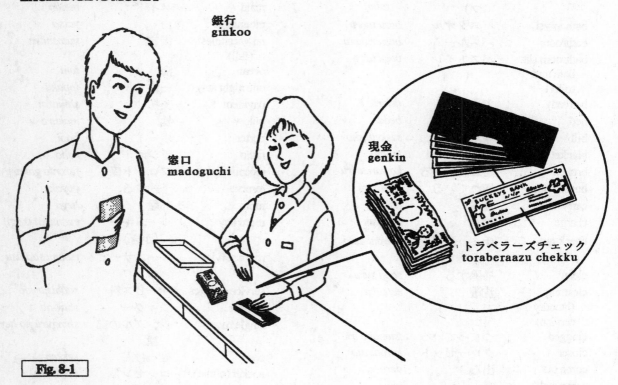

銀行
ginkoo

窓口
madoguchi

現金
genkin

トラベラーズチェック
toraberaazu chekku

Fig. 8-1

銀行はどこですか。	bank
Ginkoo wa doko desu ka.	
外国為替のカウンターはどこにありますか。	foreign exchange counter
Gaikoku kawase no kauntaa wa doko ni arimasu ka.	
日本のお金(円)がいります。	Japanese yen
Nihono no okane (En) ga irimasu.	
500 ドルを円に替えます。	exchange 500 dollars into yen
Gohyaku doru o en ni kaemasu.	
今日の為替レートはいくらですか。	exchange rate
Kyoo no *kawase reeto* wa ikura desu ka.	
トラベラーズチェックですか、現金ですか。	traveler's check, cash
Toraberaazu chekku desu ka, *genkin* desu ka.	
1 ドル105円です。	105 yen to the dollar
Ichi doru hyakugo en desu.	
手数料はいくらですか。	commission charges
Tesuuryoo wa ikura desu ka.	

あちらの**窓口**へどうぞ。   cashier's window

Achira no *madoguchi* e doozo.

1. Complete.

ジョーンズさんは日本に来ましたが、まだ日本の＿**1**＿を持っていません。500 ドルを＿**2**＿に替えたい

Joonzu san wa Nihon ni kimashita ga, mada Nihon no ＿**1**＿ o motte imasen. Gohyaku doru o ＿**2**＿ ni kaetai

です。でも、ホテルでは替えたくありません。ホテルは＿**3**＿料が高いからです。＿**4**＿で替えるつもり

desu. Demo, hoteru de wa kaetaku arimasen. Hoteru wa ＿**3**＿ ryoo ga takai kara desu. ＿**4**＿ de kaeru tsumori

です。

desu.

2. Complete.

- 500 ドルを円に＿**1**＿ください。

  Gohyaku doru o en ni ＿**1**＿ kudasai.

- はい。

  Hai.

- 為替＿**2**＿はいくらですか。

  Kawase ＿**2**＿ wa ikura desu ka.

- トラベラーズチェックですか、＿**3**＿ですか。

  Toraberaazu chekku desu ka, ＿**3**＿ desu ka.

- トラベラーズチェックです。

  Toraberaazu chekku desu.

- 今日の為替＿**4**＿は1＿**5**＿105 円です。

  Kyoo no kawase ＿**4**＿ ha ichi ＿**5**＿ hyakugo en desu.

- どうも。

  Doomo.

MAKING CHANGE

<店で>

<Mise de>

現金でお願いします。   cash

Genkin de onegaishimasu.

今、トラベラーズチェックしか持っていません。

Ima, toraberaazu chekku shika motte imasen.

トラベラーズチェックを現金にします。   cash the traveler's check

Toraberaazu chekku o genkin ni shimasu.

大きいお札しかありません。   large bills

Ookii osatsu shika arimasen.

小銭（小さいお金）がありません。   small change

Kozeni (Chiisai okane) ga arimasen.

この一万円札をくずしてもらえませんか。   break the 10,000 yen bill

Kono ichiman en satsu o kuzushite moraemasen ka.

3. Complete.

その店はトラベラーズチェックが使えなかったので、＿1＿で払いました。だから、今＿2＿がありません。

Sono mise wa toraberaazu cheeku ga tsukaenakatta node, ＿1＿ de haraimashita. Dakara, ima ＿2＿ ga arimasen.

銀行へ行ってトラベラーズチェックを＿3＿。

Ginkoo e itte toraberaazu chekku o ＿3＿.

4. Complete.

すみません。＿1＿が全然ないんですが、この千円＿2＿を＿3＿もらえませんか。

Sumimasen. ＿1＿ ga zenzen nai n desu ga, kono sen en ＿2＿ o ＿3＿ moraemasen ka.

5. Complete.

＜銀行で＞

＜Ginkoo de＞

- ＿1＿を現金にしたいんですが。＿2＿レートはいくらですか。

  ＿1＿ o genkin ni shitai n desu ga. ＿2＿ reeto wa ikura desu ka.

- 1ドル105＿3＿です。

  Ichi doru hyakugo ＿3＿ desu.

＜窓口で＞

＜Madoguchi de＞

五万円ですね。一万円＿4＿五枚でよろしいですか。

Goman en desu ne. Ichiman en ＿4＿ go mai de yoroshii desu ka.

この一万円＿5＿を＿6＿もらえませんか。

Kono ichiman en ＿5＿ o ＿6＿ moraemasen ka.

はい。＿7＿が十枚です。

Hai. ＿7＿ ga juu mai desu.

何度もすみませんが、＿8＿が全然ないんです。この千円札をくずしてください。

Nando mo sumimasen ga, ＿8＿ ga zenzen nai ndesu. Kono senen satsu o kuzushite kudasai.

OPEN AN ACCOUNT

普通預金の口座が開きたいです。   ordinary deposit, account,

Futsuu yokin no kooza ga hirakitai desu.   want to open

預金をします。   make a deposit

Yokin o shimasu.

1,000 ドル**預けます**。   deposit

Sen doru *azukemasu.*

預金の窓口の人にお金と**通帳**と**印鑑**を**渡**します。   bankbook, name seal (inkan),

Yokin no madoguchi no hito ni okane to *tsuuchoo* to *inkan* o *watashimasu.*   give

私の通帳の**預金残高**はいくらですか。   balance

Watashi no tsuuchoo no *yokin zandaka* wa ikura desu ka.

銀行には **ATM（現金自動預け払い機）**があります。   ATM

Ginkoo ni wa *ee-ti- emu (genkin jidoo azukebaraii ki)* ga arimasu.

ATM でお金を**おろ**したり、預けたり、預金残高を**調べ**たりすること   withdraw, check

Ee-tii-emu de okane o *oroshita*ri, azuketari, yokin zandaka o *shirabeta*ri suru koto

ができます。

ga dekimasu.

ATM を使うには**キャッシュカード**と**暗証番号**が必要です。   cash card, PIN

Ee-tii-emu o tsukau ni wa *kyasshu kaado* to *anshoo bangoo* ga hitsuyoo desu.

6. Complete.

私は銀行に普通＿＿1＿＿の口座があります。明日、私の＿＿2＿＿に 1,000 ドル預けに行きます。

Watashi wa ginkoo ni futsuu ＿1＿ no kooza ga arimasu. Ashita, watashi no ＿2＿ ni sen doru azuke ni ikimasu.

銀行で預金の＿＿3＿＿へ行きます。そこでお金と＿＿4＿＿と＿＿5＿＿を渡します。銀行の＿＿6＿＿を使う

Ginkoo de yokin no ＿3＿ e ikimasu. Soko de okane to ＿4＿ to ＿5＿ o watashimasu. Ginkoo no ＿6＿ o tsukau

時は印鑑はいりませんが、銀行の＿＿7＿＿と暗証番号がいります。

toki wa inkan wa irimasen ga, ginkoo no ＿7＿ to anshoo bangoo ga irimasu.

7. Complete each item with an appropriate verb.

1. 日本のお金がいります。トラベラーズチェックを＿＿＿＿。

   Nihon no okane ga irimasu. Toraberaazu chekku o ＿＿.

2. 今使わないお金がたくさんあります。銀行の口座に＿＿＿＿。

   Ima tsukawanai okane ga takusan arimasu. Ginkoo no kooza ni ＿＿.

3. 小銭がありません。お札を＿＿＿＿。

   Kozeni ga arimasen. Osatsu o ＿＿.

4. 今、現金がいります。ATM でお金を＿＿＿＿。

   Ima, genkin ga irimasu. Ee-tii-emu de okane o ＿＿.

5. ドルを円に＿＿＿＿。

   Doru o en ni ＿＿.

Key Words

account	口座	*kooza*	exchange rate	為替レート	*kawase reeto*
ATM	ATM（現金自動預け払い機)	*ee-tii-emu (genkin jidoo azukebarai ki)*	foreign exchange	外国為替	*gàikoku kawase*
			give	渡す	*watasu*
balance	預金残高	*yokin zandaka*	Japanese yen	日本のお金（円)	*Nihon no okane (en)*
bank	銀行	*ginkoo*			
bankbook	通帳	*tsuuchoo*	make a deposit	預金をする	*yokin o suru*
bill	お札	*osatsu*	name seal (inkan)	印鑑	*inkan*
break money bill	くずす	*kuzusu*	open	開く	*hiraku*
cash	現金にする	*genkin ni suru*	ordinary deposit	普通預金	*futsuu yokin*
cash	現金	*genkin*			
cash card	キャッシュカード	*kyasshu kaado*	PIN	暗証番号	*anshoo bangoo*
			small change	小銭（小さいお金)	*kozeni (chiisai okane)*
cashier's window	窓口	*madoguchi*			
			traveler's check	トラベラーズチェック	*toraberaazu chekku*
check	調べる	*shiraberu*			
counter	カウンター	*kauntaa*	withdraw	おろす	*orosu*
deposit	預ける	*azukeru*	yen	円	*en*
dollars	ドル	*doru*			
exchange	替える	*kaeru*			

Chapter 9: At the post office
第9章：郵便局で
Yuubinkyoku de

SENDING A LETTER

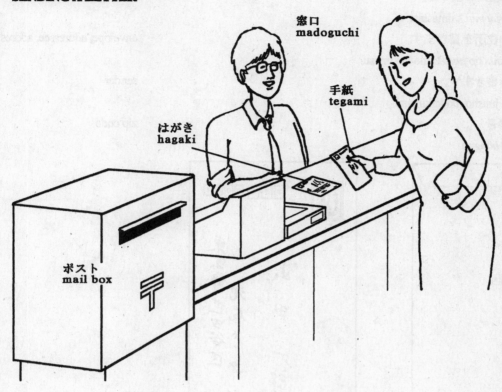

窓口
madoguchi

手紙
tegami

はがき
hagaki

ポスト
mail box

Fig. 9-1

手紙を書きました。	letter
Tegami o kakimashita.	
はがき	postcard
Hagaki	
でも、**切手**がないから、**出す**ことができません。	stamps, send out
Demo, *kitte* ga nai kara, *dasu* koto ga dekimasen.	
郵便局へ行きます。	post office
Yuubinkyoku e ikimasu.	
この手紙を出したいんですが、**いくらかかりますか**。	How much does it cost?
Kono tegami o dashitai n desu ga, *ikura kakarimasu ka.*	
速達で送ります。	by express mail, send
Sokutatsu de okurimasu.	
書留	registered mail
Kakitome	

普通郵便   regular

Futsuu yuubin

切手の**自動販売機**でも切手を買うことができます。   vending machine

Kitte no *jidoo hanbaiki* de mo kitte o kau koto ga dekimasu.

100 円切手を十枚買いました。   ten 100 yen stamp

Hyaku en kitte o juu mai kaimashita.

封筒に**受取人**の**住所**を書きます。   envelope, addressee, address

Fuutoo ni *uketorinin* no *juusho* mo kakimasu.

差出人の住所も書きます。   sender

Sashidashinin no juusho mo kakimasu.

　　　　　　　郵便番号   zip code

　　　　　　　yuubin bangoo

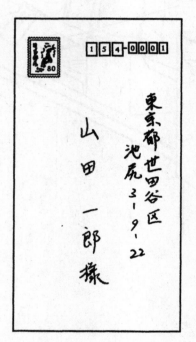

Fig. 9-2

1. Complete.

この＿_1_＿を出したいですが、＿_2_＿に入れる前に**切手**を買わなくてはいけません。いくら＿_3_＿か

Kono ＿_1_＿ o dashitai desu ga, ＿_2_＿ ni ireru mae ni kitte o kawanakute wa ikemasen. Ikura ＿_3_＿ ka

分からないから、＿_4_＿へ行かなくてはなりません。

wakaranai kara, ＿_4_＿ e ikanakute wa narimasen.

2. Complete.

- この＿_1_＿を出したいんですが、いくらですか。

  Kono ＿_1_＿ o dashitai ndesu ga, ikura desu ka.

- 普通郵便ですか、__2__ですか。

  Futsuu yuubin desu ka, __2__ desu ka.

- 速達でお願いします。

  Sokutatsu de onegai shimasu.

- 350 円です。

  Sanbyaku gojuu en desu.

- はい。それから、80 円__3__を二枚ください。

  Hai. Sorekara, hachijuu en __3__ o ni mai kudasai.

- はい。

  Hai.

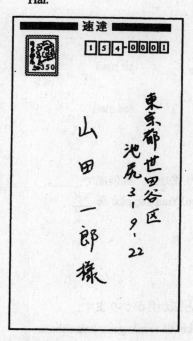

Fig. 9-3

3. Answer on the basis of Fig. 9-3.

1. この手紙を出すのにはいくらかかりますか。

   Kono tegami o dasu no ni wa ikura kakarimasu ka.

2. この手紙は普通郵便ですか、速達ですか。

   Kono tegami wa futsuu yuubin desu ka, sokutatsu desu ka.

3. 受取人の郵便番号はいくつですか。

   Uketorinin no yuubin bangoo wa ikutsu desu ka.

SENDING A PACKEGE

この**荷物**を送ります。   package, send

Kono *nimotsu* o *okurimasu.*

重さはどのぐらいですか。	weight, how much
Omosa wa *donogurai* desu ka.	
さあ、分かりません。計ってくれませんか。	weigh
Saa, wakarimasen. *Hakatte* kuremasen ka.	
保険をかけますか。	insure
Hoken o kakemasu ka.	
こわれものですか。	fragile article
Koearemono desu ka.	
この用紙に記入してください。	form, fill in
Kono *yooshi* ni *kinyuu shite* kudasai.	
着くのにどのぐらいかかりますか。	arrive
Tsuku no ni donogurai kakarimasu ka.	
航空便だと一週間ぐらいです。	air mail
Kookuubin da to isshuukan gurai desu.	
船便だと二ヶ月ぐらいです。	sea mail
Funabin da to nikagetsu gurai desu.	

4. Complete.

1. この＿＿＿をアメリカに送りたいですが、＿＿＿がどのぐらいか分かりません。郵便局で＿＿＿。

   Kono ＿＿ o Amerika ni okuritai desu ga, ＿＿ ga donogurai ka wakarimasen. Yuubinkyoku de ＿＿.

2. この荷物は高いものじゃありません。＿＿＿はかけなくていいです。

   Kono nimotsu wa takai mono ja arimasen. ＿＿ wa kakenakute ii desu.

3. この荷物は＿＿＿です。陶器(chinaware)が入っています。

   Kono nimotsu wa ＿＿ desu. Tooki ga haitte imasu.

4. この荷物を＿＿＿便で送れば一週間しかかかりませんが、＿＿＿便だと二か月かかります。

   Kono nimotsu o ＿＿ bin de okureba isshuukan shika kakarimasen ga, ＿＿ bin da to nikagetsu kakarimasu.

   もちろん、＿＿＿便は＿＿＿便よりずっと安いです。

   Mochiron, ＿＿ bin wa ＿＿ bin yori zutto yasui desu.

OTHER WORDS YOU MAY NEED

私に郵便物は来ていませんか。	mail
Watashi ni *yuubinbutsu* wa kite imasen ka.	
郵便物は日曜日を除いて毎日配達されます。	except, delivered
Yuubin butsu wa nichiyoobi *o nozoite* mainichi *haitatsu saremasu*.	
郵便配達員が郵便物を配達します。	mail carrier
Yuubin haitatsuin ga yuubinbutsu o haitatsu shimasu.	
私書箱を持っていますか。	post office box
Shishobako o motte imasu ka.	
郵便為替はどこで買えますか。	postal money order
Yuubin kawase wa doko de kaemasu ka.	

5. Complete.

1. ＿＿ をもらうのに郵便局へ行く必要はありません。＿＿＿が家まで配達してくれます。

　　 ___ o morau no ni yuubinkyoku e iku hitsuyoo wa arimasen. ___ ga uchi made haitatsu shite kuremasu.

2. 郵便物をたくさんもらう人は郵便局に＿＿＿を持つことができます。

　　 Yuubin butsu o takusan morau hito wa yuubinkyoku ni ___ o motsu koto ga dekimasu.

3. お金が送りたい時は、郵便＿＿＿を買って送ることができます。

　　 Okane ga okuritai toki wa, yuubin ___ o katte okuru koto ga dekimasu.

Key Words

address	住所	juusho
addressee	受取人	uketorinin
air mail	航空便（エアメール）	kookuubin (eameeru)
arrive	着く	tsuku
be delivered	配達される	haitatsu sareru
cashier's window	窓口	madoguchi
cost	かかる	kakaru
envelope	封筒	fuutoo
except ~	～を除いて	~ o nozoite
express mail	速達	sokutatsu
fill in	記入する	kinyuu suru
form,	用紙	yooshi
fragile article	こわれもの	kowaremono
how much	いくら	ikura
how much	どのぐらい	donogurai
insure	保険をかける	hoken o kakeru
letter	手紙	tegami
mail	郵便物	yuubinbutsu
mail carrier	郵便配達員	yuubin haitatsuin
mailbox	ポスト	posuto
package	荷物	nimotsu
post office	郵便局	yuubinkyoku
post office box	私書箱	shishobako
postal money order	郵便為替	yuubin kawase
postcard	はがき	hagaki
registered mail	書留	kakitome
regular mail	普通郵便	futsuu yuubin
sea mail	船便	hunabin
send	送る	okuru
send out	出す	dasu
sender	差出人	sashidashinin
stamp	切手	kitte
vending machine	自動販売機	jidoo hanbaiki
weigh	計る	hakaru
weight	重さ	omosa
zip code	郵便番号	yuubin bangoo

Chapter 10: Making a telephone call
第10章：電話をかける
Denwa o kakeru

MAKING A TELEPHONE CALL

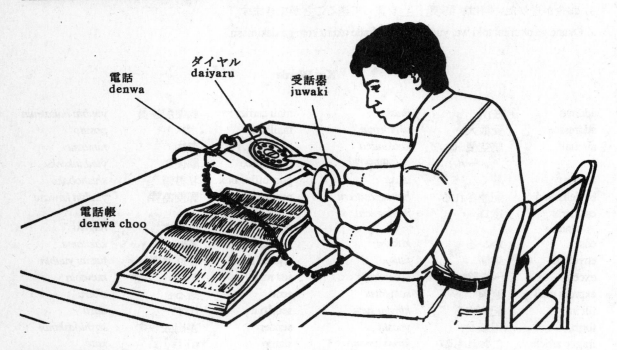

電話
denwa

ダイヤル
daiyaru

受話器
juwaki

電話帳
denwa choo

Fig. 10-1

電話をかけます（します）。	call
Denwa o kakemasu.	
電話番号が分かりません。	phone number
Denwa bangoo ga wakarimasen.	
電話帳を見なくてはいけません。	phone book
Denwachoo o minakutewa ikemasen.	
市外局番は何番ですか。	area code, what number
Shigai kyokuban wa *nan ban* desu ka.	
市内通話なら、市外局番はいりません。	local call
Shinai tsuuwa nara, shigai kyokuban wa irimasen.	
受話器をとります。	receiver
Juwaki o torimasu.	
発信音が聞こえたら、電話番号をダイヤルします。	dial tone, dial
Hasshin on ga kikoetara, denwa bangoo o *daiyaru shimasu*.	
呼び出し音が鳴ります。	ringing tone, sound
Yobidashion ga *narimasu*.	

相手が出ます。   the other party, answer (lit. appear)

Aite ga demasu.

1. Complete.

田中さんに＿1＿がかけたいです。でも＿2＿が分かりません。＿3＿を見ます。番号がありました。

Tanaksan ni ＿1＿ ga kaketai desu. Demo ＿2＿ ga wakarimasen. ＿3＿ o mimasu. Bangoo ga arimashita.

03-3312-2468 です。田中さんは市内に住んでいるので、これは市内＿4＿です。

Zero san no san san ichi ni no ni yon roku hachi desu. Tanaka san wa shinai ni sunde iru node, kore wa shinai ＿4＿ desu.

市内＿5＿の時には、＿6＿はいりません。＿7＿をとります。＿8＿を聞いてから、番号を＿9＿します。

Shinai ＿5＿ no toki ni wa, ＿6＿ wa irimasen. ＿7＿ o torimasu. ＿8＿ o kiite kara, bangoo o ＿9＿ shimasu.

＿10＿が聞こえます。田中さんが＿11＿。

＿10＿ ga kikoemasu. Tanaka san ga ＿11＿.

CELLULAR PHONES

携帯電話
keetai denwa

コードレス電話
koodoresu denwa

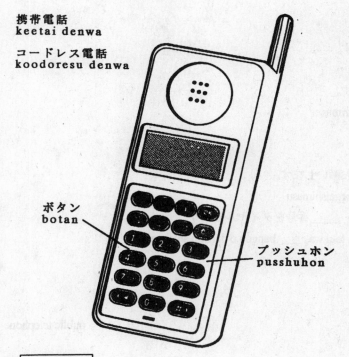

ボタン
botan

プッシュホン
pusshuhon

Fig. 10-2

2. Complete.

1. プッシュホンをかける時に、＿＿＿を押します。

   Pusshu hon o kakeru toki ni, ＿＿ o oshimasu.

2. ＿＿＿電話はコードがありません。

   ＿＿ denwa wa koodo ga arimasen.

3. 歩きながら＿＿＿電話をかけている人がよくいます。

   Aruki nagara ＿＿ denwa o kakete iru hito ga yoku imasu.

MAKING A LONG DISTANCE CALL

長距離電話をかけます。　　　　　　　　　　　　long distance call
Chookyori denwa o kakemasu.

市外電話　　　　　　　　　　　　　　　　　　out-of-town call
Shigai denwa

国際電話をかける時は、国番号を押して直接ダイヤルすることができます。　international call,
Kokusai denwa o kakeru toki wa, *kuni bangoo* o *oshite chokusetsu* daiyaru suru koto ga dekimasu.　country code, directly

指名通話の時は、初めに交換手（オペレーター）と話します。　person-to-person call,
Shimee tsuuwa no toki wa, hajime ni *kookanshu (opereetaa)* to hanashimasu.　operator

料金を払わないで電話をかけます。コレクトコールでかけます。　fare, collect call
Ryookin o harawanaide denwa o kakemasu. *Korekuto kooru* de kakemaseu.

もしもし。　　　　　　　　　　　　　　　　Hello.
Moshi moshi.

3. Complete.
1. 市内通話じゃありません。＿＿＿通話です。
   Shinai tsuuwa ja arimasen. ＿＿ tsuuwa desu.
2. 市外通話の時は、初めに＿＿＿がいります。
   Shigai tsuuwa no toki wa, hajime ni ＿＿ ga irimasu.
3. お金がありません。＿＿＿でかけます。
   Okane ga arimasen. ＿＿ de kakemasu.
4. 田中さんとだけ話したいです。＿＿＿をお願いします。
   Tanaka san to dake hanashitai desu. ＿＿ o onegaishimasu.
5. 直接アメリカに＿＿＿電話をかける時は、＿＿＿番号をダイヤルします。
   Chokusetsu Amerika ni ＿＿ denwa o kakeru toki wa, ＿＿ bangoo o daiyaru shimasu.

USING A PUBLIC TELEPHONE

公衆電話はどこにありますか。　　　　　　　　public telephone
Kooshuu denwa wa doko ni arimasu ka.

電話ボックスはどこですか。　　　　　　　　　telephone booth
Denwa bokkusu wa doko desu ka.

テレホンカードはありますか。　　　　　　　　prepaid telephone card
Terehon kaado wa arimasu ka.

番号が分からない時は、番号案内に電話するといいでしょう。　directory assistance
Bangoo ga wakaranai toki wa, *bangoo an-nai* ni denwa suru to ii deshoo.

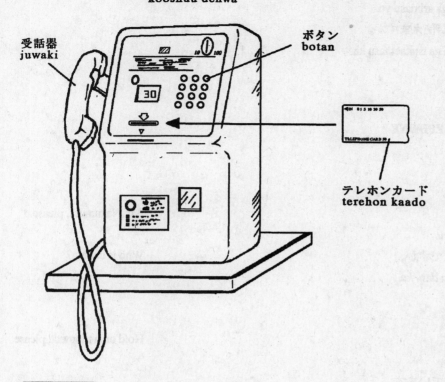

公衆電話
kooshuu denwa

受話器
juwaki

ボタン
botan

テレホンカード
terehon kaado

Fig. 10-3

<電話のかけ方>

<Denwa no kakekata>

1. 受話器を取ります。

   Juwaki o torimasu.

2. テレホンカードを入れます。

   Terehon kaado o iremasu.

3. 発信音を聞きます。

   Hasshin-on o kikimasu.

4. 番号をダイヤルします。

   Bangoo o daiyaru shimasu.

4. Complete.

- 森さんの電話番号を知っていますか。

  Mori san no denwa bangoo o shitte imasu ka.

- いいえ、知りません。番号__1__に電話して聞いたらどうですか。

  Iie, shirimasen. Bangoo __1__ ni denwa shite kiitara doo desu ka.

- このへんに__2__電話はありませんか。

  Kono hen ni __2__ denwa wa arimasen ka.

- 駅の前に電話 __3__ がありますよ。

　Eki no mae ni denwa _3_ ga arimasu yo.

- その電話は __4__ カードが使えますか。

　Sono denwa wa _4_ kaado ga tsukaemasu ka.

- はい、使えますよ。

　Hai, tsukaemasu yo.

SPEAKING ON THE TELEPHONE

もしもし。
Moshi moshi.

中村さん、お願いします。   Mr. Nakamura, please.
Nakamura san, onegaishimasu.

どなたですか／どちらさまですか。   Who is calling?
Donata desu ka/Dochira sama desu ka.

ブラウンです。
Buraun desu.

少々お待ちください。   Hold on a moment, please.
Shoo shoo omachi kudasai.

すみませんが、今、出かけています。
Sumimasen ga, ima, dekakete imasu.

何か伝えましょうか。   Would you like to leave a
Nanika tsutaemashoo ka.   message? (Lit. Shall I tell him a
                                                                    message?)

ええ、お願いします。
Ee, onegaishimasu.

5. Use the following as a guide to make up your own telephone conversation.

- もしもし。

　Moshi moshi.

- __1__。 __2__ さん、お願いします。

　_1_. _2_ san, onegaishimasu.

- __3__ ですか。

　_3_ desu ka.

- __4__ です。

　_4_ desu.

- 少々 __5__。

　Shoo shoo _5_.

- __6__ が、今、出かけています。何か伝えましょうか。

　_6_ ga, ima, dekakete imasu. Nanika tsutaemashoo ka.

- ええ、＿＿７＿＿。

Ee, _7_.

SOME THINGS THAT MAY GO WRONG

発信音が聞こえません。	dial tone, doesn't ring
Hasshin-on ga *kikoemasen.*	
この電話は故障しています。	out of order
Kono denwa wa *koshoo shite imasu*	
電話がつながりません。	can't be connected
Denwa ga *tsunagarimasen.*	
話し中です。	The line is busy.
Hanashichuu desu.	
雑音が入ります。	noise
Zatsuon ga hairimasu.	
電話が切れてしまいました。	cut off
Denwa ga *kirete* shimaimashita.	
誰も電話に出ません。	No one answers.
Dare mo denwa ni demasen.	
番号を間違えました。	dial a wrong number
Bangoo o machigaemashita.	
後でかけ直してみます。	call back
Ato de *kakenaoshite* mimasu.	

6. Complete.

1. 受話器を取りましたが、＿＿＿音が聞こえません。

   Juwaki o torimashita ga, ＿＿＿ on ga kikoemasen.

2. テレホンカードを入れることができません。この電話は＿＿＿しているようです。

   Terehon kaado o ireru koto ga dekimasen. Kono denwa wa ＿＿＿ shite iru yoo desu.

3. 何度かけても＿＿＿中です。誰と話しているんでしょうか。

   Nando kaketemo ＿＿＿ chuu desu. Dare to hanashite iru ndeshoo ka.

4. - 吉田という人はここにはいませんが。

   Yoshita to yuu hito wa koko ni wa imasen ga.

   - すみません。番号を＿＿＿。

   Sumimasen. Bangoo o ＿＿＿.

5. 誰も電話に出ません。後で＿＿＿みます。

   Dare mo denwa ni demasen. Ato de ＿＿＿ mimasu.

6. ＿＿＿が入って、よく聞こえません。

   ＿＿＿ ga haitte, yoku kikoemasen.

7. 話していたら、急に(suddenly)聞こえなくなりました。電話が＿＿しまいました。

   Hanashite itara, kyuu ni kikoenaku narimashita. Denwa ga ___ shimaimashita.

7. Put the following in the proper order for making a phone call.

(a) 受話器を取る

   juwaki o toru

(b) 電話を切る

   denwa o kiru

(c) 番号をダイヤルする

   bangoo o daiyaru suru

(d) 電話帳で相手の電話番号を調べる

   denwachoo de aite no denwa bangoo o shiraberu

(e) 発信音を聞く

   hasshin-on o kiku

(f) 相手が電話に出るのを待つ

   aite ga denwa ni deru no o matsu

(g) 話す

   hanasu

Key Words

answer (lit. appear)	出る	*deru*	fare	料金	*ryookin*
area code	市外局番	*shigai kyokuban*	Hello. [on the phone]	もしもし	*Moshi moshi.*
be connected	つながる	*tsunagaru*	Hold on a moment, please.	少々お待ちください。	*Shoo shoo omachi kudasai.*
button	ボタン	*botan*			
call	電話をかける（する）	*denwa o kakeru (suru)*	international call	国際電話	*kokusai denwa*
call back	かけ直す	*kakenaosu*	line is busy	話し中	*hanashichuu*
cellular phone	携帯電話	*keetai denwa*	local call	市内通話	*shinai tsuuwa*
collect call	コレクトコール	*korekuto kooru*	long distance call	長距離電話	*chookyori denwa*
cordless	コードレス電話	*koodoresu denwa*	noise	雑音	*zatsuon*
			operator	交換手（オペレーター）	*kookanshu (opereetaa)*
country code	国番号	*kuni bangoo*			
cut off	切れる	*kireru*	out of order	故障している	*koshoo shite iru*
dial	ダイヤル	*daiyaru*	out-of-town call	市外電話	*shigai denwa*
dial	ダイヤルする	*daiyaru suru*	person-to-person call,	指名通話	*shimee tsuuwa*
dial a wrong number	番号を間違える	*bangoo o machigaeru*	phone book	電話帳	*denwachoo*
dial tone	発信音	*hasshin-on*	phone number	電話番号	*denwa bangoo*
directly	直接	*chokusetsu*	prepaid telephone card	テレホンカード	*terehon kaado*
directory assistance	番号案内	*bangoo an-nai*			

public telephone	公衆電話	*kooshuu denwa*	telephone	電話	*denwa*
push-button phone (touch-tone phone)	プッシュホン	*pusshuhon*	telephone booth	電話ボックス	*denwa bokkusu*
			tell a message	伝える	*tsutaeru*
receiver	受話器	*juwaki*	the other party	相手	*aite*
ringing tone	呼び出し音	*yobidashi-on*	what number	何番	*nanban*
sound, ring	鳴る	*naru*	who	どなた（どちらさま）	*donata (dochira sama)*

Chapter 11: At the hairdresser
第11章：床屋／美容院で
Tokoya/Biyooin de

FOR MEN

髪が伸びたので、切りたいです。　　　　　　　　　　　　　hair, grow long,
Kami ga nobita no de, *kir tai* desu.　　　　　　　　　　　want to have my hair cut

床屋で髪を切ります。　　　　　　　　　　　　　　　　　barber shop
Tokoya de kami o kirimasu.

かみそりでそりますか、はさみで切りますか。　　　　　razor, shave, scissors
Kamisori de *sorimasu* ka, *hasami* de kirimasu ka?

そろえるだけでいいです。　　　　　　　　　　　　　　trim
Soroeru dake de ii desu.

短くしすぎないでください。　　　　　　　　　　　　　Don't cut it too short.
Mijikaku shisuginaide kudasai.

あごひげをそろえてください。　　　　　　　　　　　　beard
Agohige o soroete kudasai.

口ひげ　　　　　　　　　　　　　　　　　　　　　　　mustache
Kuchihige

もみあげ　　　　　　　　　　　　　　　　　　　　　　sideburns
Momiage

ひげをそってください。　　　　　　　　　　　　　　　shave my beard
Hige o sotte kudasai.

後ろをもう少し短くしてください。　　　　　　　　　　in the back, a little shorter
Ushiro o moo sukoshi mijikaku shite kudasai.

横　　　　　　　　　　　　　　　　　　　　　　　　　on the side
Yoko

前　　　　　　　　　　　　　　　　　　　　　　　　　on the top
Mae

えりあし　　　　　　　　　　　　　　　　　　　　　　on the neck
Eriashi

シャンプーをしてください。　　　　　　　　　　　　　shampoo
Shanpuu o shite kudasai.

髪を洗ってください。　　　　　　　　　　　　　　　　wash my hair
Kami o aratte kudasai.

ヘアリキッドもヘアスプレーもいりません。　　　　　hair lotion, hair spray
Hea rikiddo mo *hea supuree* mo irimasen.

1. Complete.

1. ＿＿＿が長くなりました。＿＿＿を切りに行きたいです。

   ___ ga nagaku narimashita. ___ o kiri ni ikitai desu.

2. まだあまり長くありません。＿＿＿だけでいいです。

   Mada amari nagaku arimasen. ___ dake de ii desu.

3. 髪を洗ってきたから、＿＿＿はしなくてもいいです。

   Kami o aratte kita kara, ___ wa shinakute mo ii desu.

4. ＿＿＿ひげも＿＿＿ひげもそろえてほしいです。

   ___ hige mo ___ hige mo soroete hoshii desu.

5. もみあげが長すぎるから、＿＿＿もらえますか。

   Momiage ga nagasugiru kara, ___ moraemasu ka.

6. あまり短い髪は好きじゃありません。＿＿＿しすぎないでください。

   Amari mijikai kami wa suki ja arimasen. ___ shisuginaide kudasai.

7. 床屋は髪を切るのに＿＿＿と＿＿＿を使います。

   Tokoya wa kami o kiru no ni ___ to ___ o tsukaimasu.

8. 私は自分でひげをそります。＿＿＿に行ってそってもらうのは好きじゃありません。

   Watashi wa jibun de hige o sorimasu. ___ ni itte sotte morau no wa suki ja arimasen.

2. Complete this exercise on the basis of Fig. 11-1.

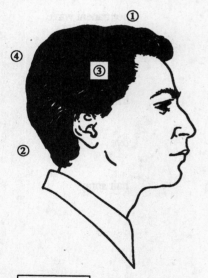

Fig. 11-1

1. ＿＿＿をもう少し短くしてください。

   ___ o moo sukoshi mijikaku shite kudasai.

2. ＿＿＿

3. ＿＿＿

4. ＿＿＿

3. Match.

1. 髪が伸びてきました。

   Kami ga nobite kimashita.

2. 髪が洗いたいです。

   Kami ga araitai desu.

3. 私の髪はあまり長くありません。

   Watashi no kami wa amari nagaku arimasen.

4. もみあげがとても長いです。

   Momiage ga totemo nagai desu.

5. かみそりでそりますか。

   Kamisori de sorimasu ka.

(a) そろえるだけでいいです。

   Soroeru dake de ii desu.

(b) そってください。

   Sotte kudasai.

(c) 床屋に行かなくてはなりません。

   Tokoya ni ikanakute wa narimasen.

(d) シャンプーをしてください。

   Shanpuu o shite kudasai.

(e) いいえ、はさみで切ってください。

   Iie, hasami de kitte kudasai.

FOR WOMEN

美容院で髪を切ります。

Biyooin de kami o kirimasu.

カットをしてください。

Katto o shite kudasai.

シャンプーとセットをしてください。

Shanpuu to setto o shite kudasai.

パーマをかけてください。

Paama o kakete kudasai.

くしでといてください。

Kushi de *toite* kudasai.

そろえてください。

Soroete kudasai.

染めてください。

Somete kudasai.

ヘアスプレーはしないでください。

Hea supuree wa shinaide kudasai.

beauty salon

cut

shampoo and set

permanent wave

comb, comb out

trim

dye

hair spray

4. Complete.

- 今日はどうしましょうか。　_1_ をかけますか。

  Kyoo wa doo shimashoo ka. _1_ o kakemasu ka.

- いいえ、シャンプーと_2_だけでいいです。

  Iie, shanpuu to _2_ dake de ii desu.

- 髪がちょっと伸びてきたようですが、_3_はしなくていいですか。

  Kami ga chotto nobitekita yoo desu ga, _3_ wa shinakute ii desu ka.

- ええ、この長さでいいです。

  Ee, kono nagasa de ii desu.

- ___4___ か。
  ___4___ ka.

- いいえ、今の色(color)でいいです。
  Iie, ima no iro de ii desu.

TYPES OF HAIR AND STYLES

ウェーブ
weebu

ストレートヘア
sutoreeto hea

前髪
maegami

ボブ
bobu

シニヨン
shiniyon

カール
kaaru

カーリーヘア
kaarii hea

分け目
wakeme

ポニーテール
ponii teeru

三つ編み
mitsuami

Fig. 11-2

5. Answer.

1. あなたはストレートヘアですか、カーリーヘアですか。

　　Anata wa sutoreeto hea desu ka, kaarii hea desu ka.

2. 分け目はありますか。

　　Wakeme wa arimasu ka.

3. 分け目はどこにありますか。右ですか、左ですか、真ん中(center)ですか。

　　Wakeme wa doko ni arimasu ka. Migi desu ka, hidari desu ka, man-naka desu ka.

6. Identify the hairstyle. (Fig. 11-3)

Fig. 11-3

1.
2.
3.
4.
5.

MATERIALS

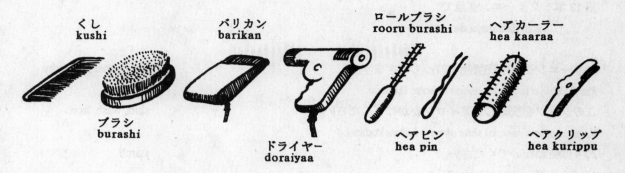

くし
kushi

バリカン
barikan

ロールブラシ
rooru burashi

ヘアカーラー
hea kaaraa

ブラシ
burashi

ドライヤー
doraiyaa

ヘアピン
hea pin

ヘアクリップ
hea kurippu

Fig. 11-4

Key Words

bang	前髪	*maegami*	hair spray	ヘアスプレー	*hea supuree*
barbershop	床屋	*tokoya*	in the back	後ろ	*ushiro*
beard	あごひげ	*agohige*	mustache	口ひげ	*kuchihige*
beauty salon	美容院	*biyooin*	on the neck	えりあし	*eriashi*
bob	ボブ	*bobu*	on the side	横	*yoko*
bobby pin	ヘアピン	*hea pin*	on the top	前	*mae*
braid	三つ編み	*mitsuami*	part	分け目	*wakeme*
brush	ブラシ	*burashi*	permanent wave	パーマ	*paama*
bun	シニヨン	*shiniyon*			
comb	くし	*kushi*	pony tail	ポニーテール	*ponii teeru*
comb out	とく	*toku*	razor	かみそり	*kamisori*
curl	カール	*kaaru*	roller	ヘアカーラー	*hea kaaraa*
curl (style)	カーリーヘア	*kaarii hea*	scissors	はさみ	*hasami*
curler	ロールブラシ	*rooru burashi*	set	セット	*setto*
cut	カット	*katto*	shampoo	シャンプー	*shanpuu*
cut	切る	*kiru*	shave	そる	*soru*
dryer	ドライヤー	*doraiyaa*	shave my beard	ひげをそる	*hige o soru*
dye	染める	*someru*	sideburns	もみあげ	*momiage*
grow long	伸びる	*nobiru*	straight hair	ストレートヘア	*sutoreeto hea*
hair	髪	*kami*			
hair clip	ヘアクリップ	*hea kurippu*	trim	そろえる	*soroeru*
hair clipper	バリカン	*barikan*	wash	洗う	*arau*
hair lotion	ヘアリキッド	*hea rikiddo*	wave	ウェーブ	*weebu*

Chapter 12: At the dry cleaner
第12章：クリーニング屋で
Kuriininguya de

クリーニング屋に洗濯物を持って行きます。	dry cleaner's, laundry
Kuriininguya ni *sentakumono* o motte ikimasu.	
このシャツを洗濯してアイロンをかけてください。	shirt, wash, iron
Kono *shatsu* o *sentaku shite airon o kakete* kudasai.	
のりは使わないでください。	starch
Nori wa tsukawanaide kudasai.	
このジャケットをドライクリーニングしてください。	jacket, dry-clean
Kono *jaketto* o *dorai kuriiningu shite* kudasai.	
いつできますか。	ready
Itsu *dekimasu* ka.	
このシャツは洗うと縮みますか。	shrink
Kono shatsu wa arau to *chijimimasu* ka.	
このしみは取れますか。	stain, come out (lit. remove)
Kono *shimi* wa *toremasu* ka.	
ここで服の修繕（直し）はお願いできますか。	clothes, mend (repair)
Koko de *fuku no shuuzen (naoshi)* wa onegai dekimasu ka.	
ここに穴があいています。	There is a hole
Koko ni *ana ga aite imasu.*	
つくろってください。	mend
Tsukurotte kudasai.	
ボタンが取れてしまいました。	button is missing
Botan ga torete shimaimashita.	
ボタンを付けてください。	sew (attatch)
Botan o *tsukete* kudasai.	
裏の縫い目がほころびてしまいました。	lining, seam, torn
Ura no *nuime* ga *hokorobite* shimaimashita.	
つくろってください。	sew
Tsukurotte kudasai.	

1. Complete.

1. このウール(wool)のセーターは水で洗濯すると＿＿＿でしょう。クリーニング屋で＿＿＿をしてもらった

   Kono uuru no seetaa wa mizu de sentaku suru to ＿＿ deshoo. Kuriininguya de ＿＿ o shite moratta

方がいいです。

hoo ga ii desu.

2. このシャツはきれいじゃありません。＿＿＿しなければなりません。その後で＿＿＿をかけます。

Kono shatsu wa kiree ja arimasen. ___ shinakereba narimasen. Sono ato de ___ o kakemasu.

3. 私はシャツを洗濯する時、＿＿＿を使うのはあまり好きじゃありません。

Watashi wa shatsu o sentaku suru toki, ___ o tsukau no wa amari suki ja arimasen.

4. このジャケットの＿＿＿がほころびてしまいました。＿＿＿もらえますか。

Kono jaketto no ___ ga hokorobite shimaimashita. ___ moraemasu ka.

5. スカートに＿＿＿があいてしまいました。＿＿＿もらえますか。

Sukaato ni ___ ga aite shimaimashita. ___ moraemasu ka.

6. このとれた＿＿＿を付けてもらえますか。

Kono toreta ___ o tsukete moraemasu ka.

7. シャツに何かこぼした(spilled)ようです。この＿＿＿は取れますか。

Shatsu ni nanika koboshita yoo desu. Kono ___ wa toremasu ka.

2. Complete.

<クリーニング屋で>

<Kuriininguya de>

- すみません。このシャツを洗濯してアイロンを＿1＿もらえませんか。

  Sumimasen. Kono shatsu o sentaku shite airon o _1_ moraemasen ka.

- はい。＿2＿は使ってもいいですか。

  Hai. _2_ wa tsukatte mo ii desu ka.

- ええ、でも少しにしてください。それから、ここにしみがあるんですが、＿3＿でしょうか。

  Eee, demo sukoshi ni shite kudasai. Sorekara, koko ni shimi ga aru ndesu ga, _3_ deshoo ka.

- これは何のしみか分かりますか。

  Kore wa nan no shimi ka wakarimasu ka.

- ええ、コーヒーです。

  Ee, koohii desu.

- やってみますが、＿4＿かどうか分かりません。コーヒーのしみはなかなか取れないんです。

  Yatte mimasu ga, _4_ ka dooka wakarimasen. Koohii no shimi wa nakanaka torenai ndesu.

- そうですか。それと、このセーターもお願いします。

  Soo desu ka. Soreto, kono seetaa mo onegaishimasu.

- はい。これはウールですね。ウールは＿5＿から＿6＿しますね。

  Hai. Kore wa uuru desu ne. Uuru wa _5_ kara _6_ shimasu ne.

- お願いします。明日までに＿7＿か。

  Onegaishimasu. Ashita made ni _7_ ka.

- シャツはできます。でもセーターは二日かかりますね。

  Shatsu wa dekimasu. Demo seetaa wa futsuka kakari masu ne.

Key Words

button	ボタン	*botan*	lining	裏	*ura*
clothes	服	*fuku*	mend (repair)	修繕（直し）	*shuuzen (naoshi)*
come out (lit. remove)	取れる	*toreru*	mend, sew	つくろう	*tsukurou*
			ready	できる	*dekiru*
dry cleaner's	クリーニング屋	*kuriininguya*	seam	縫い目	*nuime*
			sew (attach)	付ける	*tsukeru*
dry-clean	ドライクリーニング	*dorai kuriiningu*	shirt	シャツ	*shatsu*
			shrink	縮む	*chijimu*
hole	穴	*ana*	stain	しみ	*shimi*
iron	アイロンをかける	*airon o kakeru*	starch	のり	*nori*
			torn	ほころびる	*hokorobiru*
jacket	ジャケット	*jaketto*	wash	洗濯する	*sentaku suru*
laundry	洗濯物	*sentakumono*			

Chapter 13: At the restaurant

第13章：レストランで

Resutoran de

GETTING SETTLED

窓
mado

ウエイター
weitaa

メニュー
menyuu

お盆（トレイ）
obon (toree)

Fig. 13-1

ここは**高級**レストランです。 Koko wa *kookyuu resutoran* desu.	luxurious, restaurant
高い *takai*	expensive
安い *yasui*	inexpensive
ファミリーレストラン *famirii resutoran*	family restaurant
居酒屋 *izakaya*	izakaya (Japanese style bar)
予約したスミスですが。 *Yoyaku* shita Sumisu desu ga.	reservation

四名で予約したんですが。   table for four

Yon mee de yoyaku shita ndesu ga.

奥の席（テーブル）がいいんですが。   back, table

Oku no seki (teeburu) ga ii ndesu ga.

窓際の   near the window

Mado giwa no

外の   outside

Soto no

ウエーターが来ました。   waiter

Ueetaa ga kimashita.

ウエートレス   waitress

Ueetoresu

メニューを持って来てもらえますか。   menu

Menyuu o motte kite moraemasu ka.

1. Complete.

1. ＿＿＿＿していないんですが、席があいているといいですね。

　　＿＿ shite inai ndesu ga, seki ga aite iru to ii desu ne.

2. このレストランは高くてとてもおいしいメニューがたくさんあります。＿＿＿＿レストランです。

　　Kono resutoran wa takakute totemo oishii menyuu ga takusan arimasu. ＿＿ resutoran desu.

3. 今日はとてもいい天気ですね。＿＿＿＿のテーブルに座りましょう。

　　Kyoo wa totemo ii tenki desu ne. ＿＿ no teeburu ni suwari mashoo.

2. Complete.

＜レストランで＞

- いらっしゃいませ。何名様(how many)ですか。

　　Irasshaimase. Nan mee sama desu ka.

- 三名です。＿1＿しましたが。

　　San mee desu. ＿1＿ shimashita ga.

- お名前は。

　　Onamae wa.

- 鈴木です。

　　Suzuki desu.

- こちらの＿2＿と奥の＿3＿とどちらがよろしいですか。

　　Kochira no ＿2＿ to oku no ＿3＿ to dochira ga yoroshii desu ka.

- ここでいいです。

　　Koko de ii desu.

3. Complete.

やきとりが食べたかったから、＿1＿へ行きました。私達は＿2＿際の席に座りました。

Yakitori ga tabetakatta kara, ___ e ikimashita. Watashi tachi wa ___ giwa no seki ni suwarimashita.

＿3＿が水と＿4＿を持って来ました。

＿3＿ ga mizu to ＿4＿ o motte kimashita.

LOOKING AT THE MENU

前菜 *zensai*	hors d'oeuvres
スープ *suupu*	soup
サラダ *sarada*	salad
パン *pan*	bread
シーフード *shiifuudo*	sea food dish
魚 *sakana*	fish
貝 *kai*	shellfish
えび *ebi*	lobster, prawn, shrimp
かに *kani*	crab
いか *ika*	squid
たこ *tako*	octopus
肉料理 *niku ryoori*	meat and fowl dish
牛肉 *gyuuniku*	beef
豚肉 *butaniku*	pork
鶏肉 *toriniku*	chicken
羊の肉 *hitsuji no niku*	mutton, lamb

野菜	vegetable
yasai	
デザート	desserts
dezaato	
おつまみ	Japanese style hors d'oeuvre
otsumami	
ご飯	cooked rice
gohan	
みそ汁	miso soup
misoshiru	
お決まりですか。	Have you decided?
Okimari desu ka.	
〜をお勧めします。	I suggest (recommend)
〜o osusume shimasu.	
フルコースのメニューは何ですか。	full-course meal
Furu koosu no menyuu wa nan desu ka	
セットメニュー	set meal
Setto menyuu	
ランチ	lunch
Ranchi	
スープが飲みたいです。	want to eat (lit. drink) soup
Suupu ga nomitai desu.	
このお店のお勧め料理は何ですか。	house specialty
Kono *omise no osusume ryoori* wa nan desu ka.	
ワインリストを見せてください。	wine list
Wain risuto o misete kudasai.	

4. Answer on the basis of Fig. 13-2.

1. テーブルには人が何人いますか。

   Teeburu ni wa hito ga nan-nin imasu ka.

2. 立っている人はだれですか。

   Tatte iru hito wa dare desu ka.

3. お盆の上には何がありますか。

   Obon no ue ni wa nani ga arimasu ka.

4. ウエーターはお盆のほかに何を持っていますか。

   Ueetaa wa obon no hoka ni nani o motte imasu ka.

5. Complete.

1. フランス料理屋やイタリア料理屋で、前菜からデザートまでがついているものは____といいます。

   Furansu ryoori ya ya Itaria ryoori ya de, zensai kara dezaato made ga tsuite iru mono wa ___ to iimasu.

Fig. 13-2

2. 西洋（Western）料理の____はメーン料理の前に飲みますが、日本料理の____はご飯や他の

   Seeyoo ryoori no ___ wa meen ryoori no mae ni nomimasu ga, nihon ryoori no ___ wa gohan ya hoka no

   ものを食べながら飲みます。

   mono o tabenagara nomimasu.

3. ワインが飲みたいです。____を持ってきてください。

   Wain ga nomitai desu. ___ o mottekite kudasai.

4. 客：どれを頼んだらいいか分からないんですが。

   Kyaku: Dore o tanondara ii ka wakaranai ndesu ga.

   ウエーター：それでは、ハウスワインを____します。

   Ueetaa: Sore dewa, hausu wain o ___ shimasu.

ORDERING MEAT OR FOWL

私は肉は**焼いた**のが好きです。   broild, grilled

Watashi wa niku wa *yaita* no ga suki desu.

       炒めた   pan-fried

       itameta

       蒸した   steamed

	mushita	
ゆでた		boiled
yudeta		
揚げた		deep-fried
ageta		
ソテーした		sauteed
sotee shita		
煮込んだ		slowly cooked, simmered
nikonda		

私はステーキにします。   steak
　　　　suteeki

肉の焼き具合はどうしますか。   How would you like your meat?
Niku no yaki guai wa doo shimasu ka.

レアでお願いします。   rare
Rea

ミディアムレア   medium-rare
Midiamu rea

ミディアム（普通）   medium
Midiamu (futsuu)

ウェルダン   well-done
Weru dan

私は鳥のもも肉が好きです。   chicken thigh
Watashi wa tori no momo niku ga suki desu.

　　　　胸肉   breast
　　　　muneniku

　　　　内臓（臓物）   giblets
　　　　naizoo (zoomotsu)

私はひき肉の料理が好きです。   minced (ground) meat
Watashi wa hikiniku no ryoori ga suki desu.

私はポークソテーにします。   sauteed pork
Watashi wa pooku sotee ni shimasu.

　　　　とんかつ   breaded pork cutlet
　　　　tonkatsu

6. Complete.

ステーキを頼むとウエーターは客に焼き具合を聞きます。私はほとんど生(uncooked)の肉が好きなので、
Suteeki o tanomu to ueetaa wa kyaku ni yaki guai o kikimasu . Watashi wa hotondo nama no niku ga suki na node,

　__1__ を頼みますが、もう少しよく焼いた__2__ が好きな人も多いです。鶏肉は骨(bone)のない__3__ より
__1__ o tanomimasu ga, moo sukoshi yoku yaita __2__ ga suki na hito mo ooi desu. Tori niku wa hone no nai __3__ yori

骨のある＿4＿の方がおいしくて好きです。とんかつのような肉を＿5＿のはあまり好きじゃありません。

hone no aru ＿4＿ no hoo ga oishikute suki desu. Tonkatsu no yoona niku o ＿5＿ no wa amari suki ja arimasen.

ORDERING SEAFOOD

私は魚は蒸したのが好きです。	steamed
Watashi wa sakana wa *mushita* no ga suki desu.	
ゆでた	boiled
yudeta	
焼いた	broiled, grilled
yaita	
揚げた	deep-fried
ageta	
ソテーした	sateed
sotee shita	
干したの（干物）	dried
hoshita no (himono)	
生（刺身）が好きです。	raw (sashimi)
nama (sashimi)	
骨が多い魚もあります。	fishbone
Hone ga ooi sakana mo arimasu.	

7. Complete.

日本料理は油(oil)を使わないで、生で食べたり、＿1＿り、＿2＿りする料理が多いです。＿3＿は、

Nihon ryoori wa abura o tsukawanaide, nama de tabetari, ＿1＿ ri, ＿2＿ ri suru ryoori ga ooi desu. ＿3＿ wa

魚を調理しない(uncooked)で作ります。

sakana o choori shinaide tsukurimasu.

SOME PROBLEMS YOU MAY HAVE

はしがありません	chopsticks
Hashi ga arimasen.	
ナイフ	knife
Naifu	
フォーク	fork
Fooku	
スプーン	spoon
Supuun	
ティースプーン	teaspoon

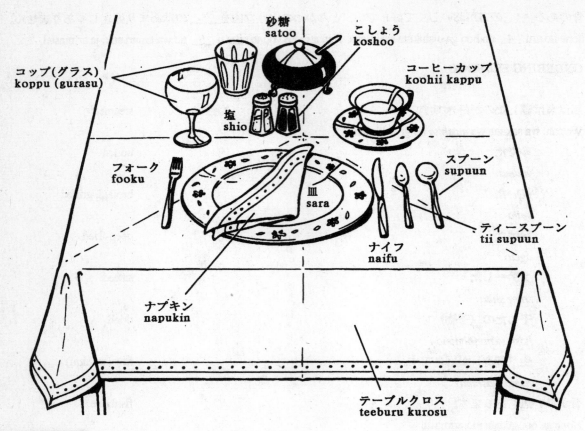

砂糖
satoo

こしょう
koshoo

コーヒーカップ
koohii kappu

コップ（グラス）
koppu (gurasu)

塩
shio

フォーク
fooku

スプーン
supuun

皿
sara

ティースプーン
tii supuun

ナイフ
naifu

ナプキン
napukin

テーブルクロス
teeburu kurosu

Fig. 13-3

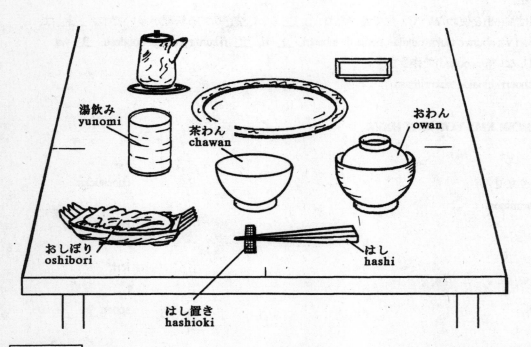

湯飲み
yunomi

茶わん
chawan

おわん
owan

おしぼり
oshibori

はし
hashi

はし置き
hashioki

Fig. 13-4

Tii supuun

ナプキン napkin

Napukin

コップ（グラス）をもうひとつください。 glass

Koppu (Gurasu) o moo hitotsu kudasai.

おしぼり small damp towel

Oshibori

塩をください。 salt

Shio

こしょう pepper

Koshoo

お水 water

Omizu

砂糖 suger

Satoo

このテーブルクロスは汚れています。 tablecloth, dirty

Kono teeburu kurosu wa yogorete imasu.

この肉は よく焼けていません。 underdone

Kono niku wa yoku yakete imasen.

焼きすぎです。 overdone

yakisugi desu.

固すぎます。 too hard

katasugimasu.

このスープはぬるいです。 cold (not warm enough)

Kono suupu wa nurui desu.

この料理はからすぎます。 too spicy, too salty

Kono ryoori wa karasugimasu.

8. Complete.

1. 西洋(Western)料理のテーブルセッティングはフォークと＿＿＿と＿＿＿です。

   Seeyoo ryoori no teeburu settingu wa fooku to ___ to ___ desu.

2. はしは＿＿＿の上に置きます。

   Hashi wa ___ no ue ni okimasu.

3. このソースは＿＿＿を入れすぎです。からすぎます。

   Kono soosu wa ___ o iresugi desu. Karasugimasu.

4. この肉はナイフで切れません。＿＿＿＿。

   Kono niku wa naifu de kiremasen. ___.

9. Identify each item in Figs. 13-5 and 13-6.

Fig. 13-5

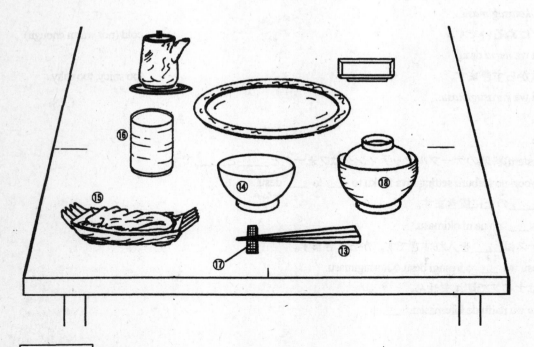

Fig. 13-6

GETTING THE CHECK

お勘定、お願いします。 *Okanjoo,* onegaishimasu.	bill, check
サービス料は含まれていますか。 *Saabisu ryoo* wa *fukumarete* imasu ka.	service charge, included
チップはいりません。 *Chippu* wa irimasen.	tips
お金はレジ（会計）で払います。 Okane wa *reji (kaikee)* de haraimasu.	cashier
クレジットカードが使えますか。 *Kurejitto kaado* ga tsukaemasu ka.	credit card
領収書（レシート）をください。 *Ryooshuusho (Reshiito)* o kudasai.	receipt

10. Complete.

日本では＿1＿料は＿2＿に含まれていて、＿3＿を払う習慣(custom)はありません。お金はテーブルでは
Nihon de wa ＿1＿ ryoo wa ＿2＿ ni fukumarete ite, ＿3＿ o harau shuukan wa arimasen. Okane wa teeburu de wa
なくて＿4＿で払います。＿5＿はたいていのレストランで使えますが、使えないところもあります。
nakute ＿4＿ de haraimasu. ＿5＿ wa taitee no resutoran de tsukaemasu ga, tsukaenai tokoro mo arimasu.

先週、私は友達と四人でレストランへ行きました。席は予約してありました。
Senshuu, watashi wa tomodashi to yonin de resutoran e ikimashita. Seki wa yoyaku shite arimashita.
私達は奥のいい席に座りました。そのレストランは外の席もありますが、その日は少し
Watashi tachi wa oku no ii seki ni suwarimashita. Sono resutoran wa soto no seki mo arimasu ga, sono hi wa sukoshi
寒かったので、外のテーブルには誰もいませんでした。ウエートレスがメニューとお水を持って来て、
samukatta no de, soto no teeburu ni wa dare mo imasen deshita. Ueetoresu ga menyuu to omizu o motte kite,
飲み物は何がいいか聞きました。私達はビールを二本頼みました。メニューには、あまり
nomimono wa nani ga ii ka kikimashita. Watashi tachi wa biiru o nihon tanomimashita. Menyuu ni wa, amari
おいしそうなものがありませんでしたが、私達はみんなで四つ注文しました。
oishisoo na mono ga arimasen deshita ga, watashi tachi wa min-na de yottsu chuumon shimashita.
ビールはすぐ来ましたが、グラスがひとつ足りなかったので、ウエートレスを呼んで、もうひとつ
Biiru wa sugu kimashita ga, gurasu ga hitotsu tarinakatta node, ueetoresu o yonde, moo hitotsu
持って来てもらいました。料理が来た時、今度ははしがありませんでした。でも料理は悪くありません
mottekite moraimashita. Ryoori ga kita toki, kondo wa hashi ga arimasen deshita. Demo ryoori wa waruku arimasen
でした。私達四人は、みんな違うものを注文したのですが、どれも全部おいしかったです。
deshita. Watashi tachi yo nin wa, min-na chigau mono o chuumon shita no desu ga, dore mo zenbu oishikatta desu.
ウエートレスがデザートはどうかと聞きに来ましたが、私達はみんなもうおなかがいっぱいでした。
Ueetoresu ga dezaato wa dooka to kiki ni kimashita ga, watashi tachi wa min-na moo onaka ga ippai deshita.

デザートは食べないで、コーヒーだけ飲みました。コーヒーも飲み終わって、私達はレジでお金を払って
Dezaato wa tabenaide, koohii dake nomimashita. Koohii mo nomi owatte, watashi tachi wa reji de okane o haratte
帰りました。日本のレストランはお勘定にサービス料が含まれているので、チップはいりません。
kaerimashita. Nihon no resutoran wa o kanjoo ni saabisuryoo ga fukumarete iru node, chippu wa irimasen.

11. Complete.

1. この人と友達は＿＿＿で食事をしました。

   Kono hito to tomodachi wa ___ de shokuji o shimashita.

2. 行く前に、四人の席を＿＿＿しておきました。

   Iku mae ni, yo nin no seki o ___ shite okimashita.

3. ＿＿＿に座りました。

   ___ ni suwarimashita.

4. 寒かったから＿＿＿には座りませんでした。

   Samukatta kara ___ ni wa suwarimasen deshita.

5. まず、＿＿＿を二本注文しました。

   Mazu, ___ o ni hon chuumon shimashita.

6. ＿＿＿がメニューを持って来ました。

   ___ ga menyuu o motte kimashita.

7. ＿＿＿にはあまりおいしそうなものはありませんでした。

   ___ ni wa amari oishisoo na mono wa arimasen deshita.

12. Answer.

1. 料理が来た時、何がありませんでしたか。

   Ryoori ga kita toki, nani ga arimasen deshita ka.

2. 料理はどうでしたか。

   Ryoori wa doo deshita ka.

3. デザートは食べましたか。

   Dezaato wa tabemashita ka.

4. 食事の後で、何を飲みましたか。

   Shokuji no ato de, nani o nomimashita ka.

5. サービス料はお勘定に含まれていましたか。

   Saabisuryoo wa okanjoo ni fukumarete imashita ka.

6. チップは払いましたか。

   Chippu wa haraimashita ka.

Key Words

back	奥	*oku*		bill, check	お勘定	*okanjoo*
beef	牛肉	*gyuuniku*		boiled	ゆでた	*yudeta*

bread	パン	pan	Japanese tea cup	湯のみ	yunomi
breaded pork cutlet	とんかつ	tonkatsu	knife	ナイフ	naifu
breast	胸肉	muneniku	lobster, prawn, shrimp	えび	ebi
broiled, grilled	焼いた	yaita	lunch	ランチ	ranchi
cashier	レジ（会計）	reji (kaikee)	luxurious	高級	kookyuu
chicken	鶏肉	toriniku	meat and fowl dish	肉料理	niku ryoori
chicken thigh	鳥のもも肉	tori no momoniku	medium	ミディアム（普通）	midiamu (futsuu)
chopstick	はし	hashi			
chopstick rest	はし置き	hashi oki	medium-rare	ミディアムレア	midiamu rea
coffee cup	コーヒーカップ	koohii kappu	menu	メニュー	menyuu
			minced (ground) meat	ひき肉	hikiniku
cold (not warm enough)	ぬるい	nurui	miso soup	みそ汁	misoshiru
cooked rice	ご飯	gohan	mutton, lamb	羊の肉	hitsuji no niku
crab	かに	kani	napkin	ナプキン	napukin
credit card	クレジットカード	kurejitto kaado	near the window	窓際	madogiwa
deep-fried	揚げた	ageta	octopus	たこ	tako
desserts	デザート	dezaato	outside	外	soto
dirty	汚れている	yogorete iru	overdone	焼きすぎ	yakisugi
dried	干したの（干物）	hoshita no (himono)	pan-fried	炒めた	itameta
			pepper	こしょう	koshoo
eat (lit. drink soup etc.)	飲む	nomu	plate	皿	sara
expensive	高い	takai	pork	豚肉	butaniku
family restaurant	ファミリーレストラン	famirii resutoran	rare	レア	rea
			raw (sashimi)	生（刺身）	nama (sashimi)
fish	魚	sakana	receipt	領収書（レシート）	ryooshuusho (reshiito)
fishbone	骨	hone			
fork	フォーク	fooku			
full-course meal	フルコースのメニュー	furu koosu no menyuu	reservation	予約	yoyaku
			reserve	予約する	yoyaku suru
giblets	内臓（臓物）	naizoo (zoomotsu)	restaurant	レストラン	resutoran
glass	コップ（グラス）	koppu (gurasu)	rice bowl	茶わん	chawan
			salad	サラダ	sarada
Have you decided?	お決まりですか。	Okimari desu ka.	salt	塩	shio
hors d'oeuvres	前菜	zensai	sauteed	ソーした	sotee shita
house specialty	お店のお勧め料理	omise no osusume ryoori	sauteed pork	ポークソテー	pooku sotee
			sea food dish	シーフード	shiifuudo
I suggest ~ (recommend)	～をお勧めします	~ o osusume shimasu	service charge	サービス料	saabisuryoo
			set meal	セットメニュー	setto menyuu
inexpensive	安い	yasui			
izakaya (Japanese style bar)	居酒屋	izakaya	shellfish	貝	kai
			slowly cooked, simmered	煮込んだ	nikonda
Japanese style hors d'oeuvre	おつまみ	otsumami	small damp towel	おしぼり	oshibori

soup	スープ	*suupu*	tray	お盆（トレー）	*obon (toree)*
spoon	スプーン	*supuun*	underdone	よく焼けていない	*yoku yakete inai*
squid	いか	*ika*			
steak	ステーキ	*suteeki*	vegetable	野菜	*yasai*
steamed	蒸した	*mushita*	waiter	ウエーター	*ueetaa*
sugar	砂糖	*satoo*	waitress	ウエートレス	*ueetoresu*
table	席（テーブル）	*seki (teeburu)*	water	お水	*omizu*
tablecloth	テーブルクロス	*teeburu kurosu*	well-done	ウェルダン	*werudan*
			window	窓	*mado*
teaspoon	ティースプーン	*tii supuun*	wine list	ワインリスト	*wain risuto*
			wooden soup bowl	おわん	*owan*
tips,	チップ	*chippu*			
too hard	固すぎる	*katasugiru*			
too spicy, too salty	からすぎる	*karasugiru*			

Chapter 14: Shopping for food
第 14 章：食料品　（食べ物）を買う
Shokuryoohin (Tabemono) o kau

TYPES OF STORES

肉屋に行きます。	meat shop
Nikuya ni ikimasu.	
魚屋	fish market
Sakanaya	
八百屋	green grocer
Yaoya	
パン屋	bakery
Pan-ya	
ケーキ屋	pastry shop
Keekiya	
豆腐屋	tofu seller
Toofuya	
酒屋	liquor store
Sakaya	
米屋	rice shop
Komeya	
スーパーに食料（食べ物）を買いに行きます。	supermarket, foodstuffs
Suupaa ni *shokuryoo (tabemono)* o kai ni ikimasu.	
入口にあるかごに買った物を入れながら買い物をします。	entrance, basket
Iriguchi ni aru *kago* ni katta mono o irenagara kaimono o shimasu.	
カート	shopping cart
kaato	
買ったものをビニール袋に入れて持って帰ります。	plastic bag
Katta mono o biniirubukuro ni irete motte kaerimasu.	

1. Complete.

1. ケーキやクッキーは＿＿＿にあります。

   Keeki ya kukkii wa ___ ni arimasu.

2. 豚肉や牛肉は＿＿＿にあります。

   Butaniku ya gyuuniku wa ___ ni arimasu.

3. 果物や野菜は＿＿＿にあります。

   Kudamono ya yasai wa ___ ni arimasu.

4. 魚や貝は＿＿＿にあります。

   Sakana ya kai wa ___ ni arimasu.

105

5. パンは＿＿＿＿＿にあります。

Pan wa ___ ni arimasu.

6. 豆腐は＿＿＿＿＿にあります。

Toofu wa ___ ni arimasu.

7. ワインは＿＿＿＿＿にあります。

Wain wa ___ ni arimasu.

2. Identify the stores where you would find the following.

1. ほうれん草 (spinach)

hoorensoo

2. ロールパン (dinner role)

roorupan

3. 鶏肉 (chicken)

toriniku

4. えび (shrimp)

ebi

5. りんご (apple)

ringo

6. チョコレートケーキ

chokoreeto keeki

7. 米

kome

3. Complete.

　_1_ で買い物をする時は入口にある_2_か_3_に買った食料を入れます。買った物は_4_に

　_1_ de kaimono o suru toki wa, iriguchi ni aru _2_ ka _3_ ni katta shokuryoo o iremasu. Katta mono wa _4_ ni

入れて持って帰ります。

irete motte kaerimasu.

Key Words

apple	りんご	*ringo*	liquor store	酒屋	*sakaya*
bakery	パン屋	*pan-ya*	meat shop	肉屋	*nikuya*
basket	かご	*kago*	pastry shop	ケーキ屋	*keekiya*
chicken	鶏肉	*toriniku*	plastic bag	ビニール袋	*beniirubukuro*
chocolate cake	チョコレート	*chokoreeto keeki*	rice	米	*kome*
	ケーキ		rice shop	米屋	*komeya*
dinner role	ロールパン	*roorupan*	shopping cart	カート	*kaato*
entrance	入口	*iriguchi*	shrimp	えび	*ebi*
fish market	魚屋	*sakanaya*	spinach	ほうれんそう	*hoorensoo*
foodstuffs	食料 (食べ物)	*shokuryoo*	supermarket	スーパー	*suupaa*
		(tabemono)	tofu seller	豆腐屋	*toofuya*
green grocer	八百屋	*yaoya*			

Chapter 15: Buying clothing and shoes
第15章：洋服／靴を買う
Yoohuku/Kutsu o kau

BUYING SHOES

靴
kutsu

靴ひも
kutsu himo

底
soko

ヒール（かかと）
hiiru (kakato)

幅
haba

Fig. 15-1

いらっしゃいませ。	May I help you? (lit. Welcome)
Irasshaimase.	
何をお探しですか。	What can I help you?
Nani o osagashi desu ka.	(lit. What are you looking for?)
靴がほしいんですが。	shoes
Kutsu	
ブーツ	boots
Buutsu	
サンダル	sandals
Sandaru	
スリッパ	slippers
Surippa	
スニーカー	sneakers

Suniikaa

靴のサイズはいくつですか。   shoe size

Kutsu no saizu wa ikutsu desu ka.

24.5 センチです。   24.5 centimeter

Nijuuyon ten go senchi desu.

茶色[ベージュ、白、黒]の皮のがいいです。   brown [beige, white, black],

Chairo [beeju, shiro, kuro] no kawa no ga ii desu.   leather

これはヒール（かかと）が高すぎます。   heels, too high

Kore wa hiiru (kakato) ga takasugimasu.

ハイヒールは好きじゃありません。   high heels

Haihiiru wa suki ja arimasen.

ゴム底は好きじゃありません。   rubber soles

Gomuzoko wa suki ja arimasen.

サイズがあっていません。   size doesn't fit

Saizu ga atte imasen.

小さすぎます。   too small

Chiisasugmasu.

大きすぎます。   too big

Ookisugimasu.

幅が広すぎます。   width, too wide

Haba ga hirosugimasu.

狭すぎます。   too narrow

semasugimasu.

つま先が痛いです。   toes, painful

Tsumasaki ga itai desu.

靴ひもと靴墨もください。   shoelaces, shoe polish

Kutsuhimo to kutsuzumi mo kudasai.

1. Answer on basis of Fig. 15-2.

Fig. 15-2

1. これは靴ですか、サンダルですか、ブーツですか。
   Kore wa kutsu desu ka, sandaru desu ka, buutsu desu ka.

2. かかとは高いですか、低いですか。
   Kakato wa takai desu ka, hikui desu ka.

3. 靴ひもはついていますか。
   Kutsuhimo wa tsuite imasu ka.

2. Complete.

- ___1___。何をお探しですか。
   _1_. Nani o osagashi desu ka.

- 靴がほしいんですが。
   Kutsu ga hoshii ndesu ga.

- はい。___2___はおいくつですか。
   Hai. _2_ wa oikutsu desu ka.

- 24 ___3___です。
   Nijuuyon _3_ desu.

- ___4___が高いのと低いのとどちらがよろしいですか。
   _4_ ga takai no to hikui no to dochira ga yoroshii desu ka.

- 低い方がいいです。___5___は好きじゃないんです。
   Hikui hoo ga ii desu. _5_ wa suki ja nai ndesu.

- では、これはいかがですか。
   Dewa, kore wa ikaga desu ka.

- いいんですが、___6___があっていないようです。つま先が痛いです。
   Ii ndesu ga, _6_ ga atte inai yoo desu. Tsumasaki ga itai desu.

- それは___7___すぎますね。今、同じのでもう少し大きいのを持って来ます。
   Sore wa _7_ sugimasu ne. Ima, onaji no de moo sukoshi ookii no o motte kimasu.

BUYING MEN'S CLOTHING

いらっしゃいませ。何をお探しですか。
Irasshaimase. Nani o osagashi desu ka.

ジーンズ（ジーパン）がほしいんですが。   jeans
Jiinzu (Jiipan) ga hoshii ndesu ga.

ズボン（パンツ）   pants,
Zugon (Pantsu)

スラックス   trousers
Surakkusu

半ズボン   shorts
Hanzubon

ワイシャツ *Waishatsu*	dress shirt
Tシャツ *Tiishatsu*	T-shirt
下着 *Shitagi*	underwear
パンツ(ブリーフ・トランクス) *Pantsu (Buriifu, Torankusu)*	underpants (brief, boxer shorts)
シャツ *Shatsu*	shirt, undershirt
靴下 *Kutsushita*	socks
セーター *Seetaa*	sweater
スーツ *Suutsu*	suit
ジャケット *Jaketto*	jacket
オーバー *Oobaa*	overcoat
コート *Kooto*	coat
レインコート *Reinkooto*	raincoat
水着 *Mizugi*	bathing suit
ベルト *Beruto*	belt
ネクタイ *Nekutai*	necktie
ハンカチ *Hankachi*	handkerchief
帽子 *Booshi*	hat, cap
木綿（コットン）のシャツがいいんですが。 *Momen (Kotton) no shatsu ga ii ndesu ga.*	cotton
フランネル Furan-neru	flannel
シルク（絹） *Shiruku (Kinu)*	silk

ウール
Uuru   wool

ナイロン
Nairon   nylon

合繊（合成繊維）
Goosen (Gooseesen-i)   synthetic material

長袖
Nagasode   long sleeves

半袖
Hansode   short sleeves

しわになりにくいシャツ
Shiwa ni narinikui shatsu   wrinkle-resistant

コーデュロイのジャケットはありますか。
Koodyuroi no jaketto wa arimasu ka.   corduroy

デニム
Denimu   denim

皮
Kawa   leather

スエード
Sueedo   suede

ストライプ（縞）のシャツは好きじゃありません。
Sutoraipu (Shima) no shatsu wa suki ja arimasen.   striped

チェック
Chekku   checked (checkered)

無地
Muji   solid colored

このネクタイはこのチェックのシャツに合いません。
Kono nekutai wa kono chekku no shatsu ni *aimasen*   don't match

サイズはいくつですか。
Saizu wa ikutsu desu ka.

分かりません。計ってください。
Wakarimasen. *Hakatte* kudasai.   measure

サイズが合っていないようです。ちょっときついです。
Saizu ga atte inai yoo desu. Chotto *kitsui* desu.   size doesn't fit, tight

ファスナー（チャック、ジッパー）がいいですか。
Fasunaa (chakku, jippaa) ga ii desu ka.   zipper

ボタンがいいですか。
Botan ga ii desu ka.   button

3. List the items in a complete outfit of clothing for a man.

4. Complete.

- いらっしゃいませ。何をお探しですか。

    Irasshaimase. Nani o osagashi desu ka.

- シャツを見せてもらえませんか。

    Shatsu o misete moraemasen ka.

- 木綿のがよろしいですか。

    Momen no ga yoroshii desu ka.

- いえ、木綿は__1__になりますよね。__2__になりにくいのがいいんですが。

    Ie, momen wa __1__ ni narimasu yo ne. __2__ ni narinikui no ga ii ndesu.

- そうですか。今は夏ですので、__3__も__4__もありません。合繊のシャツはいかがでしょうか。

    Soo desu ka. Ima wa natsu desu node, __3__ mo __4__ mo arimasen. Goosen no shatsu wa ikaga deshoo ka.

- ええ、それでいいです。

    Ee, sore de ii desu.

- __5__はおいくつですか。

    __5__ wa oikutsu desu ka.

- Mです。

    Emu desu.

- 半袖でよろしいですか。

    Hansode de yoroshii desu ka.

- いえ、__6__の方がいいです。

    Ie, __6__ no hoo ga ii desu.

- ストライプとチェックとどちらがよろしいですか。

    Sutoraipu to chekku to dochira ga yoroshii desu ka.

- いえ、どちらもあまり好きじゃないんです。白か青の__7__のシャツがいいです。

    Ie, dochira mo amari suki ja nai ndesu. Siro ka ao no __7__ no shatsu ga ii desu.

5. Complete.

1. この縞のシャツは私のチェックのジャケットに全然____。

    Kono shima no shatsu wa watashi no chekku no jaketto ni zenzen __.

2. 昨日買ったズボンの____がこわれていました(broken)。

    Kinoo katta zubon no __ ga kowarete imashita.

3. このズボンは大きすぎるので、____がいります。

    Kono zubon wa ookisugiru node, __ ga irimasu.

4. 雨の日は____を着ます。

    Ame no hi wa __ o kimasu.

5. 下着がいります。____を六枚とパンツを六枚買います。

    Shitagi ga irimasu. __ o roku mai to pantsu o roku mai kaimasu.

6. 自分の服の_____が分かりません。店員に_____もらいます。

   Jibun no fuku no ___ ga wakarimasen. Ten-in ni ___ moraimasu.

7. コットンは好きじゃありません。_____の方がしわになりにくいから好きです。

   Kotton wa suki ja arimasen. ___ no hoo ga shiwa ni narinikui kara suki desu.

8. この帽子は_____すぎます。もう少し小さいのを見せてください。

   Kono booshi wa ___ sugimasu. Moo sukoshi chiisai no o misete kudasai.

BUYING WOMEN'S CLOTHING

いらっしゃいませ。どんなものをお探しですか。

Irasshaimase. Don-na mono o osagashi desu ka.

スカーフが欲しいんですが。	scarf
Sukaafu ga hoshii ndesu ga.	
コート	coat
Kooto	
ブラウス	blouse
Burausu	
スカート	skirt
Sukaato	
ジーンズ（ジーパン）	jeans
Jiinzu (Jiipan)	
パンツ	pants
Pantsu	
セーター	sweater
Seetaa	
スーツ	suit
Suutsu	
ワンピース	dress (one-piece dress)
Wanpiisu	
下着	underwear
Shitagi	
ショーツ	panties (underpants)
Shootsu	
スリップ	slip
Surippu	
ブラジャー	brassiere
Burajaa	
ガードル	girdle
Gaadoru	

ストッキング   panty hose
Sutokkingu

タイツ   tights
Taitsu

靴下   socks
Kutsushita

ハンカチ   handkerchief
Hankachi

帽子   cap or hat
Booshi

手袋   gloves
Tebukuro

マフラー   muffler, scarf
Mafuraa

ハンドバッグ   handbag
Handobaggu

水着   bathing suit
Mizugi

レーンコート   raincoat
Reen kooto

木綿（コットン）のブラウスがいいんですが。   cotton
Momen (Kotton) no burausu ga ii ndesu ga.

シルク（絹）   silk
Shiruku (Kinu)

ナイロン   nylon
Nairon

合繊（合成繊維）   synthetic material
Goosen (Gooseesen-i)

しわになりにくいブラウス   wrinkle-resistant
Shiwa ni narinikui burausu

長袖と半袖とどちらの方がいいですか。   long sleeves, short sleeves
Nagasode to hansode to dochira no hoo ga ii desu ka.

ストライプ（縞）のブラウスが欲しいです。   striped
Sutoraipu (Shima) no burausu ga hoshii desu.

チェック   checked (checkered)
Chekku

水玉模様   polka-dotted
Mizutama moyoo

レース	lace
Reesu	
コーデュロイのスカートが欲しいです。	corduroy
Koodyuroi no sukaato ga hoshii desu.	
ウール	wool
Uuru	
スエード	suede
Sueedo	
サイズはいくつですか。	size
Saizu wa ikutsu desu ka.	
11 号です。	size 11
Juuichi goo desu.	
分かりません。計っていただけますか。	measure
Wakarimasen. Hakatte itadakemasu ka.	

6. List the items in a complete outfit of clothing for a woman.

7. Answer based on Fig. 15-3.

Fig. 15-3

1. この長袖のシャツは＿＿＿です。

   Kono nagasode no shatsu wa ___ desu.

2. この半袖のシャツは＿＿＿です。

   Kono hansode no shatsu wa ___ desu.

3. このスカーフは＿＿＿です。

   Kono sukaafu wa ___ desu.

8. Complete.

1. コットンのシャツは＿＿＿になりやすいから好きじゃありません。＿＿＿の方がいいです。

   Kotton no shatsu wa ___ ni nariyasui kara suki ja arimasen. ___ no hoo ga ii desu.

2. ストライプのシャツはチェックのスカートに＿＿＿。

   Sutoraipu no shatsu wa chekku no sukaato ni ___.

3. サイズが分かりません。＿＿＿に計ってもらいます。

   Saizu ga wakarimasen. ___ ni hakatte moraimasu.

9. Choose the appropriate word.

1. ＿＿＿のシャツが欲しいです。 (a) 皮　　(b) 合成繊維

   ___ no shatsu ga hoshii desu.　　(a) Kawa　(b) Gooseesen-i

2. スカートより＿＿＿の方が好きです。 (a) パンツスーツ　　(b) スカーフ

   Sukaato yori ___ no hoo ga suki desu.　　(a) pantsu suutsu　　　(b) sukaafu

3. スエードの＿＿＿はありますか。 (a) 靴　　(b) 靴下

   Sueedo no ___ wa arimasen ka.　　(a) kutsu　(b) kutsushita

4. ＿＿＿のスカーフを買いました。 (a) シルク　　(b) 皮

   ___ no sukaafu o kaimashta.　　(a) Shiruku　　(b) Kawa

5. 寒いです。＿＿＿がいります。　　(a) セーター　　(b) 水着

   Samui desu. ___ ga irimasu.　　(a) Seetaa　　(b) Mizugi

Key Words

bathing suit	水着	mizugi	checked (checkered)	チェック	chekku
beige	ベージュ	beeju	clothing	洋服	yoofuku
belt	ベルト	beruto	coat	コート	kooto
black	黒	kuro	corduroy	コーデュロイ	koodyuroi
blouse	ブラウス	burausu	cotton	木綿（コットン）	momen (kotton)
boots	ブーツ	buutsu			
boxer shorts	トランクス	torankusu	denim	デニム	denimu
brassiere	ブラジャー	burajaa	dress (one-piece dress)	ワンピース	wanpiisu
brief	ブリーフ	buriifu			
brown	茶色	chairo	dress shirt	ワイシャツ	waishatsu
buttons	ボタン	botan	fit	合う	au
cap, hat	帽子	booshi	flannel	フランネル	furan-neru
centimeter	センチ	senchi			

girdle	ガードル	gaadoru	shorts	半ズボン	hanzubon
gloves	手袋	tebukuro	silk	シルク（絹）	shiruku (kinu)
handbag	ハンドバッグ	handobaggu	size	号	goo
handkerchief	ハンカチ	hankachi	size	サイズ	saizu
heels	ヒール（かかと）	hiiru (kakato)	skirt	スカート	sukaato
			slip	スリップ	surippu
high heels	ハイヒール	haihiiru	slippers	スリッパ	surippa
jacket	ジャケット	jaketto	sneakers	スニーカー	suniikaa
jeans	ジーンズ（ジーパン）	jiinzu (jiipan)	socks	靴下	kutsushita
			soles	底	soko
lace	レース	reesu	solid colored	無地	muji
leather	皮	kawa	striped	ストライプ（縞）	sutoraipu (shima)
long sleeves	長袖	nagasode			
look for	探す	sagasu	suede	スエード	sueedo
match	合う	au	suit	スーツ	suutsu
May I help you? (lit. Welcome)	いらっしゃいませ	irasshaimase	sweater	セーター	seetaa
			synthetic material	合繊（合成繊維）	goosen (goosee sen-i)
measure	計る	hakaru	tight	きつい	kitsui
muffler, scarf	マフラー	mahuraa	tights	タイツ	taitsu
necktie	ネクタイ	nekutai	toes	つま先	tsumasaki
nylon	ナイロン	nairon	too big	大きすぎる	ookisugiru
overcoat	オーバー	oobaa	too high	高すぎる	takasugiru
painful	痛い	itai	too narrow	狭すぎる	semasugiru
panties (underpants)	ショーツ	shootsu	too small	小さすぎる	chiisasugiru
			too wide	広すぎる	hirosugiru
pants	ズボン（パンツ）	zubon (pantsu)	trousers	スラックス	surakkusu
			T-shirt	Tシャツ	tiishatsu
panty hose	ストッキング	sutokkingu	underpants	パンツ	pantsu
polka-dotted	水玉模様	mizutama moyoo	underwear	下着	shitagi
raincoat	レーンコート	reen kooto	white	白	shiro
rubber soles	ゴム底	gomuzoko	width	幅	haba
sandals	サンダル	sandaru	wool	ウール	uuru
scarf	スカーフ	sukaafu	wrinkle-free	しわになりにくい	shiwa ni narinikui
shirt, undershirt	シャツ	shatsu			
shoe polish	靴墨	kutsuzumi	zipper	ファスナー（チャック、ジッパー）	fasunaa (chakku, jippaa)
shoelace	靴ひも	kutsuhimo			
shoes	靴	kutsu			
short sleeves	半袖	hansode			

Chapter 16: At home
第16章：家で
Uchi de

THE KITCHEN

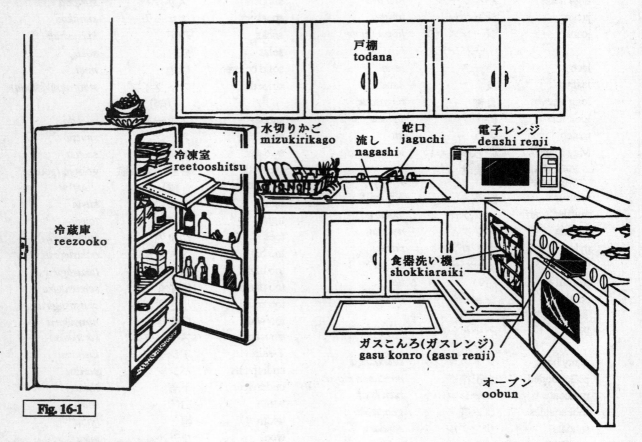

戸棚
todana

水切りかご
mizukirikago

流し
nagashi

蛇口
jaguchi

電子レンジ
denshi renji

冷凍室
reetooshitsu

冷蔵庫
reezooko

食器洗い機
shokkiaraiki

ガスこんろ（ガスレンジ）
gasu konro (gasu renji)

オーブン
oobun

Fig. 16-1

WASHING THE DISHES

流しで食器を洗います。	sink, dishes, wash
Nagashi de *shokki* o *araimasu.*	
蛇口をひねって、水を出します。	faucet, turn on, water
Jaguchi o hinette, mizu o dashimasu.	
スポンジに洗剤をつけます。	sponge, liquid detergent
Suponji ni *senzai* o tsukemasu.	
そのスポンジで食器を洗います。	
Sono suponji de shokki o araimasu.	
食器を水ですすぎます。	rinse
Shokki o mizu de *susugimasu.*	
お湯	hot water
oyu	

118

洗った食器は**水切りかご**に入れます。　　　　　　　　dish drainer
Aratta shokki wa *mizukiri kago* ni iremasu.

食器を**ふきん**で**ふきます**。　　　　　　　　　　dish towel, dry (lit. wipe)
Shokki o *fukin* de *fukimasu*.

1. Complete.

晩ご飯が終わって、今から＿1＿を洗います。まず、＿2＿をひねって水を出します。スポンジに＿3＿を
Bangohan ga owatte, ima kara ＿1＿ o araimasu. Mazu, ＿2＿ o hinette mizu o dashimasu. Suponji ni ＿3＿ o

少しつけます。そのスポンジで＿4＿を洗って、水で＿5＿。洗った食器は＿6＿に入れて、ふきんで
sukoshi tsukemasu. Sono suponji de ＿4＿ o aratte, mizu de ＿5＿. Aratta shokki wa ＿6＿ ni irete, fukin de

ふきます。
fukimasu.

COOKING

料理をします。　　　　　　　　　　　　　　cooking
Ryoori o shimasu.

鍋で**肉**と**野菜**を**煮ます**。　　　　　　stew pan, meat, vegetable, cook
Nabe de *niku* to *yasai* o *nimasu*.

鍋で**卵**を**ゆでます**。　　　　　　　　　　egg, boil
Nabe de *tamago* o *yudemasu*.

フライパンで**ステーキ**を**焼きます**。　　　frying pan, steak, grill
Furaipan de *suteeki* o *yakimasu*.

フライパンで野菜を**炒めます**。　　　　　　fry
Furaipan de yasai o *itamemasu*.

オーブンで**パン**を焼きます。　　　　　　oven, bread, bake
Oobun de *pan* o *yakimasu*.

炊飯器で**ご飯**を**炊きます**。　　　　　　rice cooker, rice, cook
Suihanki de *gohan* o *takimasu*.

てんぷらを**揚げます**。　　　　　　　　tempura, deep-fry
Tenpura o *agemasu*.

バターを**溶かします**。　　　　　　　　butter, melt
Bataa o *tokashimasu*.

シチューを**煮込みます**。　　　　　stew, simmer (boil for a long time)
Shichuu o *nikomimasu*.

ふたをします。　　　　　　　　　　lid
Futa o shimasu.

沸騰させます。　　　　　　　　　　heat to boiling
Futtoo sasemasu.

じゃがいもの**皮**を**むきます**。　　　potato, skin, peel
Jagaimo no *kawa* o *mukimasu*.

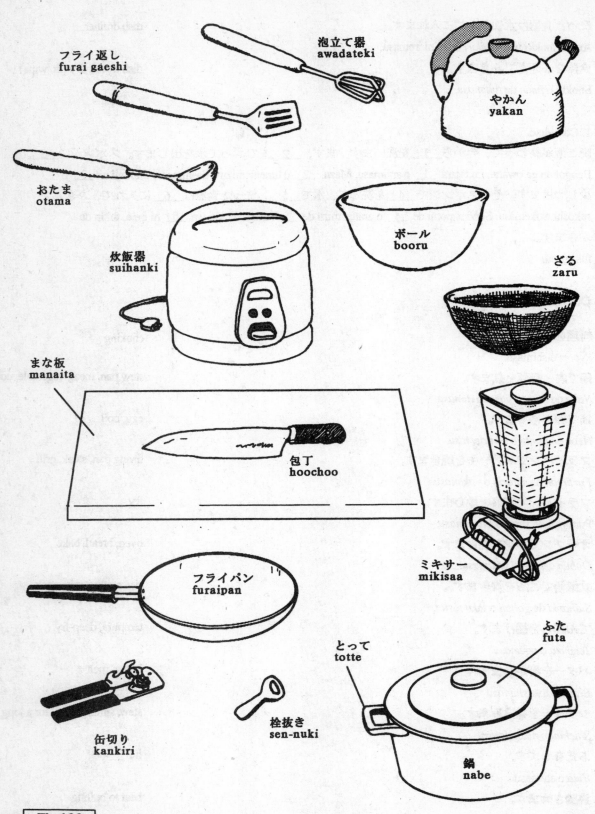

フライ返し
furai gaeshi

泡立て器
awadateki

やかん
yakan

おたま
otama

炊飯器
suihanki

ボール
booru

ざる
zaru

まな板
manaita

包丁
hoochoo

ミキサー
mikisaa

フライパン
furaipan

とって
totte

ふた
futa

缶切り
kankiri

栓抜き
sen-nuki

鍋
nabe

Fig. 16-2

包丁で肉を切ります。

Hoochoo de niku o *kirimasu.*

まな板の上で野菜を切ります。

Manaita no ue de yasai o kirimasu.

ざるで野菜の水気を切ります。

Zaru de yasai no *mizuke o kirimasu.*

米をとぎます。

Kome o *togimasu.*

泡だて器で卵を泡立てます。

Awadateki de tamago o *awadatemasu.*

フライ返しで肉をひっくり返します。

Furaigaeshi de niku o *hikkurikaeshimasu.*

やかんでお湯をわかします。

Yakan de *oyu o wakashimasu.*

kitchen knife, cut	
cutting board	
colander, drain	
rice, rinse (wash)	
whisk, whip	
turner, turn over	
kettle, boil the water	

2. Tell which utensil you need.

1. トマトを切る

   tomato o kiru

2. 缶詰を開ける

   kanzume o akeru

3. 水気を切る

   mizuke o kiru

4. フライパンの中の魚をひっくり返す

   furaipan no naka no sakana o hikkurikaesu

5. 卵を泡立てる

   tamago o awadateru

6. お茶を入れるためにお湯をわかす

   ocha o ireru tame ni oyu o wakasu

7. ご飯を炊く

   gohan o taku

8. ミックスジュースを作る

   mikkusu juusu o tsukuru

3. Identify each item in Fig. 16-3.

4. Complete.

1. ＿＿＿で玉ねぎ(onion)の＿＿＿をむいて、＿＿＿の上で切ります。

   ___ de tamanegi no ___ o muite, ___ no ue de kirimasu.

2. 鍋に＿＿＿をわかして、卵を入れて＿＿＿。

   Nabe ni ___ o wakashite, tamago o irete ___.

Fig. 16-3

3. サラダを作ります。野菜を＿＿＿から、ざるに入れて、野菜の＿＿＿をよく切ります。

   Sarada o tsukurimasu. Yasai o ＿＿ kara, zaru ni irete, yasai no ＿＿ o yoku kirimasu.

4. ご飯を炊く時は、まず米を＿＿＿、それを＿＿＿に入れてスイッチを入れます。

   Gohan o taku toki ha, mazu kome o ＿＿, sore o ＿＿ ni irete suicchi o iremasu.

5. Give the Japanese verb for:

1. bake something in the oven

2. boil something such as potatoes

3. melt butter

4. whip

5. fry something in a frying pan

6. deep-fry

THE BATHEROOM AND TOILET

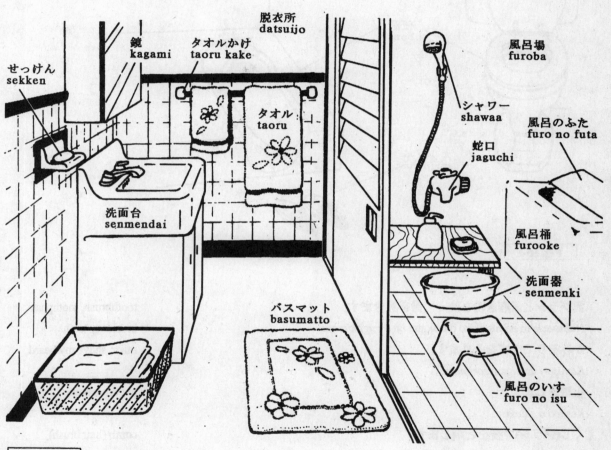

せっけん
sekken

鏡
kagami

タオルかけ
taoru kake

脱衣所
datsuijo

風呂場
furoba

タオル
taoru

シャワー
shawaa

蛇口
jaguchi

風呂のふた
furo no futa

洗面台
senmendai

風呂桶
furooke

洗面器
senmenki

バスマット
basumatto

風呂のいす
furo no isu

Fig. 16-4

<朝>

<Asa>

シャワーを浴びます。   take a shower

Shawaa o abimasu.

せっけんで顔を洗います。   soap, wash my face

Sekken de kao o araimasu.

お手洗い(トイレ)
otearai (toire)

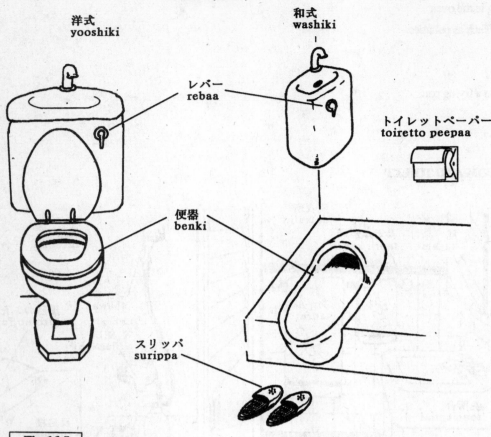

洋式
yooshiki

和式
washiki

レバー
rebaa

トイレットペーパー
toiretto peepaa

便器
benki

スリッパ
surippa

Fig. 16-5

歯ブラシと歯磨き粉を使って歯を磨きます。

Haburashi to *hamigakiko* o tsukatte *ha o migakimasu.*

かみそりでひげをそります。

Kamisori de hige o sorimasu.

化粧をします。

Keshoo o shimasu.

くし(ブラシ)で髪をとかします。

Kushi (Burashi) de kami o tokashimasu.

<夜>

<Yoru>

お風呂に入ります。

Ofuro ni hairimasu.

髪を洗います（シャンプーをします）。

Kami o araimasu (Shanpuu o shimasu).

toothbrush, toothpaste,

brush my teeth

razor, shave my beard

put on makeup

comb (hair brush),

comb my hair

take a bath

wash my hair (shampoo)

タオルで体をふきます。

Taoru de karada o fukimasu.

ドライヤーで髪を乾かします。

Doraiyaa de kami o kawakashimasu.

towel, dry (lit. wipe) my body

dryer, dry my hair

6. Complete.

1. 外から帰ったら手を洗います。＿＿＿を使ってよく洗います。

   Soto kara kaettara te o araimasu. ＿＿ o tsukatte yoku araimasu.

2. 日本では、たいていの人は夜＿＿＿に入りますが、朝、＿＿＿を浴びる人もいます。

   Nihon de wa, taitee no hito wa yoru ＿＿ ni hairimasu ga, asa, ＿＿ o abiru hito mo imasu.

3. ＿＿＿で服を脱いでから、風呂場に入ります。

   ＿＿ de fuku o nuide kara, furoba ni hairimasu.

4. シャワーを浴びたら、タオルで体を＿＿＿。

   Shawaa o abitara, taoru de karada o ＿＿.

5. 化粧をする時、＿＿＿で顔を見てします。

   Keshoo o suru toki, ＿＿ de kao o mite shimasu.

6. ＿＿＿で歯を磨きます。

   ＿＿ de ha o migakimasu.

7. 日本のトイレには＿＿＿式と＿＿＿式があります。

   Nihon no toire ni wa ＿＿ shiki to ＿＿ shiki ga arimasu.

7. Label each item in Fig. 16-6.

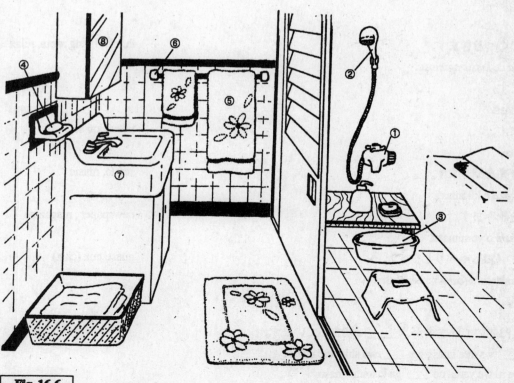

Fig. 16-6

THE LIVING ROOM

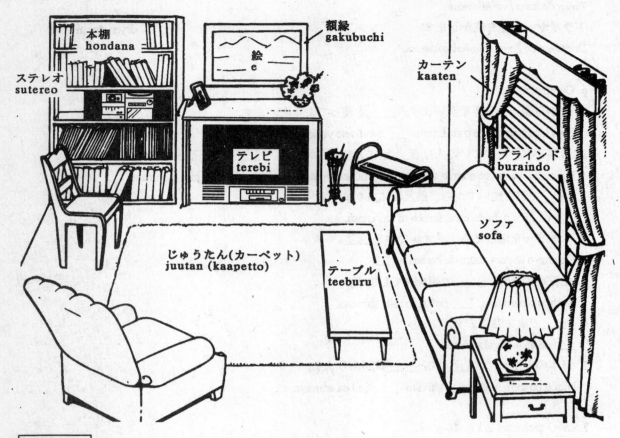

Fig. 16-7

家族は居間でくつろぎます。   family, living room, relax
Kazoku wa *ima* de *kutsurogimasu.*

お茶を飲みます。   tea
Ocha o nomimasu.

テレビを見ます。   television set
Terebi o mimasu.

ステレオで音楽を聞きます。   stereo, music
Sutereo de *ongaku* o kikimasu.

新聞や雑誌を読みます。   newspaper , magazine
Shinbun ya *zasshi* o yomimasu.

客と話します（おしゃべりします）。   guest, talk (chat)
Kyaku to *hanashimasu (oshaberishimasu).*

8. Complete.

1. 窓の＿＿＿は開いていますが、＿＿＿は閉まっています。

   Mado no ＿＿ wa aite imasu ga, ＿＿ wa shimatte imasu.

   Ima no kabe ni wa yama no ＿＿ ga kakatte imasu.

2. ＿＿＿に本がたくさんあります。

　　___ ni hon ga takusan arimasu.

3. 居間の＿＿＿に座って、＿＿＿したり、お茶を飲んだりします。

　　Ima no ___ ni suwatte, ___ shitari, ocha o nondari shimasu.

4. 夜、時々＿＿＿を見たり、＿＿＿で音楽を聞いたりします。

　　Yoru, tokidoki ___ o mitari, ___ de ongaku o kiitari shimasu.

5. 今日、家にいるのは家族だけです。＿＿＿はいません。

　　Kyoo, uchi ni iru no wa kazoku dake desu. ___ wa imasen.

6. 居間の壁(wall)には山の＿＿＿がかかっています。

　　Ima no kabe ni wa yama no ＿＿＿ ga kakatte imasu.

THE JAPANESE-STYLE ROOM

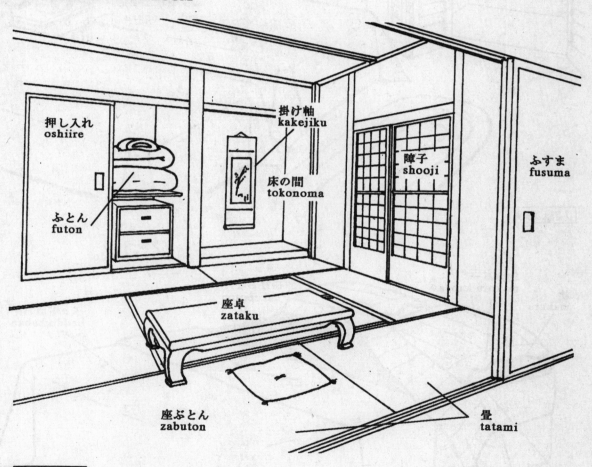

押し入れ oshiire
掛け軸 kakejiku
床の間 tokonoma
障子 shooji
ふすま fusuma
ふとん futon
座卓 zataku
座ぶとん zabuton
畳 tatami

Fig. 16-8

THE BEDROOM

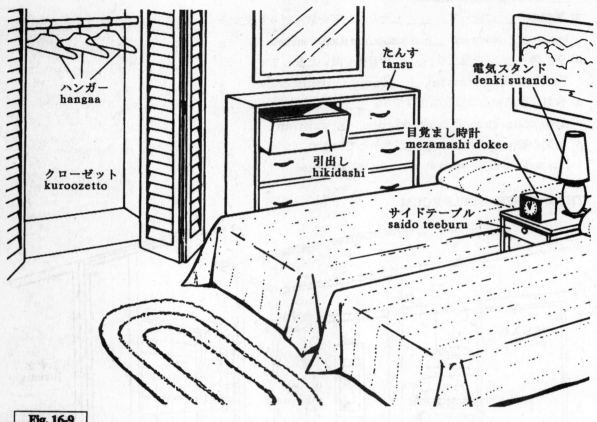

ハンガー
hangaa

クローゼット
kuroozetto

たんす
tansu

電気スタンド
denki sutando

目覚まし時計
mezamashi dokee

引出し
hikidashi

サイドテーブル
saido teeburu

Fig. 16-9

ダブルベッド
daburu beddo

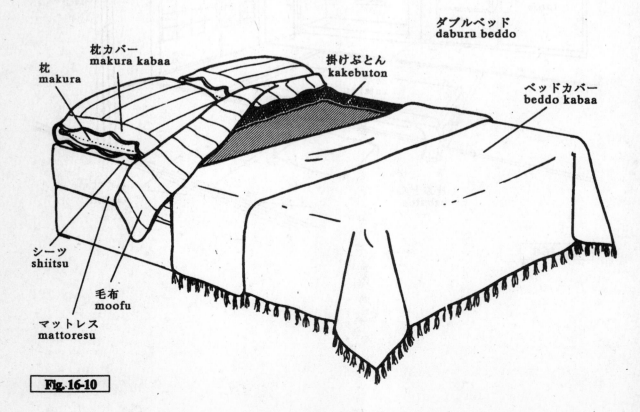

枕
makura

枕カバー
makura kabaa

掛けぶとん
kakebuton

ベッドカバー
beddo kabaa

シーツ
shiitsu

毛布
moofu

マットレス
mattoresu

Fig. 16-10

Japanese	Romaji	English

もう 11 時です。寝室（ベッドルーム）に行って、寝ます。 — **bedroom, go to bed**
Moo juuichiji desu. *Shinshitsu (Beddo ruumu)* ni itte, *nemasu.*

目覚し時計を七時にセットします。 — **alarm clock, set**
Mezamashidokee o shichiji ni *setto shimasu.*

私は毎日八時間寝ます。 — **sleep**
Watashi wa mainichi hachijikan *nemasu.*

寝つきがいいです。 — **get to sleep easily**
Netsuki ga ii desu.

　　悪いです — **don't get to sleep easily**
　　warui desu.

七時に起きます。 — **wake up**
Shichiji ni *okimasu.*

ベッドを整えます。 — **make the bed**
Beddo o totonoemasu.

ふとんを敷きます。 — **futon , spread out**
Futon o shikimasu.

　　たたみます。 — **fold up**
　　tatamimasu.

9. Complete.

1. ＿＿＿にベッドが二つあります。ベッドの間に＿＿＿があって、その上に＿＿＿と＿＿＿があります。
   ___ ni beddo ga futatsu arimasu. Beddo no aida ni ___ ga atte, sono ue ni ___ to ___ ga arimasu.

2. 二人で寝るベッドを＿＿＿といいます。
   Futari de neru beddo o ___ to iimasu.

3. ダブルベッドにはたいてい＿＿＿が二つあります。
   Daburu beddo ni wa taitee ___ ga futatsu arimasu.

4. このたんすには＿＿＿が五つあります。
   Kono tansu ni wa ___ ga itsutsu arimasu.

5. クローゼットの中に＿＿＿があります。そこに洋服をかけます。
   Kuroozetto no naka ni ___ ga arimasu. Soko ni yoofuku o kakemasu.

6. 日本式(style)のふとんに寝る時は、＿＿＿からふとんを出して、ふとんを＿＿＿。そして、朝起きたら
   Nihon shiki no futon ni neru toki wa, ___ kara futon o dashite, futon o ___. Soshite, asa okitara
   ふとんを＿＿＿。
   futon o ___.

10. Name six items that go on a bed.

11. Answer.

1. あなたはたいてい何時に寝ますか。
   Anata wa taitee nanji ni nemasu ka.

2. 寝る前に目覚し時計をセットしますか。

   Neru mae ni mezamashidokee o setto shimasu ka.

3. 何時間ぐらい寝ますか。

   Nanjikan gurai nemasu ka.

4. 寝つきはいいですか、悪いですか。

   Netsuki wa ii desu ka, warui desu ka.

5. たいてい何時に起きますか。

   Taitee nanji ni okimasu ka.

HOUSEWORK

汚れた服を洗います。   dirty clothes, wash

Yogoreta fuku o araimasu.

洗濯をします。   do the laundry

Sentaku o shimasu.

洗濯物を洗濯機に入れます。   laundry, washing machine

Sentakumono o sentakuki ni iremasu.

      乾燥機   dryer

      kansooki

      干します。   hung out to dry

      hoshimasu.

アイロンをかけます。   iron

Airon o kakemasu.

アイロンとアイロン台はどこにありますか。   iron, ironing board

Airon to airondai wa doko ni arimasu ka.

掃除をします。   clean

Sooji o shimasu.

家具のほこりをはらいます。   furniture, dust, brush off

Kagu no hokori o haraimasu.

ぞうきんで窓ガラスをふきます。   cleaning rag, windowpane, wipe

Zookin de madogarasu o fukimasu.

ほうきとちりとりを使って、床をはきます。   broom, dustpan, floor, sweep

Hooki to chiritori o tsukatte, yuka o hakimasu.

掃除機をかけます。   vacuum

Soojiki o kakemasu.

モップをかけます。   mop

Moppu o kakemasu.

ブラシで便器をみがきます。   brush, toilet, scrub

Burashi de benki o migakimasu.

スポンジで風呂桶を洗います。   sponge, bathtub
Suponji de *furo-oke* o araimasu.

ごみを捨てます。   garbage, throw away
Gomi o *sutemasu.*

　　　出します。   take out
　　dashimasu.

12. Complete.

今日はすることがたくさんあります。洗濯物がたくさんあるから、__1__ をしましょう。洗濯物を
Kyoo wa suru koto ga takusan arimasu. Sentakumono ga takusan aru kara, __1__ o shimashoo. Sentakumono o
__2__ に入れます。洗濯が終わったら__3__ に入れます。それから__4__ の上で、シャツにアイロンを__5__ 。
__2__ ni iremasu. Sentaku ga owattara, __3__ ni iremasu. Sorekara, __4__ no ue de, shatsu ni airon o __5__.
次は居間の掃除をします。居間のじゅうたんに__6__ をかける前に、家具の__7__ をはらいます。
Tsugi wa ima no sooji o shimasu. Ima no juutan ni __6__ o kakeru mae ni, kagu no __7__ o haraimasu.
時間があったら、窓ガラスも__8__ 。
Jikan ga attara, madogarasu mo __8__.

13. Match.

1. アイロンをかける   (a) ぞうきん
   airon o kakeru   zookin

2. はく   (b) アイロン台
   haku   airondai

3. 便器をみがく   (c) スポンジ
   benki o migaku   suponji

4. 窓ガラスをふく   (d) ほうき
   madogarasu o fuku   hooki

5. 風呂桶を洗う   (e) ブラシ
   furo-oke o arau   burashi

SOME MINOR PROBLEMS AROUND THE HOME

部屋の電気をつけます。   turn on the light
Heya no *denki o tsukemasu.*

電気がつきません。   it won't go on
Denki ga *tsukimasen.*

電球が切れたんでしょうか。   light bulb, burned out
Denkyuu ga *kireta* ndeshoo ka.

いいえ、プラグがはずれていました。   plug is off (is not inserted)
Iie, *puragu* ga *hazurete imashita.*

プラグを**コンセント**に**差しこみます**。 — wall-outlet, plug in

Puragu o *konsento* ni *sashikomimasu.*

電気を消していないのに、**電気が消えました**。 — turn off the light, it went off

Denki o keshite inai noni , *denki ga kiemashita.*

ヒューズがとんだようです。 — fuse blew

Hyuuzu ga tonda yoo desu.

ヒューズボックスを**チェック**します。 — fuse box, check

Hyuuzu bokkusu o *chekku* shimasu.

電気の**スイッチ**はどこですか。 — switch

Denki no *suicchi* wa doko desu ka.

洗面台の水が**流れません**。 — washbasin, won't drain

Senmendai no mizu ga *nagaremasen.*

詰まってしまったようです。 — clogged up

Tsumatte shimatta yoo desu.

パイプ(水道管)から水が**漏れて**います。 — pipes, leaking

Paipu (Suidookan) kara mizu ga *morete imasu.*

修理の人を呼びます。 — repairman

Shuuri no hito o yobimasu.

14. Complete.

テレビがつきません。どうしたんでしょうか。あ、テレビのプラグが__1__からはずれていました。

Terebi ga tsukimasen. Doo shita ndeshoo ka. A, terebi no puragu ga __1__ kara hazurete imashita.

プラグを__2__に__3__。あ、つきました。

Puragu o __1__ ni __3__. A, tsukimashita.

15. Complete.

電気が__1__。どうしたんでしょうか。私は消していませんよ。__2__がとんだかもしれません。

Denki ga __1__. Doo shita ndeshoo ka. Watashi wa keshite imasen yo. __2__ ga tonda kamo shiremasen.

ヒューズボックスを__3__します。でも、よく分かりません。これは__4__の人を呼んだ方がいいですね。

Hyuuzu bokkusu o __3__ shimasu. Demo, yoku wakarimasen. Kore wa __4__ no hito o yonda hoo ga ii desu ne.

16. Complete.

- トイレの水が__1__。どうしたんでしょうか。

  Toire no mizu ga __1__. Doo shita ndeshoo ka.

- __2__しまったようですね。

  __2__ shimatta yoo desu ne.

- 修理の人を呼んで、見てもらいましょう。

  Shuuri no hito o yonde, mite moraimashoo.

Key Words

alarm clock	目覚し時計	*mezamashidokee*
bath	お風呂	*ofuro*
bathmat	バスマット	*basumatto*
bathroom	風呂場	*furoba*
bathroom chair	風呂の椅子	*furo no isu*
bathtub	風呂桶	*furooke*
bathtub cover	風呂桶のふた	*furooke no futa*
beard	ひげ	*hige*
bed	ベッド	*beddo*
bedroom	寝室（ベッドルーム）	*shinshitsu (beddo ruumu)*
bedspread	ベッドカバー	*beddo kabaa*
blanket	毛布	*moofu*
blender	ミキサー	*mikisaa*
blind	ブラインド	*buraindo*
blow (fuse)	とぶ	*tobu*
body	体	*karada*
boil	ゆでる	*yuderu*
boil the water	湯をわかす	*yu o wakasu*
bookshelf	本棚	*hondana*
bottle opener	栓抜き	*sen-nuki*
bowl	ボール	*booru*
bread	パン	*pan*
bread, bake, grill	焼く	*yaku*
broom	ほうき	*hooki*
brush my	磨く	*migaku*
brush off	はらう	*haru*
brush, hair brush	ブラシ	*burashi*
burn out	切れる	*kireru*
butter	バター	*bataa*
can opener	缶切り	*kankiri*
canned food	缶詰	*kanzume*
carpet	じゅうたん（カーペット）	*juutan (kaapetto)*
changing room	脱衣所	*datsuijo*
check	チェックする	*chekku suru*
chest, wardrobe	たんす	*tansu*
clean	掃除をする	*sooji o suru*
cleaning rag,	ぞうきん	*zookin*
clogged up	詰まる	*tsumaru*
closet	クローゼット	*kuroozetto*
clothes	服	*fuku*
colander	ざる	*zaru*
comb	くし	*kushi*
comb one's hair	髪をとかす	*kami o tokasu*
comforter quilt	掛けぶとん	*kakebuton*
cook	煮る	*niru*
cook (rice)	炊く	*taku*
cooked rice	ご飯	*gohan*
cooking	料理	*ryoori*
cupboard	戸棚	*todana*
curtain	カーテン	*kaaten*
cut	切る	*kiru*
cutting board	まな板	*manaita*
deep-fry	揚げる	*ageru*
desk lamp	電気スタンド	*denki sutando*
dirty	汚れている	*yogorete iru*
dish drainer	水切りかご	*mizukiri kago*
dish towel	ふきん	*fukin*
dishes	食器	*shokki*
do the laundry	洗濯をする	*sentaku o suru*
don't get to sleep easily	寝つきが悪い	*netsuki ga warui*
double bed	ダブルベッド	*daburu beddo*
drain	水気を切る	*mizuke o kiru*
drain	流れる	*nagareru*
drawer	引き出し	*hikidashi*
dry	乾かす	*kawakasu*
dry (lit. wipe)	ふく	*fuku*
dryer	ドライヤー	*doraiyaa*
dryer	乾燥機	*kansooki*
dust	ほこり	*hokori*
dustpan	ちりとり	*chiritori*
egg	卵	*tamago*
face	顔	*kao*
family	家族	*kazoku*
faucet	蛇口	*jaguchi*
floor	床	*yuka*
floor cushion	座布団	*zabuton*
fold up	たたむ	*tatamu*
freezer	冷凍庫	*reetooko*
fry	炒める	*itameru*
frying pan	フライパン	*furaipan*
furniture	家具	*kagu*
fuse	ヒューズ	*hyuuzu*
fuse box	ヒューズボックス	*hyuuzu bokkusu*
fusuma, Japanese sliding door	ふすま	*fusuma*
futon	ふとん	*futon*
garbage	ごみ	*gomi*

gas cooker	ガスこんろ (ガスレンジ)	gasu konro (gasu renji)	oven	オーブン	oobun
			peel	むく	muku
get to sleep easily	寝つきがいい	netsuki ga ii	picture	絵	e
			picture frame	額縁	gakubuchi
go off	消える	kieru	pillow	枕	makura
guest	客	kyaku	pillowcase	枕カバー	makura kabaa
hair	髪	kami	pipes	パイプ(水道管)	paipu (suidookan)
handle	とって	totte			
hanger	ハンガー	hangaa	plug	プラグ	puragu
hanging scroll	掛け軸	kakejiku	plug	風呂桶の栓	furooke no sen
heat to boiling	沸騰させる	futtoo saseru	plug in	差しこむ	sashikomu
home	家	uchi	potato	じゃがいも	jagaimo
hot water	お湯	oyu	razor	かみそり	kamisori
hung out to dry	干す	hosu	refrigerator	冷蔵庫	reezooko
iron	アイロン	airon	relax	くつろぐ	kutsurogu
iron	アイロンをかける	airon o kakeru	repairman	修理の人	shuuri no hito
			rice	米	kome
ironing board	アイロン台	airon dai	rice cooker	炊飯器	suihanki
is off	はずれている	hazurete iru	rinse	すすぐ	susugu
Japanese futon	布団	futon	rinse rice	米をとぐ	kome o togu
Japanese style	和式	washiki	scrub	みがく	migaku
kettle	やかん	yakan	set	セット	setto
kitchen knife	包丁	hoochoo	shampoo	シャンプー	shanpuu
ladle	おたま	otama	shave	そる	soru
laundry	洗濯物	sentaku mono	sheet	シーツ	shiitsu
leak	漏れる	moreru	shoji, Japanese sliding paper screen	障子	shooji
lever	レバー	rebaa			
lid	ふた	futa			
light	電気	denki	shower	シャワー	shawaa
light bulb	電球	denkyuu	side table	サイドテーブル	saido teeburu
liquid detergent	洗剤	senzai			
living room	居間	ima	simmer (boil for a long time)	煮込む	nikomu
low table	座卓	zataku			
magazine	雑誌	zasshi			
make the bed	ベッドを整える	beddo o totonoeru	sink	流し	nagashi
			skin	皮	kawa
makeup	化粧	keshoo	sleep, go to bed	寝る	neru
mattress	マットレス	mattoresu	slippers	スリッパ	surippa
meat	肉	niku	soap	せっけん	sekken
melt	溶かす	tokasu	sofa	ソファ	sofa
microwave oven	電子レンジ	denshi renji	sponge	スポンジ	suponji
			spread out	敷く	shiku
mirror	鏡	kagami	steak	ステーキ	suteeki
mop	モップをかける	moppu o kakeru	stereo	ステレオ	sutereo
			stew	シチュー	shichuu
music	音楽	ongaku	stew pan	鍋	nabè
newspaper	新聞	shinbun	sweep	はく	haku
oshi-ire, Japanese style built-in closet	押し入れ	oshiire	switch	スイッチ	suicchi
			table	テーブル	teeburu
			take a bath	お風呂に入る	ofuro ni hairu

take a shower	浴びる	*abiru*		turn on	ひねる	*hineru*
take out	出す	*dasu*		turn on, go on	つく	*tsuku*
talk (chat)	話す（おしゃべりする）	*hanasu (oshaberi suru)*		turn over	ひっくり返す	*hikkurikaesu*
				turner	フライ返し	*furaigaeshi*
tatami mat	畳	*tatami*		vacuum	掃除機をかける	*soojiki o kakeru*
tea	お茶	*ocha*				
teeth	歯	*ha*		vegetable	野菜	*yasai*
television set	テレビ	*terebi*		wake up	起きる	*okiru*
tempura	てんぷら	*tenpura*		wall-outlet	コンセント	*konsento*
throw away	捨てる	*suteru*		wash	洗う	*arau*
toilet	お手洗い（トイレ）	*otearai (toire)*		washbasin	洗面台	*senmendai*
				washbowl	洗面器	*senmenki*
toilet	便器	*benki*		washing machine	洗濯機	*sentakuki*
toilet paper	トイレットペーパー	*toiretto peepaa*		washroom	洗面所	*senmenjo*
tokonoma, alcove	床の間	*toko no ma*		waste basket	ごみ箱	*gomibako*
				water	水	*mizu*
toothbrush	歯ブラシ	*haburashi*		Western style	洋式	*yooshiki*
toothpaste	歯磨き粉	*hamigakiko*		whip	泡立てる	*awadateru*
towel	タオル	*taoru*		whisk	泡だて器	*awadateki*
towel bar	タオルかけ	*taorukake*		windowpane	窓ガラス	*madogarasu*
turn off	消す	*kesu*				

Chapter 17: At the hospital

第 17 章 : 病院で

        Byooin de

ADMITTANCE

<病院の受付で>	hospital (clinic), reception
<Byooin no *uketsuke* de>	
診察をお願いします。	medical examination
Shinsatsu o onegaishimasu.	
診てもらいたいんですが。	want to see a doctor
Mite moraitai ndesu ga.	
この用紙に記入してください。	form, fill in
Kono *yooshi* ni *kinyuu shite* kudasai.	
保険証はありますか。	health insurance card
Hokenshoo wa arimasu ka.	
診察券はありますか。	appointment card (patient
Shinsatsuken wa arimasu ka.	registration card)

1. Complete.

初めての病院で＿1＿をしてもらう時は、まず＿2＿に行きます。そこで＿3＿をもらって名前などを

Hajimete no byooin de ＿1＿ o shite morau toki wa, mazu ＿2＿ ni ikimasu. Soko de ＿3＿ o moratte namae nado o

書きます。そして、その用紙と＿4＿を受付に出します。＿5＿券があれば、それも出します。

kakimasu. Soshite, sono yooshi to ＿4＿ o uketsuke ni dashimasu. ＿5＿ ken ga areba, sore mo dashimasu.

I HAVE A COLD

<患者が言います>	patient
<Kanja ga iimasu>	
具合が悪いんです。	I don't feel well.
Guai ga warui ndesu.	
気持ちが悪いです。	I feel sick (nauseated).
Kimochi ga warui desu.	
かぜをひいた（かぜだ）と思います。	have a cold
Kaze o hiita (Kaze da) to omoimasu.	
インフルエンザ（流感）でしょうか。	flu
Infuruenza (Ryuukan) deshoo ka.	
のどが痛いんです。	throat, hurts
Nodo ga *itai* n desu.	
耳	ears
Mimi	

頭
Atama

head

熱があります。
Netsu ga arimasu.

have a fever

寒気がします。
Samuke ga shimasu.

have a chill

せきが出ます。
Seki ga demasu.

cough

鼻がつまっています。
Hana ga tsumatte imasu.

nose, is stuffed

鼻水が出ます。
Hanamizu ga demasu.

I have a runny nose.

<医者が言います>
<Isha ga iimasu>

doctor

どんな症状ですか。
Don-na *shoojoo* desu ka.

symptoms

めまいがしますか。
Memai ga shimasu ka.

dizzy

吐き気がしますか。
Hakike ga shimasu ka.

nauseated, nausea

口を開けてください。
Kuchi o akete kudasai.

Open your mouth.

のどを診てみましょう。
Nodo o *mite* mimashoo.

throat, examine

大きく息を吸ってください。
Ookiku iki o sutte kudasai.

Take a deep breath

はいてください。
Haite kudasai.

breathe out

胸が苦しいですか。
Mune ga kurushii desu ka.

chest, hurt (feel pressure)

熱（体温）を測ります。
Netsu (Taion) o *hakarimasu.*

temperature, take (lit. measure)

ペニシリンなどの薬にアレルギーがありますか。
Penishirin nado no *kusuri* ni *arerugii* ga arimasu ka.

penicillin, medicine, allergic

注射を打ちます（します）。
Chuusha o *uchimasu (shimasu).*

injection, give (lit. shoot)

そでをまくってください。
Sode o *makutte* kudasai.

sleeve, roll up

服の前を開けてください。

Fuku no mae o akete kudasai.

Open your shirt

(lit. the front of your clothes)

かぜ薬と抗生物質を出しておきます。

Kazegusuri to *kooseebusshitsu* o dashite okimasu.

cold medicine, antibiotic

食後に二錠飲んでください。

Shokugo ni *nijoo* nonde kudasai.

after meals, two pills

食前に

Shokuzen ni

before meals

2. Complete.

伊藤さんは今朝から__1__が悪いです。のどが赤くて__2__です。顔は熱いのに、とても寒いです。

Itoo san wa kesa kara __1__ ga warui desu. Nodo ga akakute __2__ desu. Kao wa atsui no ni, totemo samui desu.

__3__ がします。せきも出ます。__4__ をひいたようです。それで、__5__ に診てもらいに行きました。

__3__ ga shimasu. Seki mo demasu. __4__ o hiita yoo desu. Sorede, __5__ ni mite morai ni ikimashita.

3. Complete.

<病院で>

<Byooin de>

- よろしくお願いします。

  Yoroshiku onegaishimasu.

- はい、どうしましたか。

  Hai, doo shimashita ka.

- 今朝から__1__が悪くて。かぜでしょうか。

  Kesa kara __1__ ga warukute. Kaze deshoo ka.

- どんな__2__ですか。

  Don-na __2__ desu ka.

- のどが痛くて、__3__がするんです。

  Nodo ga itakute, __3__ ga suru ndesu.

- そうですか。じゃ、のどをちょっと見てみましょう。__4__を大きく開けてください。

  Soo desu ka. Ja, nodo o chotto mite mimashoo. __4__ o ookiku akete kudasai.

  ああ、本当に赤いですね。

  Aa, hontoo ni akai desu ne.

- そうですか。

  Soo desu ka.

- 今度は__5__を見ますから、服の前を__6__ください。大きく__7__を吸ってください。__8__ください。

  Kondo wa __5__ o mimasu kara, fuku no mae o __6__ kudasai. Ookiku __7__ o sutte kudasai. __8__ kudasai.

  息を吸ったりはいたりすると、胸が__9__ですか。

  Iki o suttari haitari suru to, mune ga __9__ desu ka.

- ええ、少しだけ。

  Ee, sukoshi dake.

- せきは出ますか。

  Seki wa demasu ka.

- ええ、たくさん出ます。

  Ee, takusan demasu.

- __10__ は測りましたか。

  __10__ wa hakari mashita ka.

- ええ、38度(38 degree)でした。

  Ee, sanjuuhachi do deshita.

- ちょっと熱がありますね。何かの薬に__11__はありますか。

  Chotto netsu ga arimasu ne. Nani ka kusuri ni __11__ wa arimasu ka.

- いいえ、ないと思いますが。

  Iie, nai to omoimasu ga.

- じゃ、__12__を打ちますので、__13__をまくってください。薬は風邪薬と__14__を出しておきます。

  Ja, __12__ o uchimasu node, __13__ o makutte kudasai. Kusuri wa kazegusuri to __14__ o dashite okimasu.

  食後に一__15__ずつ飲んでください。二、三日でよくなるはずです。

  Shokugo ni ichi __15__ zutsu nonde kudasai. Ni, san nichi de yoku naru hazu desu.

A PHYSICAL EXAMINATION

<病歴>   medical history

<*Byoorekt*>

あなたか家族の誰かがアレルギー体質ですか。   someone in your family; allergic

Anata ka *kazoku no dare ka ga arerugii taishitsu* desu ka.

リューマチにかかったことがありますか。   rheumatism, get (suffer from)

ryuumachi ni kakatta koto ga arimasu ka.

ぜんそく   asthma

zensoku

がん   cancer

gan

糖尿病   diabetes

toonyoobyoo

心臓病   cardiopathy

shinzoobyoo

精神病   mental illness

seeshinbyoo

性病   venereal disease

seebyoo

結核   tuberculosis

kekkaku

てんかんをおこしたことがありますか。   have an epileptic seizure

tenkan o okoshita koto ga arimasu ka.

子供の時、ポリオにかかりましたか。   polio
Kodomo no toki, *porio* ni kakarimashita ka.

　　　はしか   measles
　　　hashika

　　　水ぼうそう   chicken pox
　　　mizuboosoo

　　　おたふくかぜ   mumps
　　　otafukukazse

THE VITAL ORGANS

あなたの血液型は何ですか。   blood type
Anata no *ketsuekigata wa nan desu ka.*

生理は順調ですか。   menstrual periods, regular
Seeri wa *junchoo* desu ka.   (smooth)

手術を受けたことがありますか。   operation, have (lit. receive)
Shujutsu o uketa koto ga arimasu ka.

扁桃腺を取りましたか。   tonsils, remove
Hentoosen o *torimashita ka.*

盲腸   appendix
Moochoo

血圧を測ります。   blood pressure, measure
Ketsuatsu o *hakarimasu.*

採血をします。   collect blood
Saiketsu o shimasu.

血液検査をします。   blood test
Ketsueki kensa o shimasu.

脈拍を測ります。   pulse
Myakuhaku o hakarimasu.

肺のレントゲン写真をとります。   lungs, x-ray
Hai no *rentogen shashin* o torimasu.

聴診をします。   listen to your chest (auscultate)
Chooshin o shimasu.

心電図をとります。   electrocardiogram
Shindenzu o torimasu.

尿検査をします。   urine test
Nyoo kensa o shimasu.

検便をします。   analysis of the feces
Kenben o shimasu.

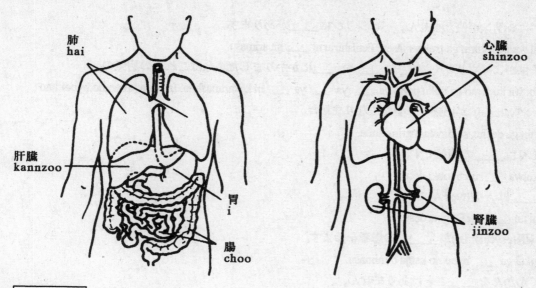

Fig. 17-1

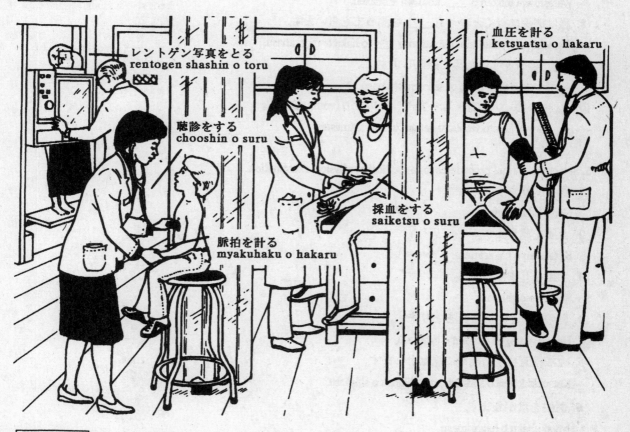

Fig. 17-2

4. Complete.

1. ＿＿＿病の人は発作(heart attack)をおこすことがあります。

　＿＿ byoo no hito wa hossa o okosu koto ga arimasu.

2. 私はペニシリンが使えません。ペニシリンに＿＿＿があります。

Watashi wa penishirin ga tsukaemasen. Penishirin ni ___ ga arimasu.

3. 昔は子供がよくポリオや＿＿や＿＿や＿＿にかかりました。今はこれらの病気の

Mukashi wa kodomo ga yoku porio ya ___ ya ___ ya ___ ni kakarimashita. Ima wa korerano byooki no

ワクチン(vaccine) が出来て、少なくなりました。

wakuchin ga dekite, sukunaku narimashita.

4. ぜんそくは＿＿＿の病気です。

Zensoku wa ___ no byooki desu.

5. 私の＿＿＿はＡ型(type A)です。

Watashi no ___ wa Ee gata desu.

6. 精神科医(psychiatrist)が＿＿＿病の患者を診ます。

Seeshinkai ga ___ byoo no kanja o mimasu.

7. 私はてんかんを＿＿＿ことはありません。

Watashi wa tenkan o ___ koto wa arimasen.

8. 私は病院に行くといつも＿＿＿を測ってもらいます。

Watashi wa byooin ni iku to itsumo ___ o hakatte moraimasu.

9. ＿＿＿検査をするために採血します。

___ kensa o suru tame ni saiketsu shimasu.

10. ＿＿＿が悪い人は痛くなったり、吐いたり(vomit)します。

___ ga warui hito wa itaku nattari, haitari shimasu.

5. Select the normal procedures for a medical or physical examination.

1. 熱を測ります。

Netsu o hakarimasu.

2. 血圧を測ります。

Ketsuatsu o hakarimasu.

3. 手術をします。

Shujutsu o shimasu.

4. 肺のレントゲン写真をとります。

Hai no rentogen shashin o torimasu.

5. 血液検査をするために採血をします。

Ketsueki kensa o suru tame ni saiketsu o shimasu.

6. 脈拍をはかります。

Myakuhaku o hakarimasu.

7. ペニシリン注射をします。

Penishirin chuusha o shimasu.

8. 心電図をとります。

Shindenzu o torimasu.

9. 抗生物質を処方(prescribe)します。

Koosee busshitsu o shohoo shimasu.

10. 聴診をします。

    Chooshin o shimasu.

11. 尿検査をします。

    Nyoo kensa o shimasu.

I HAD AN ACCIDENT

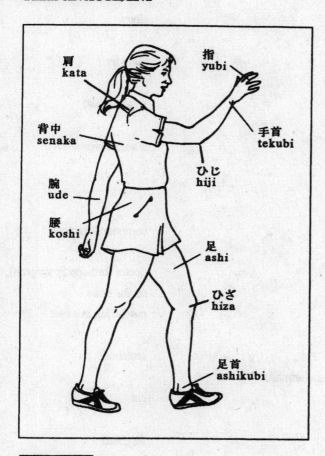

肩 kata

指 yubi

背中 senaka

手首 tekubi

ひじ hiji

腕 ude

腰 koshi

足 ashi

ひざ hiza

足首 ashikubi

Fig. 17-3

指を骨折しました。   finger, have a fracture

Yubi o *kossetsu shimashita.*

指の骨が折れました   bone, break

Yubi no *hone* ga *oremashita.*

腕   arm

Ude

手首   wrist

Tekubi

足   leg, foot

Ashi

足首 *Ashikubi*	ankle
腰 *Koshi*	hip
ひざ *Hiza*	knee
ひじ *Hiji*	elbow
肩 *Kata*	shoulder
手首をひねりました。 Tekubi o *hinerimashita*.	sprain (twist)
ここが痛いです。 *Koko ga itai desu.*	It hurts here.
医者は足のレントゲン写真をとりました。 Isha wa ashi no rentogen shashin o torimashita.	
複雑骨折です。 *Fukuzatsu kossetsu* desu.	compound fracture
医者（整形外科医）は骨をつなぎました。 *Isha (Seekeegekai)* wa hone o *tsunagimashita*.	doctor (orthopedic surgeon), set the bone
足にギプスをはめました。 *Ashi* ni *gipusu* o *hamemashita*.	put the leg in a cast
患者は松葉杖を使わなければならないこともあります。 Kanja wa *matsubazue* o tsukawanakereba naranai koto mo arimasu.	crutches
指を切りました。 Yubi o *kirimashita*.	cut
ひたい *Hitai*	forehead
医者は傷口を縫います。 Isha wa *kizu guchi* o *nuimasu*.	cut, stitch
それから包帯を巻きます。 Sorekara *hootai* o *makimasu*.	bandage, bind up
五日後に抜糸をします。 Itsukago ni *basshi o shimasu*.	take out the stitches

6. Complete.

吉田さんは転んで(fell down)、足を__1__してしまいました。それで、友達に病院へ連れて行ってもらい
Yoshida san wa koronde, ashi o __1__ shite shimaimashita. Sorede, tomodachi ni byooin e tsurete itte morai
ました。医者は初めに__2__写真をとりました。それから折れた__3__をつないで、そこに__4__をはめ

mashita. Isha wa hajime ni __2__ shashin o torimashita. Sorekara oreta __3__ o tsunaide, soko ni __4__ o hame
ました。吉田さんはこれから一か月ぐらい、__5__ を使って歩かなければなりません。

mashita. Yoshida san wa kore kara ikkagetsu gurai, __6__ o tsukatte arukanakereba narimasen.

7. Identify each item in Fig. 17-4.

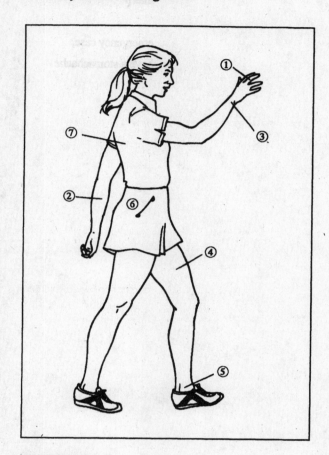

Fig. 17-4

IN THE EMERGENCY ROOM

救急車が救急病院に着きました。   ambulance, emergency hospital
Kyuukyuusha ga *kyuukyuu byooin* ni tsukimashita.
患者は担架で運ばれてきました。   stretcher, be carried
Kanja wa *tanka* de *hakobarete* kimashita.
車いすではありません。   wheelchair
Kurumaisu dewa arimasen.
すぐに看護婦が脈拍を測ります。   nurse, pulse, measure
Sugu ni *kangofu* ga *myakuhaku* o *hakarimasu*.

血圧も測ります。   blood pressure
Ketsuatsu mo hakarimasu.
当直医が診察をします。   doctor on duty, examine
Toochokui ga *shinsatsu* o shimasu.
当直医は研修医（インターン）のこともあります。   intern
Toochokui wa *kenshuu i (intaan)* no koto mo arimasu.
この急患はおなかが痛いと言っています。   emergency case,
Kono kyuukan wa *onaka ga itai* to itte imasu.   have a stomachache

8. Answer.
1. この患者は何で病院まで来ましたか。
   Kono kanja wa nan de byooin made kimashita ka.
2. ここはどんな病院ですか。
   Koko wa don-na byooin desu ka.
3. 患者は車いすで運ばれてきましたか。
   Kanja wa kurumaisu de hakobarete kimashita ka.
4. 看護婦は何を測りましたか。
   Kangofu wa nani o hakarimashita ka.
5. 誰が患者を診察しましたか。
   Dare ga kanja o shinsatsu shimashita ka.
6. 患者はどこが痛いと言っていますか。
   Kanja wa doko ga itai to itte imasu ka.

9. Complete.
1. ＿＿病院には急患がたくさん来ます。
   ___ byooin ni wa kyuukan ga takusan kimasu.
2. ＿＿に乗ってくる患者もいます。
   ___ ni notte kuru kanja mo imasu.
3. 救急車から病院の中まで、患者はたいてい＿＿か＿＿で運ばれます。
   Kyuukyuusha kara byooin no naka made, kanja wa taitee ___ ka ___ de hakobaremasu.
4. ＿＿はまず患者の脈拍と血圧を測ります。
   ___ wa mazu kanja no myakuhaku to ketsuatsu o hakarimasu.
5. 救急病院で働いている医者は＿＿といいます。
   Kyuukyuu byooin de hataraite iru isha wa ___ to iimasu.

SURGERY

手術をします。   operation
Shujutsu o shimasu.

患者を**病室**から**手術室**まで運びます。　　　　　　　　　　ward, operating room

Kanja o *byooshitsu* kara *shujutsushitsu* made hakobimasu.

患者を**手術台**にのせます。　　　　　　　　　　　　　　　operating table

Kanja o *shujutsudai* ni nosemasu.

麻酔医が患者に**麻酔**をします。　　　　　　　　　　　　anesthesiologist, anesthesia

Masuii ga kanja ni *masui* o shimasu.

外科医が手術をします。　　　　　　　　　　　　　　　　surgeon

Gekai ga shujutsu o shimasu.

これは**盲腸（虫垂炎）**の手術です。　　　　　　　　　　　appendicitis

Kore wa *moochoo (chuusuien)* no shujutsu desu.

盲腸を取ります。

Moochoo o torimasu.

10. Complete.

医者はこの患者に手術をすることを決めました。手術の日、＿＿1＿＿が患者を＿＿2＿＿まで

Isha wa kono kanja ni shujutsu o suru koto ni kimemashita. Shujutsu no hi, ＿1＿ ga kanja o ＿2＿ made

運びました。そして患者を＿＿3＿＿にのせました。＿＿4＿＿が患者に麻酔をして、＿＿5＿＿が手術を

hakobimashita. Soshite kanja o ＿3＿ ni nosemashita. ＿4＿ ga kanja ni masui o shite, ＿5＿ ga shujutsu o

始めました。

hajimemashita.

IN THE RECOVERY ROOM

手術を受けた患者は**回復室**に運ばれます。　　　　　　　　recovery room

Shujutsu o uketa kanja wa *kaifukushitsu* ni hakobaremasu.

回復室で**酸素マスク**と**点滴**をします。　　　　　　　　　oxygen mask,

Kaifukushitsu de *sansomasuku* to *tenteki* o shimasu.　　　intravenous feeding

酸素テントは使いません。　　　　　　　　　　　　　　　oxygen tent

Sansotento wa tsukaimasen.

医者は患者に**手術後の経過**を説明します。　　　　　　　　prognosis

Isha wa kanja ni *shujutsugo no keeka* o setsumee shimasu.　　(progress after an operation)

経過がよくない時は、**集中治療室(ICU)**に運んで、　　　　ICU

Keeka ga yokunai toki wa, *shuuchuu chiryooshitsu (ai-shii-yuu)* ni hakonde

そこで**治療**をします。　　　　　　　　　　　　　　　　　treat

soko de *chiryoo* o shimasu.

11. Complete.

1. 患者は手術を受けた後で、＿＿＿＿に運ばれます。

　Kanja wa shujutsu o uketa ato de, ＿＿ ni hakobaremasu.

2. 早く回復するように、＿＿＿マスクと＿＿＿をします。

   Hayaku kaifuku suru yoo ni, ___ masuku to ___ o shimasu.

3. 医者に手術後の＿＿＿がいいと言われたので、この患者はよろこんでいます(is glad)。

   Isha ni shujutsugo no ___ ga ii to iwareta node, kono kanja wa yorokonde imasu.

IN THE DELIVERY ROOM

私は**妊娠**しています。   pregnant
Watashi wa *ninshin shite imasu.*

子供が**生まれます**。   be born
Kodomo ga *umaremasu.*

子供を**産みます**（**出産します**）   give birth
Kodomo o *umimasu (shussan shimasu).*

陣痛が始まりました。   labor pains
Jintsuu ga hajimarimashita.

分娩室に入っています。   delivery room
Bunbenshitsu ni haitte imasu.

産婦人科医が**赤ん坊**を**とりあげます**。   obstetrician (ob-gyn), baby,
Sanfujinka i ga *akanboo* o *toriagemasu.*   deliver (lit. take out)

12. Complete.

    この女の人は＿1＿しています。もうすぐ、子供が生まれます。陣痛が始まったら、＿2＿に行きます。

    Kono on-na no hito wa _1_ shite imsu. Moosugu, kodomo ga umaremasu. Jintsuu ga hajimattara, _2_ ni ikimasu.
    そこで、＿3＿医が、子供をとりあげます。

    Sokode, _3_ i ga, kodomo o toriagemasu.

    ある日、田中さんはおなかがとても痛くなりました。痛くて歩くこともできません。どうすればいいか
    Aru hi, Tanaka san wa onaka ga totemo itaku narimashita. Itakute aruku koto mo dekimasen. Doo sureba ii ka
    分からなかったので、１１９番に電話をして、救急車を呼びました。救急車は
    wakaranakatta node, hyakujuukyuu ban ni denwa o shite, kyuukyuusha o yobimashita.   Kyuukyuusha wa
    五分ぐらいで来ました。田中さんは担架で救急車まで運ばれて、十分ぐらいで救急病院
    gofun gurai de kimashita. Tanaka san wa tanka de kyuukyuusha made hakobarete, juppun gurai de kyuukyuu byooin
    に着きました。一人の看護婦が田中さんの脈拍を測って、もう一人が血圧を
    ni tsukimashita.   Hitori no kangofu ga Tanaka san no myakuhaku o hakatte, moo hitori ga ketsuatsu o
    測りました。医者が来て、田中さんにどんな症状かと聞きました。田中さんはおなかがどのように
    hakarimashita. Isha ga kite, Tanaka san ni don-na shoojoo ka to kikimashita. Tanaka san wa onaka ga donoyooni
    痛いかを説明しました。医者は吐いたり(vomit)、下痢をしたり(diarrhea) したか聞きました。
    itai ka o setsumee shimashita. Isha wa haitari, geri o shitari shita ka kikimashita.
    田中さんは、そういうことはなかったけれど、おなかがとても痛いと言いました。医者はレントゲン
    Tanaka san wa , soo iu koto wa nakatta keredo, onaka ga totemo itai to iimashita. Isha wa rentogen

写真をとると言いました。看護婦が田中さんを車椅子に乗せて、レントゲン室(room)まで運びました。

shashin o toru to iimashita. Kangofu ga Tanaka san o kurumaisu ni nosete, rentogenshitsu made hakobimashita.

そこで、おなかのレントゲン写真をとりました。医者は田中さんに「虫垂炎です。手術をして、

Soko de, onaka no rentogen shashin o torimashita. Isha wa Tanaka san ni "Chuusuien desu. Shujutsu o shite,

盲腸をとります。」と説明しました。田中さんは手術室に運ばれて、手術台の上に

moochoo o torimasu." to setsumee shimashita. Tanaka san wa shujutsushitsu ni hakobarete, shujutsudai no ue ni

乗せられました。麻酔医が田中さんの右腕に麻酔をして、1から10まで数えてください(count) と

noseraremashita. Masuii ga Tanaka san no migi ude ni masui o shite, ichi kara juu made kazoete kudasai to

言いました。外科医が手術を始めて、盲腸を取りました。手術の時間はとても短かったです。

iimashita. Gekai ga shujutsu o hajimete, moochoo o torimashta. Shujutsu no jikan wa totemo mijikakatta desu.

田中さんは起きた時、回復室にいて、酸素マスクをしていました。腕に点滴もしていました。

Tanaka san wa okita toki kaifukushitsu ni ite, sansomasuku o shite imashita. Ude ni tenteki mo shite imashita.

看護婦が来て、手術後の経過はいいと言ったので、田中さんはほっとしました(was relieved)。二日後に

Kangofu ga kite, shujutsu no keeka wa ii to itta node, Tanaka san wa hotto shimashita. Futsukago ni

病院を出て、家に帰る時は、担架や車椅子を使わないで、元気に歩いて帰ることができました。

byooin o dete, uchi ni kaeru toki wa, tanka ya kurumaisu o tsukawanaide, genki ni aruite kaeru koto ga dekimashita.

13. Complete.

1. 田中さんはおなかが＿＿＿なりました。

   Tanaka san wa onaka ga ___ narimashita.

2. 病院まで＿＿＿で行きました。

   Byooin made ___ de ikimashita.

3. 病院に着いて、救急車から病院の中まで、田中さんは＿＿＿で運ばれました。

   Byooin ni tsuite, kyuukyuusha kara byooin no naka made, Tanaka san wa ___ de hakobaremashita.

4. 看護婦が田中さんの＿＿＿と＿＿＿を測りました。

   Kangofu ga Tanaka san no ___ to ___ o hakarimashita.

5. 田中さんは医者に＿＿＿を説明しました。

   Tanaka san wa isha ni ___ o setsumee shimashita.

6. ＿＿＿をとるために、看護婦は田中さんをレントゲン室に運びました。

   ___ o toru tame ni, kangofu wa Tanaka san o rentogenshitsu ni hakobimashita.

7. 医者は＿＿＿をすることに決めました。

   Isha wa ___ o suru koto ni kimemashita.

8. 手術室で田中さんは＿＿＿の上に乗せられました。

   Shujutsushitsu de Tanaka san wa ___ no ue ni noseraremashita.

9. 麻酔医が田中さんに＿＿＿をしました。

   Masuii ga Tanaka san ni ___ o shimashita.

10. ＿＿＿が手術をして、盲腸をとりました。

    ___ ga shujutsu o shite, moochoo o torimashita.

11. 起きた時、田中さんは＿＿＿のベッドの上にいました。

    Okita toki, Tanaka san wa ___ no beddo no ue ni imashita.

12. 早く回復するように、＿＿＿と＿＿＿をしていました。

Hayaku kaifuku suru yoo ni, ___ to ___ o shite imashita.

13. 手術後の＿＿＿はよくて、田中さんは元気になりました。

Shujutsugo no ___ wa yokute, Tanaka san wa genki ni narimashita.

Key Words

after meals	食後	shokugo	cardiopathy	心臓病	shinzoobyoo
allergic	アレルギー、アレルギー体質	arerugii, arerugii taishitsu	chest	胸	mune
			chicken pox	水ぼうそう	mizuboosoo
			clothes	服	fuku
ambulance	救急車	kyuukyuusha	cold	かぜ	kaze
analysis of the feces	検便	kenben	cold medicine	かぜ薬	kazegusuri
			collect blood	採血	saiketsu
anesthesia	麻酔	masui	compound fracture	複雑骨折	fukuzatsu kossetsu
anesthesiologist	麻酔医	masuii			
ankle	足首	ashikubi	cough	せきが出る	seki ga deru
antibiotic	抗生物質	koosee busshitsu	counter for pills	～錠	~joo
appendicitis	盲腸（虫垂炎）	moochoo (chuusuien)	crutches	松葉杖	matsubazue
			cut	傷口	kizuguchi
appointment card (patient registration card)	診察券	shinsatsuken	cut	切る	kiru
			deliver (lit. take out)	とりあげる	toriageru
arm	腕	ude	delivery room	分娩室	bunbenshitsu
asthma	ぜんそく	zensoku	diabetes	糖尿病	toonyoobyoo
auscultation; listen to one's chest	聴診する	chooshin suru	dizzy	めまいがする	memai ga suru
			doctor	医者	isha
			doctor on duty	当直医	toochokui
baby	赤ん坊	akanboo	ears	耳	mimi
back	背中	senaka	elbow	ひじ	hiji
bandage	包帯	hootai	electrocardiogram	心電図	shindenzu
be born	生まれる	umareru	emergency case	急患	kyuukan
be carried	運ばれる	hakobareru	emergency hospital	救急病院	kyuukyuu byooin
before meals	食前	shokuzen			
bind up	巻く	maku	examine	診る	miru
blood pressure	血圧	ketsuatsu	examine	診察をする	shinsatsu o suru
blood test	血液検査	ketsueki kensa	family	家族	kazoku
blood type	血液型	ketsuekigata	feel sick (nauseated)	気持ちが悪い	kimochi ga warui
bone	骨	hone			
bowels	腸	choo	fill in	記入する	kinyuu suru
break	折れる	oreru	finger	指	yubi
breathe in	息を吸う	iki o suu	flu	インフルエンザ（流感）	infuruenza (ryuukan)
breathe out	息をはく	iki o haku			
cancer	がん	gan	forehead	ひたい	hitai

form	用紙	*yooshi*	mouth	口	*kuchi*
get (suffer from)	かかる	*kakaru*	mumps	おたふくかぜ	*otafukukaze*
give (lit. shoot)	打つ（する）	*utsu (suru)*	nauseated, nausea	吐き気がする	*hakike ga suru*
give birth	産む（出産する）	*umu (shussan suru)*	nose	鼻	*hana*
			not feel well	具合が悪い	*guai ga warui*
have (lit. receive)	受ける	*ukeru*	nurse	看護婦	*kangofu*
have a chill	寒気がする	*samuke ga suru*	obstetrician (ob-gyn)	産婦人科医	*sanfujinkai*
have a cold	かぜをひく	*kaze o hiku*	open	開ける	*akeru*
have a fever	熱がある	*netsu ga aru*	operating room	手術室	*shujutsushitsu*
have a fracture	骨折する	*kossetsu suru*	operating table	手術台	*shujutsudai*
have a runny nose	鼻水が出る	*hanamizu ga deru*	operation	手術	*shujutsu*
have a stomachache	おなかが痛い	*onaka ga itai*	orthopedic surgeon	整形外科医	*seekeegekai*
have an epileptic seizure	てんかんをおこす	*tenkan o okosu*	oxygen mask	酸素マスク	*sansomasuku*
			oxygen tent	酸素テント	*sansotento*
			patient	患者	*kanja*
head	頭	*atama*	penicillin	ペニシリン	*penishirin*
health insurance card	保険証	*hokenshoo*	polio	ポリオ	*porio*
			pregnant	妊娠している	*ninshin shite iru*
heart	心臓	*shinzoo*	prognosis (progress after an operation)	手術後の経過	*shujutsugo no keeka*
hip	腰	*koshi*			
hospital (clinic)	病院	*byooin*			
hurt (feel pressure)	苦しい	*kurushii*	pulse	脈拍	*myakuhaku*
			put the leg in a cast	ギプスをはめる	*gipusu o hameru*
hurts	痛い	*itai*			
ICU	集中治療室（ICU）	*shuuchuu chiryoo shitsu (ai-shii-yuu)*	reception	受付	*uketsuke*
			recovery room	回復室	*kaifuku shitsu*
			regular (smooth)	順調	*junchoo*
injection	注射	*chuusha*	remove	取る	*toru*
intern	研修医（インターン）	*kenshuui (intaan)*	rheumatism	リューマチ	*ryuumachi*
			roll up	まくる	*makuru*
intravenous feeding	点滴	*tenteki*	see a doctor (have a doctor examine)	診てもらう	*mite morau*
is stuffed	つまっている	*tsumatte iru*			
kidneys	腎臓	*jinzoo*	set the bone	骨をつなぐ	*hone o tsunagu*
knee	ひざ	*hiza*	shoulder	肩	*kata*
labor pains	陣痛	*jintsuu*	sleeve	そで	*sode*
leg, foot	足	*ashi*	sprain	ひねる	*hineru*
liver	肝臓	*kanzoo*	stitch	縫う	*nuu*
lungs	肺	*hai*	stomach	胃	*i*
measles	はしか	*hashika*	stretcher	担架	*tanka*
measure	測る	*hakaru*	surgeon	外科医	*gekai*
medical examination	診察	*shinsatsu*	symptoms	症状	*shoojoo*
medical history	病歴	*byooreki*	take out the stitches	抜糸をする	*basshi o suru*
medicine	薬	*kusuri*	temperature	熱（体温）	*netsu (taion)*
menstrual periods	生理	*seeri*	throat	のど	*nodo*
mental illness	精神病	*seeshinbyoo*	tonsils	扁桃腺	*hentoosen*

treat	治療をする	*chiryoo o suru*	wheelchair	車いす	*kurumaisu*
tuberculosis	結核	*kekkaku*	wrist	手首	*tekubi*
urine test	尿検査	*nyoo kensa*	x-ray	レントゲン写真	*rentogen shashin*
venereal disease	性病	*seebyoo*			
ward	病室	*byooshitsu*			

Chapter 18: Entertainment
第18章：エンターテインメント
Entaateinmento

SEEING A SHOW

劇場で演劇（芝居）を見ます。 — theater, play
Gekijoo de engeki (shibai) o mimasu.

コンサートホールでコンサートを聞きます。 — concert hall, concert
Konsaato hooru de konsaato o kikimasu.

どんなジャンルが好きですか。 — kind (genre)
Don-na janru ga suki desu ka.

ドラマ — drama
Dorama

悲劇 — tragedy
Higeki

喜劇（コメディー） — comedy
Kigeki (Komedii)

ミュージカル — musical
Myuujikaru

クラシック — classical music
Kurashikku

ロック — rock
Rokku

ジャズ — jazz
Jazu

どんな俳優が出ていますか。 — actor (male or female)
Don-na haiyuu ga dete imasu ka.

男優 — actor (male)
dan-yuu

女優 — actress
joyuu

あきらの役は誰ですか。 — part (role)
Akira no yaku wa dare desu ka.

誰があきらの役をやって（演じて）いますか。 — play the part, take the role
Dare ga Akira no yaku o yatte (enjite) imasu ka.

主役は誰ですか。 — protagonist (lead)
Shuyaku wa dare desu ka.

この芝居は三幕あります。 — acts
Kono shibai wa san maku arimasu.

153

第二幕の後で、休憩があります。   the second act, intermission

Dai ni maku no ato de, *kyuukee* ga arimasu.

舞台が今、始まりました。   show

Butai ga ima, hajimarimashita.

主役が舞台（ステージ）に出てきました。   stage

Shuyaku ga *butai (suteeji)* ni dete kimashita.

観客が拍手をします。   spectators applaud

Kankyaku ga *hakushu o shimasu.*

幕が上がります。   curtain, go up

Maku ga *agarimasu.*

    下ります。   go down

    orimasu.

1. Complete.

1. 昨日、＿＿＿＿で芝居を見ました。

   Kinoo, ＿＿ de shibai o mimashita.

2. 悲劇はあまり好きじゃありません。＿＿＿＿の方が好きです。

   Higeki wa amari suki ja arimasen. ＿＿ no hoo ga suki desu.

3. 高倉健が父親の＿＿＿＿をやっていて、広末涼子がその子供の＿＿＿＿です。

   Takakura Ken ga chichioya no ＿＿ o yatte ite, Hirosue Ryooko ga sono kodomo no ＿＿ desu.

4. あの俳優が一番大切な役をやっています。この芝居の＿＿＿＿です。

   Ano haiyuu ga ichiban taisetsu na yaku o yatte imasu. Kono shibai no ＿＿ desu.

5. 芝居が始まる時、＿＿＿＿が上がります。

   Shibai ga hajimaru toki, ＿＿ ga agarimasu.

6. 第二幕と第三幕の間に 15 分の＿＿＿＿があります。

   Dai ni maku to dai san maku no aida ni juugofun no ＿＿ ga arimasu.

7. 主役が＿＿＿＿に出てきた時、＿＿＿＿が大きな拍手をしました。

   Shuyaku ga ＿＿ ni detekita toki, ＿＿ ga ookiina hakushu o shimashita.

2. Give the opposite.

1. 喜劇

   kigeki

2. 男優

   dan-yuu

3. 幕が上がる

   maku ga agaru

AT THE TICKET WINDOW

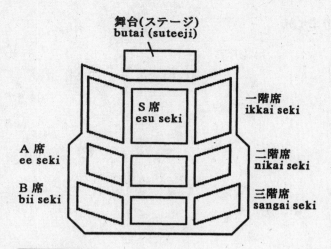

舞台（ステージ）
butai (suteeji)

S 席
esu seki

一階席
ikkai seki

A 席
ee seki

二階席
nikai seki

B 席
bii seki

三階席
sangai seki

Fig. 18-1

<劇場の切符売り場で>
<Gekijoo no *kippu uriba* de>   ticket window

今夜の公演のチケット（切符）はまだありますか。
Kon-ya no *kooen* no *chiketto (kippu)* wa mada arimasu ka.   performance, ticket

すみません。売りきれました（売り切れです）。
Sumimasen. *Urikiremashita (urikire desu).*   sold out

明日のS席の切符はありますか。
Ashita no *esu seki* no kippu wa arimasu ka.   S-seat (special seat)

オーケストラ席を二枚ください。
Ookesutora seki o nimai kudasai.   orchestra seat

私の席はD列の15番です。
Watashi no *seki* wa *dii retsu* no *juugo ban* desu.   seat, D-15. (Row-D, Number 15)

開場は何時ですか。
Kaijoo wa nanji desu ka.   What time does the door open?

開演
Kaien   What time does the performance start?

クロークにコートを預けます。
Kurooku ni *kooto* o azukemasu.   cloakroom, coat

案内係がプログラムをくれます。
An-naigakari ga *puroguramu* o kuremasu.   usher, program

3. Complete.
<劇場の切符売り場で>
<Gekijoo no kippu uriba de>

- 金曜日の公演の＿1＿はまだありますか。

  Kin-yoobi no kooen no ＿1＿ wa mada arimasu ka.

- いいえ、＿2＿。土曜日の＿3＿なら、まだありますが。

  Iie, ＿2＿. Doyoobi no ＿3＿ nara, mada arimasu ga.

- じゃ、土曜日でもいいです。

  Ja, doyoobi demo ii desu.

- ＿4＿席、＿5＿席、＿6＿席、とありますが。

  ＿4＿ seki, ＿5＿ seki, ＿6＿ seki, to arimasu ga.

- Ｓ席を二枚ください。

  Esu seki o nimai kudasai.

- はい、Ｓ席を二枚ですね。

  Hai, es seki o nimai desu ne.

- いくらですか。

  Ikura desu ka.

- 一万二千円です。

  Ichiman nisen en desu.

- すみません、これは＿7＿は何時ですか。

  Sumimasen, kore wa ＿7＿ wa nanji desu ka.

- ＿8＿は六時半で、＿9＿は七時です。

  ＿8＿ wa rokuji han de, ＿9＿ wa shichiji desu.

- どうも。

  Doomo.

4. Read the conversation and answer the questions that follow.

山田：今日、切符を買ってくれましたか。

Yamada: Kyoo, kippu o katte kuremashita ka.

青木：ええ、買いましたよ。

Aoki: Ee, kaimashita yo.

山田：じゃ、今晩行くんですね。何時ですか。

Yamada: Ja, konban iku ndesu ne. Nanji desu ka.

青木：今晩じゃないんですよ。今晩の切符は売り切れだったから、明日の切符を買ったんです。

Aoki: Konban ja nai ndesu yo. Konban no kippu wa urikire datta kara, ashita no kippu o katta ndesu.

山田：いいですよ。どんな席ですか。

Yamada: Ii desu yo. Don-na seki desu ka.

青木：Ａ席です。Ｓ席は売りきれだったんです。あまりいい席じゃないかもしれませんけど。

Aoki: Ee seki desu. Esu seki wa urikire datta ndesu. Amari ii seki ja nai kamoshiremasen kedo.

山田：いいですよ。見られればいいんですから。Ｓ席は高いし、Ａ席でいいです。

Yamada: Ii desu yo. Mirarereba ii ndesu kara. Esu seki wa takai shi, Ee seki de ii desu.

1. 青木さんは今日、どこへ行きましたか。

   Aoki san wa kyoo, doko e ikimashita ka.

2. 山田さんと青木さんは今晩、劇場に行きますか。どうしてですか。

   Yamada san to Aoki san wa konban, gekijoo ni ikimasu ka. Dooshite desu ka.

3. 明日の切符も売切れでしたか。

   Ashita no kippu mo urikire deshita ka.

4. どんな席の切符を買いましたか。

   Don-na seki no kippu o kaimashita ka.

5. それはどうしてですか。

   Sore wa dooshite desu ka.

6. S席とA席とどちらの方が高いですか。

   Esu seki to ee seki to dochira no hoo ga takai desu ka.

5. Correct each statement.

1. 切符はクロークで買います。

   Kippu wa kurooku de kaimasu.

2. A席が一番いい席です。

   Ee seki ga ichiban ii seki desu.

3. 舞台が始まると幕が下ります。

   Butai ga hajimaru to maku ga orimasu.

4. コートは切符売り場に預けます。

   Kooto wa kippu uriba ni azukemasu.

5. 開場は舞台が始まる時間のことです。

   Kaijoo wa butai ga hajimaru jikan no koto desu.

AT THE MOVIES

今、どんな映画がやっていますか。
Ima, don-na *eega* ga *yatte imasu* ka. — movie, showing

その映画には誰が出ていますか。
Sono eega ni wa dare ga *dete imasu* ka. — playing (acting)

その映画はどの映画館でやっていますか。
Sono eega wa dono *eegakan* de yatte imasu ka. — movie theater

「タイタニック」一枚ください。
"Taitanikku" *ich mai kudasai*. — One for ~, please.

大人（学生、子供）一枚ください。
Otona (Gakusee, Kodomo) ichimai kudasai. — One adult (student, child), please.

前の席には座りたくありません。スクリーンに近すぎます。
Mae no seki ni wa suwaritaku arimasen. *Sukuriin* ni *chikasugimasu*. — front seat, screen, too close

これはアメリカの映画ですが、

Kore wa Amerika no eega desu ga,

日本語に吹き替えられています（日本語吹き替えです）。   dubbed in Japanese

Nihongo ni fukikaerarete imasu (*Nihongo fukikae desu*).

日本語の**字幕つき**です。   with subtitles

Nihongo no jimaku tsuki desu.

6. Complete.

1. スピルバーグ監督(director)の新しい＿＿＿が駅の前の映画館で＿＿＿。

Supirubaagu kantoku no atarashii ___ ga eki no mae no eegakan de ___.

2. 私は吹き替えの映画は好きじゃありません。＿＿＿つきの方が好きです。

Watashi wa fukikae no eega wa suki ja arimasen. ___ tsuki no hoo ga suki desu.

3. 私は映画館で＿＿＿に近い席に座るのは好きじゃありません。

Watashi wa eegakan de ___ ni chikai seki ni suwaru no wa suki ja arimasen.

Key Words

act	幕	*maku*	go down	下りる	*oriru*
actor (male)	男優	*dan-yuu*	goes up	上がる	*agaru*
actor (male or femal)	俳優	*haiyuu*	intermission	休憩	*kyuukee*
actress	女優	*joyuu*	jazz	ジャズ	*jazu*
adult	大人	*otona*	kind (genre)	ジャンル	*janru*
applaud	拍手をする	*hakushu o suru*	movie	映画	*eega*
A-seat	A席	*ee seki*	movie theater	映画館	*eegakan*
B-seat	B席	*bii seki*	musical	ミュージカル	*myuujikaru*
child	子供	*kodomo*	number	番	*ban*
classical music	クラシック	*kurashikku*	One for ~, please.	～枚ください	*~ mai kudasai*
cloakroom	クローク	*kurooku*	orchestra	オーケストラ	*ookesutora*
coat	コート	*kooto*	orchestra seat	オーケストラ席	*ookesutoraseki*
comedy	喜劇（コメディー）	*kigeki (komedii)*	part (role)	役	*yaku*
concert	コンサート	*konsaato*	performance	公演	*kooen*
concert hall	コンサートホール	*konsaato hooru*	performance starts	開演	*kaien*
curtain	幕	*maku*	play	演劇（芝居）	*engeki (shibai)*
door opens	開場	*kaijoo*	play the part, take the role	役をやって（演じて）いる	*yaku o yatte (enjite) iru*
drama	ドラマ	*dorama*			
dubbed in Japanese	日本語に吹き替えられている（日本語吹き替え）	*nihongo ni fukikaerarete iru (nihongo fukikae)*	playing (acting)	出ている	*dete iru*
			program	プログラム	*puroguramu*
			protagonist (lead)	主役	*shuyaku*
entertainment	エンターテインメント	*entaateinmento*	rock	ロック	*rokku*
floor seats	～階席	*~ kaiseki*	row	列	*retsu*

screen,	スクリーン	sukuriin	student	学生	gakusee
seat	席	seki	the ~th act	第〜幕	dai ~ maku
show	舞台	butai	theater	劇場	gekijoo
showing	やっている	yatte iru	ticket window	切符売り場	kippu uriba
sold out	売りきれる（売り切れ)	urikireru (urikire)	tickets	チケット（切符)	chiketto (kippu)
spectators	観客	kankyaku	too close	近すぎる	chikasugiru
S-seat (special seat)	S席	esu seki	tragedy	悲劇	higeki
			usher	案内係	an-naigakari
stage	舞台（ステージ)	butai (suteeji)	with subtitles	字幕つき	jimaku tsuki

Chapter 19: Sports
第19章：スポーツ
Supootsu

SOCCER

サッカーは一つの**チーム**が 11 人です。	soccer, team
Sakkaa wa hitotsu no *chiimu* ga juuichi nin desu.	
サッカーの**試合**はサッカー場（グラウンド）でします。	game, soccer field (ground)
Sakkaa no *shiai* wa *sakkaajoo (guraundo)* de shimasu.	
選手は足で**ボール**を**蹴**ります。	player, foot, ball, kick
Senshu wa *ashi* de *booru* o *kerimasu.*	
ゴールキーパーが**ゴール**を**守**ります。	goalie, goal, defend
Goorukiipaa ga *gooru* o *mamorimasu.*	
ゴールキーパーはボールを**止**めます。	stop
Goorukiipaa wa booru o *tomemasu.*	
レフトバックは味方にボールを**パス**します。	left end, teammate, toss
Refutobakku wa *mikata* ni booru o *pasu shimasu.*	
選手が**ゴール**をしました（**決**めました）。	makes a goal
Senshu ga *gooru* o shimashita (kimemashita).	
点（**得点**）を入れました。	score
ten (tokuten) o iremashita.	
選手が**相手チーム**の選手を蹴りました。	opponent team
Senshu ga *aite chiimu* no senshu o kerimashita.	
審判員が**笛**（ホイッスル）を**吹**きます。	referee, whistle, blow
Shinpan-in ga *fue (hoissuru)* o *fukimasu.*	
反則（ファール）をとります。	foul
hansoku (faaru) o torimasu.	
前半が終わりました。	first half
Zenhan ga owarimashita.	
後半	second half
Koohan	
今は、まだ**同点**です。	tie
Ima wa, mada *dooten* desu.	
試合は**2対3**です。	a score of 2 to 3
Shiai wa *ni tai san* desu.	
A**チーム**が**勝**ちました（A チームの**勝**ちです）。	win
Ee chiimu ga *kachimashita* (Ee chiimu no *kachi desu*).	
B**チーム**が**負**けました（B チームの**負**けです）。	loose
Bii chiimu ga *makemashita* (Bii chiimu no *make desu*).	

試合は**引き分け**です。　　　　　　　　　　　　　　　　　　　　finish in a tie

Shiai wa *hikiwake* desu.

得点板（スコアボード）に**得点**が出ます。　　　　　　　　　　scoreboard, score

Tokutenban (Sukoa boodo) ni *tokuten* ga demasu.

1. Answer.

1. サッカーの試合は一つのチームに何人いますか。

　Sakkaa no shiai wa hitotsu no chiimu ni nan nin imasu ka.

2. サッカーの試合はどこでしますか。

　Sakkaa no shiai wa doko de shimasu ka.

3. 誰がゴールを守りますか。

　Dare ga gooru o mamorimasu ka.

4. どうやってボールをパスしますか。

　Dooyatte booru o pasu shimasu ka.

5. ゴールキーパーはボールをどうしますか。

　Goorukiipaa wa booru o dooshimasu ka.

6. 誰が反則をとりますか。

　Dare ga hansoku o torimasu ka.

7. 審判員は何を吹きますか。

　Shinpan-in wa nani o fukimasu ka.

8. 得点はどこに出ますか。

　Tokuten wa doko ni demasu ka.

Fig. 19-1

2. Complete.

試合が始まりました。グラウンドには二つの＿1＿ がいます。全部で＿2＿人の選手がいます。一人の

Shiai ga hajimarimashita. Guraundo ni wa futatsu no ＿1＿ ga imasu. Zenbu de ＿2＿ nin no senshu ga imasu. Hitori no

選手がボールを＿3＿。相手チームの選手がそれを止めました。そして、＿4＿の選手にボールをパス

senshu ga booru o ＿3＿. Aite chiimu no senshu ga sore o tomemashita. Soshite, ＿4＿ no senshu ni booru o pasu

しました。ボールをもらった選手はゴールの近くにいたので、ゴールに向かって(toward)ボールを蹴りました。

shimashita. Booru o moratta senshu wa gooru no chikaku ni ita node, gooru ni mukatte booru o kerimashita.

でも、＿5＿がそれを止めました。＿6＿が終わりました。試合は1＿7＿1で、まだ＿8＿です。

Demo, ＿5＿ ga sore o tomemashita. ＿6＿ ga owarimashita. Shiai wa ichi ＿7＿ ichi de, mada ＿8＿ desu.

3. Identify each item in Fig. 19-1.

BASEBALL

野球はひとつのチームが9人です。 *Yakyuu* wa hitotsu no chiimu ga kyuu nin desu.	baseball
野球の試合は野球場（グラウンド）でします。 Yakyuu no shiai wa *yakyuujoo (guraundo)* de shimasu.	baseball field
選手はグローブでボールを受けます。 Senshu wa *guroobu* de booru o *ukemasu*.	glove, catch
ピッチャーはキャッチャーにボールを投げます。 *Picchaa* wa *kyacchaa* ni booru o *nagemasu*.	pitcher, catcher, pitch
キャッチャーはミットでピッチャーからのボールを受けます。 Kyacchaa wa *mitto* de picchaa kara no booru o ukemasu.	mitt
バッターはバットでボールを打ちます。 *Battaa* wa *batto* de booru o *uchimasu*.	batter, bat, hit
キャッチャーの後ろには審判員（アンパイヤー）がいます。 Kyacchaa no ushiro ni wa *shinpan-in (anpaiyaa)* ga imasu.	referee (umpire)
審判員はストライクやアウトをとります。 Shinpan-in wa *sutoraiku* ya *auto* o torimasu.	strike, out
野球の試合は9回で、表と裏があります。 Yakyuu no shiai wa kyuu *kai* de, *omote* to *ura* ga arimasu.	innings, top, bottom
試合は3対3の同点です。 Shiai wa san tai san no *dooten* desu.	tie
Aチームのバッターがヒットを打ちました。 Ee chiimu no battaa ga *hitto o uchimashita*.	make a hit
一塁ベースへ走ります。 *Ichi rui beesu* e *hashirimasu*.	first base, run
4番バッターがホームランを打ちました。	cleanup (the fourth batter),

Yo ban battaa ga *hoomuran* o uchimashita.

Aチームが**5対3**で勝ちました。

Ee chiimu ga *go tai san* de kachimashita.

home run

won by a score of 5 to 3

4. Complete.

ジャイアンツとタイガースの＿1＿です。今、最後の回です。9回の＿2＿が終って、これから9回の＿3＿が

Jaiantsu to Taigaasu no ＿1＿ desu. Ima, saigo no kai desu. Kyuu kai no ＿2＿ ga owatte, korekara kyuu kai no ＿3＿ ga

始まります。試合は3対3の＿4＿です。ピッチャーがボールを＿5＿。ストライクです。キャッチャーはボール

hajimarimasu. Shiai wa san tai san no ＿4＿ desu. Picchaa ga booru o ＿5＿. Sutoraiku desu. Kyacchaa wa booru

を＿6＿、またピッチャーに投げました。ピッチャーはキャッチャーとサインを交換して（exchanges signals）、

o ＿6＿, mata picchaa ni nagemashita. Picchaa wa kyacchaa to sain o kookan shite,

もう一度ボールを投げました。今度はバッターは＿7＿。ホームランです。バッターはうれしそうに走って、

moo ichido booru o nagemashita. Kondo wa battaa wa ＿7＿. Hoomuran desu. Battaa wa ureshisoo ni hashitte,

ホームに戻ってきました。4＿8＿3でタイガースが勝ちました。

hoomu ni modotte kimashita. Yon ＿8＿ san de Taigaasu ga kachimashita.

TENNIS

テニスの**トーナメント**があります。

Tenisu no *toonamento* ga arimasu.

tennis, tournament

テニスの**試合**は**テニスコート**でします。

Tenisu no *shiai* wa *tenisu kooto* de shimasu.

game (match), tennis court

選手は**ラケット**とボールを使います。

Senshu wa *raketto* to booru o tsukaimasu.

racket

シングルスの試合は二人でします。

Shingurusu no shiai wa futari de shimasu.

singles match

ダブルスの試合は四人でします。

Daburusu no shiai wa yonin de shimasu.

doubles match

一人の選手が**サーブ**をします。

Hitori no senshu ga *saabu* o shimasu.

serve

相手の選手がそのボールを**打ち返します**。

Aite no senshu ga sono booru o *uchikaeshimasu*.

opponent, returns

アウトです。

Auto desu.

out

ネット（ネットボール）です。

Net (Neto booru) desu.

net ball

A選手は**3セットのうち2セット**とりました。

Ee senshu wa *san setto no uchi ni setto* torimashita.

2 sets out of 3

5. Complete.

1. ＿＿＿の試合は二人で、＿＿＿の試合は四人でします。

   ___ no shiai wa futari de, ___ no shiai wa yonin de shimasu.

2. テニスをする時、＿＿＿で＿＿＿を打ちます。

   Tenisu o suru toki, ___   de ___ o uchimasu.

3. テニスは＿＿＿でします。

   Tenisu wa ___ de shimasu.

4. ボールがコートの外に出たら、＿＿＿です。

   Booru ga kooto no soto ni detara, ___ desu.

5. 一人の選手が＿＿＿をして、相手の選手がそれを＿＿＿。

   Hitori no senshu ga ___ o shite, aite no senshu ga sore o ___.

GOLF

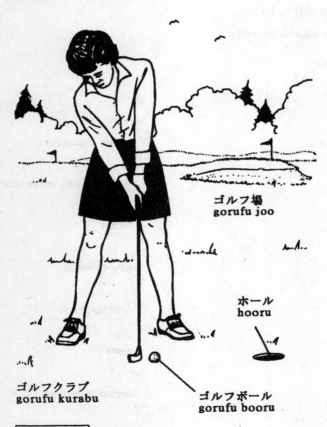

ゴルフ場
gorufu joo

ホール
hooru

ゴルフクラブ
gorufu kurabu

ゴルフボール
gorufu booru

Fig. 19-2

ゴルフはゴルフ場（コース）でします。   golf, golf course

Gorufu wa *gorufujoo (koosu)* de shimasu.

ゴルフクラブでボールを打ちます。   golf club

Gorufu kurabu de booru o uchimasu.

ボールを**ホール**に入れます。   hole

Booru o *hooru* ni iremasu.

１**ラウンド**は１８**ホール**です。   round, hole

Ichi *raundo* wa juuhachi *hooru* desu.

ゴルフ練習場で、ボールを打つ**練習**ができます。   driving range, practice

Gorufu renshuujoo de, booru o utsu *renshuu* ga dekimasu.

6. Complete.

ゴルフは__1__でします。ゴルフ選手は__2__を__3__で打って、__4__に入れます。1__5__は18__6__です。

Gorufu wa __1__ de shimasu. Gorufu senshu wa __2__ o __3__ de utte, __4__ ni iremasu. Ichi __5__ wa juuhachi __6__ desu.

私の友達もゴルフが好きですが、ゴルフ場が遠いのでいつも__7__に行って練習しています。

Watashi no tomodachi mo gorufu ga suki desu ga, gorufujoo ga tooi node itsumo __7__ ni itte renshuu shite imasu.

SUMO WRESTLING

Fig. 19-3

相撲の選手は**力士**といいます。   sumo, sumo wrestler

Sumoo no senshu wa *rikishi* to iimasu.

相撲の審判員は**行司**といいます。   gyooji (referee)

Sumoo no shinpan-in wa *gyooji* to iimàsu.

土俵で相撲をとります。   dohyoo (ring), have a sumo bout

Dohyoo de *sumoo o torimasu.*

土俵の外に出たら、負けです。

Dohyoo no soto ni detara, make desu.

土俵に**体の一部**が**触れ**ても、負けです。   a part of the body, touch

Dohyoo ni *karada no ichibu* ga *furete* mo, make desu.

相撲は一年に六**場所**あります。   regular sumo tournament

Sumoo wa ichi nen ni roku *basho* arimasu.

一場所は 15 日間です。

7. Complete.

二人の __1__ が __2__ の上で相撲をとります。 __3__ が審判をします。 __4__ の外に出たり、__5__ に __6__ の

Futari no __1__ ga __2__ no ue de sumoo o torimasu. __3__ ga shinpan o shimasu. __4__ no soto ni detari, __5__ ni __6__ no

一部が触れると負けです。 日本では相撲は一年に六 __7__ あります。

ichibu ga fureru to make desu. Nihon de wa sumoo wa ichi nen ni roku __7__ arimasu.

THE BEACH

今日の**海**はとても**静か**（**おだやか**）です。   sea, calm

Kyoo no *umi* wa totemo *shizuka (odayaka)* desu.

昨日は海が**荒れていました**   rough

Kinoo wa umi ga *arete imashita.*

波が高かったです。   wave

Nami ga takakatta desu.

潮が**満ち**ています。   tide, high

Shio ga *michite imasu.*

   引いています。   low

   hiite imasu.

満潮は何時ですか。   high tide

Manchoo wa nanji desu ka.

干潮   low tide

Kanchoo

高潮が来ました。   tidal wave

Takashio ga kimashita.

8. Complete.

1. 今日は海に波がほとんどありません。 今日の海はとても____。

   Kyoo wa umi ni nami ga hotondo arimasen. Kyoo no umi wa totemo ___.

2. 昨日は波が高かったです。昨日は海が＿＿＿。

Kinoo wa nami ga takakatta desu.　Kinoo wa umi ga ＿＿.

3. きょうの満潮は午前で、＿＿＿は午後です。

Kyoo no manchoo wa gozen de, ＿＿ wa gogo desu.

4. 台風(typhoon)の時、＿＿＿が来ます。とても危ないので、海に行ってはいけません。

Taifuu no toki, ＿＿ ga kimasu. Totemo abunai node, umi ni itte wa ikemasen.

9. Match to complete each statement.

1. 満潮というのは

Manchoo to iu no wa

2. 干潮というのは

Kanchoo to iu no wa

3. 高潮というのは

Takashio to iu no wa

(a) 潮が引いていることです。

shio ga hiite iru koto desu.

(b) 波が高いことです。

namiga takai koto desu.

(c) 潮が満ちていることです。

shio ga michite iru koto desu.

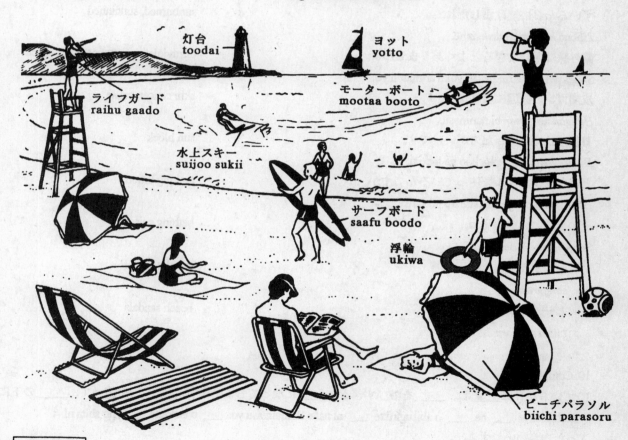

Fig. 19-4

海辺で夏休みを過ごします。

Umibe de natsuyasumi o sugoshimasu.

beach, spend

ここは人気のある**ビーチリゾート**です。   seaside resort
Koko wa ninki no aru *biichi rizooto* desu.

私は**泳ぎます**。   swim
Watashi wa *oyogimasu.*

　　スキューバダイビングをします。   scuba-diving
　　sukyuuba daibingu o shimasu.

　　サーフィンをします。   surfing
　　saafin o shimasu.

　　水上スキーをします。   water-skiing
　　suijoo sukii o shimasu.

　　海辺を**散歩**します。   take a walk
　　umibe o *sanpo shimasu.*

　　日光浴をします。   sunbathe
　　nikkooyoku o shimasu.

ずいぶん**日に焼けました**ね。   sunburned, suntanned
Zuibun *hi ni yakemashita* ne.

紫外線は**浴びすぎる**とよくありませんよ。   ultraviolet rays, exposed too much
Shigaisen wa *abisugiru* to yoku arimasen yo.

皮膚ガンの**原因**になります。   skin cancer, cause
Hifugan no *gen-in* ni narimasu.

日焼け止めを使った方がいいです。   sun block
Hiyakedome o tsukatta hoo ga ii desu.

どんな**サンオイル**を使っているんですか。   tanning lotion
Don-na *san-oiru* o tsukatte iru ndesu ka.

その**水着**、いいですね。   bathing suit
Sono *mizugi,* ii desu ne.

　　サングラス   sunglasses
　　sangurasu

　　ビーチサンダル   beach sandals
　　biichi sandaru

10. Complete.

1. ずいぶん日に＿＿ね。＿＿を浴びすぎると＿＿になってしまいますよ。＿＿を使って、＿＿の下に
　 Zuibun hi ni ＿＿ ne. ＿＿ o abisugiru to ＿＿ ni natte shimaimasu yo. ＿＿ o tsukatte, ＿＿ no shita ni
入った方がいいですよ。
haitta hoo ga ii desu yo.

2. 晩ご飯の後で、少し海辺を＿＿しませんか。
　 Ban gohan no ato de, sukoshi umibe o ＿＿ shimasen ka.

3. 私は泳げないので、＿＿を持って海に入ります。

Watashi wa oyogenai no de, ___ o motte umi ni hairimasu.

4. 泳ぐ時は＿＿＿を着ます。

Oyogu toki wa ___ o kimasu.

5. ＿＿＿をします。サーフボードを持って来ました。

___ o shimasu. Saafu boodo o motte kimashita.

11. Choose the correct ones.

泳いでもいいのは、

Oyoide mo ii no wa,

1. ライフガードがいる時

   raifu gaado ga iru toki

2. ライフガードがいない時

   raifu gaado ga inai toki

3. 波が高い時

   Nami ga takai toki

4. 海がおだやかな時

   Umi ga odayaka na toki

5. 海が荒れている時

   Umi ga arete iru toki

6. モーターボートの近く

   Mootaa booto no chikaku

SKIING

山 yama
リフト rifuto
スキー帽 sukii boo
スキー場 sukii joo
ゲレンデ gerende
手袋 tebukuro
スキーウェア sukii wea
スキーヤー sukiiyaa
ストック sutokku
スキー靴 sukii gutsu

Fig. 19-5

スキー場には初心者用のグレンデのほかに　　　　　　　　　skiing ground, for beginner, slope

Sukiijoo ni wa *shoshinsha yoo* no *gerende* no hoka ni

中級レベルのグレンデや上級レベルのグレンデもあります。　　intermediate level, advanced level

chuukyuu reberu no gerende ya *jookyuu reberu* no gerende mo arimasu.

上級者はとても難しいコースを滑ります。　　　　　　　　　expert, course, ski down

Jookyuusha wa totemo muzukashii *koosu o suberimasu.*

初心者は簡単なコースを滑ります。　　　　　　　　　　　　beginner

Shoshinsha wa kantan na koosu o suberimasu.

12. Complete.

1. コロラド州やユタ州には＿＿＿がたくさんあって、冬は人がたくさんそこへ＿＿＿をしに行きます。

　　Kororado shuu ya Yuta shuu ni wa ＿＿ ga takusan atte, fuyu wa hito ga takusan soko e ＿＿ o shi ni ikimasu.

2. スキー場には＿＿＿用のグレンデから＿＿＿用のグレンデまで、いろいろなレベルのコースがあります。

　　Sukiijoo ni wa ＿＿ yoo no gerende kara ＿＿ yoo no gerende made, iroiro na reberu no koosu ga arimasu.

3. 初めてスキーをする人は初心者用のグレンデを＿＿＿。

　　Hajimete sukii o suru hito wa shoshinsha yoo no gerende o ＿＿.

4. 山の上まで歩く必要はありません。＿＿＿で行けます。

　　Yama no ue made aruku hitsuyoo wa arimasen. ＿＿ de ikemasu.

13. Prepare a list of the equipment one needs to ski.

Key Words

a part of the body	体の一部	*karada no ichibu*	calm	静か（おだやか）	*shizuka (odayaka)*
advanced level	上級レベル	*jookyuu reberu*	catch	受ける	*ukeru*
ball	ボール	*booru*	catcher	キャッチャー	*kyacchaa*
~ base	～塁ベース	*~ rui beesu*	cause	原因	*gen-in*
baseball	野球	*yakyuu*	cleanup (the fourth batter)	４番バッター	*yoban battaa*
baseball field	野球場（グラウンド）	*yakyuujoo (guraundo)*	course	コース	*koosu*
bat	バット	*batto*	defend	守る	*mamoru*
bathing suit	水着	*mizugi*	dohyoo (ring)	土俵	*dohyoo*
batter	バッター	*battaa*	doubles match	ダブルスの試合	*daburusu no shiai*
beach	海辺	*umibe*			
beach sandals	ビーチサンダル	*biichi sandaru*	driving range	ゴルフ練習場	*gorufu renshuu joo*
beach umbrella	ビーチパラソル	*biichi parasoru*	expert	上級者	*jookyuusha*
			exposed too much	浴びすぎる	*abisugiru*
beginner	初心者	*shoshinsha*	finish in a tie	引き分け	*hikiwake*
blow (a whistle)	吹く	*fuku*	first half	前半	*zenhan*
bottom	裏	*ura*	float ring (life saver)	浮き輪	*ukiwa*

foot	足	*ashi*	practice	練習	*renshuu*
for beginner	初心者用	*shoshinsha yoo*	racket	ラケット	*raketto*
foul	反則（ファール）	*hansoku (faaru)*	referee (umpire)	審判員（アンパイヤー）	*shinpan-in (anpaiyaa)*
full	満ちている	*michite iru*	regular sumo tournament	場所	*basho*
game (match)	試合	*shiai*	returns	打ち返す	*uchikaesu*
glove	グローブ	*guroobu*	rough	荒れている	*arete iru*
gloves	手袋	*tebukuro*	round	ラウンド	*raundo*
goal	ゴール	*gooru*	run	走る	*hashiru*
goalie	ゴールキーパー	*gooru kiipaa*	score	点（得点）を入れる	*ten (tokuten) o ireru*
golf	ゴルフ	*gorufu*			
golf ball	ゴルフボール	*gorufu booru*	score	得点	*tokuten*
golf club	ゴルフクラブ	*gorufu kurabu*	score of ~ to ~	～対～	*~ tai ~*
golf course	ゴルフ場（コース）	*gorufujoo (koosu)*	scoreboard	得点板（スコアボード）	*tokutenban (sukoa boodo)*
gyooji (referee)	行司	*gyooji*	scuba-diving	スキューバダイビング	*sukyuuba daibingu*
have a sumo bout	相撲をとる	*sumoo o toru*			
			sea	海	*umi*
high tide	満潮	*manchoo*	seaside resort	ビーチリゾート	*biichi rizooto*
hit	打つ	*utsu*			
hole	ホール	*hooru*	second half	後半	*koohan*
home run	ホームラン	*hoomuran*	serve	サーブ	*saabu*
~ innings	～回	*~ kai*	set	セット	*setto*
intermediate level	中級レベル	*chuukyuu reberu*	singles match	シングルスの試合	*shingurusu no shiai*
kick	蹴る	*keru*			
left end	レフトバック	*refutobakku*	ski	スキー	*sukii*
lifeguard	ライフガード	*raifu gaado*	ski boots	スキー靴	*sukii gutsu*
lighthouse	灯台	*toodai*	ski cap	スキー帽	*sukii boo*
loose	負ける（負け）	*makeru (make)*	ski down	滑る	*suberu*
low	引いている	*hiite iru*	ski lift	リフト	*rifuto*
low tide	干潮	*kanchoo*	ski suit	スキーウエア	*sukii wea*
make a hit	ヒットを打つ	*hitto o utsu*	skier	スキーヤー	*sukiiyaa*
makes a goal	ゴールをする（決める）	*gooru o suru (kimeru)*	skiing ground	スキー場	*sukiijoo*
			skin cancer	皮膚ガン	*hifugan*
mawashi (belt)	まわし	*mawashi*	slope	ゲレンデ	*gerende*
mitt	ミット	*mitto*	soccer	サッカー	*sakkaa*
motorboat	モーターボート	*mootaa booto*	soccer field (ground)	サッカー場（グラウンド）	*sakkaajoo (guraundo)*
mountain	山	*yama*	spend	過ごす	*sugosu*
net ball	ネット（ネットボール）	*netto (netto booru)*	sports	スポーツ	*supootsu*
			stop	止める	*tomeru*
			strike	ストライク	*sutoraiku*
opponent	相手	*aite*	sumo	相撲	*sumoo*
opponent team	相手チーム	*aite chiimu*	sumo wrestler	力士	*rikishi*
out	アウト	*auto*	sun block	日焼け止め	*hiyakedome*
pitch	投げる	*nageru*	sunbathe	日光浴をする	*nikkooyoku o suru*
pitcher	ピッチャー	*picchaa*	sunburned, suntanned	日に焼ける	*hi ni yakeru*
player	選手	*senshu*			
pole	ストック	*sutokku*	sunglasses	サングラス	*san gurasu*

surfboard	サーフボード	*saafu boodo*	top	表	*omote*
surfing	サーフィン	*saafin*	toss (the ball)	パスする	*pasu suru*
swim	泳ぐ	*oyogu*	touch	触れる	*fureru*
take a walk	散歩する	*sanpo suru*	tournament	トーナメント	*toonamento*
tanning lotion	サンオイル	*sanoiru*	ultraviolet rays	紫外線	*shigaisen*
team	チーム	*chiimu*	water-skiing	水上スキー	*suijoo sukii*
teammate	味方	*mikata*	wave	波	*nami*
tennis	テニス	*tenisu*	whistle	笛（ホイッスル）	*fue (hoissuru)*
tennis court	テニスコート	*tenisu kooto*			
tidal wave	高潮	*takashio*	win	勝つ（勝ち）	*katsu (kachi)*
tide	潮	*shio*	yacht	ヨット	*yotto*
tie	同点	*dooten*			

Chapter 20: The weather
第20章：天気
Tenki

今日はいい天気です（天気がいいです）。   nice weather
Kyoo wa *ii tenki* desu (*tenki ga ii* desu).

    天気が悪いです。   bad
    tenki ga *warui* desu.

    暑いです。   hot
    atsui desu.

    寒いです。   cold
    samui desu.

    涼しいです。   cool
    suzushii desu.

    暖かいです。   warm
    atatakai desu.

    蒸し暑いです。   humid
    mushiatsui desu.

    風が強いです。   windy
    kaze ga tsuyoi desu.

明日は晴れです。   fine, clear
Ashita wa *hare* desu.

    曇りです。   cloudy
    kumori desu.

    雨です。   rain
    ame desu.

    雪です。   snow
    yuki desu.

    霧です。   fog
    kiri desu.

    雷です。   thunder
    kaminari desu.

    雷雨です。   thunderstorm
    raiu desu.

晴れています。   clear
Harete imasu.

曇っています。   cloudy
Kumotte imasu.

雨が降っています。   raining
Ame ga futte imasu.

173

小雨	drizzling
Kosame	
雪	snowing
Yuki	
ひょう	hailing
Hyoo	
霧が出ています。	foggy
Kiri ga dete imasu.	
雷が鳴っています。	thundering
Kaminari ga natte imasu.	
今日は雨が降ったり止んだりして、変な天気です。	raining on and off, strange
Kyoo wa *ame ga futtari yandari shite, hen na* tenki desu.	
にわか雨です。	shower
Niwakaame desu.	
吹雪です。	snowstorm
Fubuki desu.	
台風が来ます。	typhoon
Taifuu ga kimasu.	

1. Complete.

1. 夏は＿＿＿です。冬は＿＿＿です。

   Natsu wa ___ desu. Fuyu wa ___ desu.

2. 日本では六月ごろ、よく＿＿＿が降ります。一月ごろ、＿＿＿が降ります。

   Nihon de wa roku gatsu goro, yoku ___ ga furimasu. Ichi gatsu goro, ___ ga furimasu.

3. 今日はいい天気です。＿＿＿います。

   Kyoo wa ii tenki desu. ___ imasu.

4. 空(sky)が暗いです。＿＿＿います。

   Sora ga kurai desu. ___ imasu.

5. 夏でも日本の北の方(northern part)はあまり暑くありません。＿＿＿です。

   Natsu demo Nihon no kita no hoo wa amari atsuku arimasen. ___ desu.

6. 冬でも日本の南の方(southern part)はあまり寒くありません。＿＿＿です。

   Fuyu demo Nihon no minami no hoo wa amari samuku arimasen. ___ desu.

7. 今日は＿＿＿が出ています。何も見えません。

   Kyoo wa ___ ga dete imasu. Nani mo miemasen.

8. 雨が降っていて、気温(temperature)が高い日は、とても＿＿＿です。

   Ame ga futte ite, kion ga takai hi wa, totemo ___ desu.

9. 雪がたくさん降っていて、風が強いです。＿＿＿です。

   Yuki ga takusan futte ite, kaze ga tsuyoi desu. ___ desu.

10. ＿＿＿が鳴っている時は、金物(ironware)の近くにいてはいけません。

    ___ ga natte iru toki wa, kanamono no chikaku ni ite wa ikemasen.

2. Tell more about the weather.

1. 天気がいいです。 例えば(For example)...

    Tenki ga ii desu.   Tatoeba...

2. 天気が悪いです。 例えば...

    Tenki ga warui desu. Tatoeba...

3. 変な天気です。 例えば...

    Hen na tenki desu.   Tatoeba...

3. Give words related to each of the following.

1. ＿＿が強い

    ___ ga tsuyoi

2. ＿＿が降る

    ___ ga furu

3. ＿＿が出ている

    ___ ga dete iru

4. ＿＿が鳴っている

    ___ ga natte iru

4. Complete.

1. 明日は雨じゃありませんが、晴れでもありません。 ＿＿＿です。

    Ashita wa ame ja arimasen ga, hare demo arimasen. ___ desu.

2. 雨が少しだけ降っています。 ＿＿＿が降っています。

    Ame ga sukoshi dake futte imasu. ___ ga futte imasu.

3. 空から小さい氷(ice)が降っています。 ＿＿＿が降っています。

    Sora kara chiisai koori ga futte imasu. ___ ga futte imasu.

4. 晴れていましたが、急に(suddenly)雨が降りました。 ＿＿＿です。

    Harete imashita ga, kyuu ni ame ga furimashita. ___ desu.

5. 日本では秋によく＿＿＿が来ます。 その被害(damage)は大きいです。

    Nihon de wa aki ni yoku ___ ga kimasu. Sono higai wa ookii desu.

Key Words

bad	天気が悪い	*tenki ga warui*	fog	霧	*kiri*
clear	晴れている	*harete iru*	foggy	霧が出ている	*kiri ga deteiru*
cloudy	曇っている	*kumotte iru*	hailing	ひょう	*hyoo*
cloudy	曇り	*kumori*	hot	暑い	*atsui*
cold	寒い	*samui*	humid	蒸し暑い	*mushiatsui*
cool	涼しい	*suzushii*	nice weather	いい天気（天気がいい）	*ii tenki (tenki ga ii)*
drizzling	小雨	*kosame*			
fine, clear	晴れ	*hare*	rain	雨	*ame*

rain	雨が降る	*ame ga furu*	thunder	雷	*kaminari*
raining on and off	雨が降ったり止んだりする	*ame ga futtari yandari suru*	thundering	雷が鳴っている	*kaminari ga natte iru*
			thunderstorm	雷雨	*raiu*
shower	にわか雨	*niwakaame*	typhoon	台風	*taifuu*
snow	雪	*yuki*	warm	暖かい	*atatakai*
snow	雪が降る	*yuki ga furu*	weather	天気	*tenki*
snowstorm	吹雪	*fubuki*	windy	風が強い	*kaze ga tsuyoi*
strange	変な	*hen na*			

Appendix 1: Numbers
付録1 : 数　Kazu

一	ichi	1
二	ni	2
三	san	3
四	yon, shi	4
五	go	5
六	roku	6
七	nana, shichi	7
八	hachi	8
九	kyuu, ku	9
十	juu, too	10
十一	juuichi	11
十二	juuni	12
二十	nijuu	20
二十一	nijuu ichi	21
三十	sanjuu	30
四十	yonjuu	40
五十	gojuu	50
六十	rokujuu	60
七十	nanajuu	70
八十	hachijuu	80
九十	kyuujuu	90

百	hyaku	100
百一	hyaku ichi	101
百十一	hyaku juu ichi	111
二百	nihyaku	200
三百	sanbyaku	300
四百	yonhyaku	400
五百	gohyaku	500
六百	roppyaku	600
七百	nanahyaku	700
八百	happyaku	800
九百	kyuuhyaku	900
千	sen	1,000
二千	nisen	2,000
三千	sanzen	3,000
四千	yonsen	4,000
五千	gosen	5,000
六千	rokusen	6,000
七千	nanasen	7,000
八千	hassen	8,000
九千	kyuusen	9,000
一万	ichiman	10,000
十万	juuman	100,000
百万	hyakuman	1,000,000
一千万	issenman	10,000,000
一億	ichioku	100,000,000

Appendix 2: Time expressions
付録2：時の表現　Toki no hyoogen

DAYS OF THE WEEK

今日は何曜日ですか。   What day (of the week) is it today?
Kyoo wa *nan-yoobi* desu ka?

月曜日	*getsuyoobi*	Monday
火曜日	*kayoobi*	Tuesday
水曜日	*suiyoobi*	Wednesday
木曜日	*mokuyoobi*	Thursday
金曜日	*kin-yoobi*	Friday
土曜日	*doyoobi*	Saturday
日曜日	*nichiyoobi*	Sunday
第一日曜日	*daiichi nichiyoobi*	the first Sunday
第二土曜日	*daini doyoobi*	the second Saturday
週	*shuu*	week
週末	*shuumatsu*	weekend
平日	*heejitsu*	weekday
休日	*kyuujitsu*	holiday (day off)
祝日（祭日）	*shukujitsu (saijitsu)*	national holiday
誕生日	*tanjoobi*	birthday

HOLIDAYS

January 1	元旦	*gantan*	New Year's Day
First Monday of Januaryu	成人の日	*seejin no hi*	Coming-of-Age Day
February 11	建国記念の日	*kenkokukinen no hi*	National Foundation Day
March 21	春分の日	*shunbun no hi*	Vernal Equinox Day
April 29	みどりの日	*midori no hi*	Greenery Day
May 3	憲法記念日	*kenkoku kinen bi*	Constitution Day
May 4	国民の休日	*kokumin no kyuujitsu*	Public Holiday
May 5	子供の日	*kodomo no hi*	Children's Day
July 20	海の日	*umi no hi*	Sea Day
September 15	敬老の日	*keeroo no hi*	Respect-for-Aged Day
September 23	秋分の日	*shuubun no hi*	Autumnal Equinox Day
Second Monday of October	体育の日	*taiiku no hi*	Health-Sports Day

November 3	文化の日	*bunka no hi*	Culture Day
November 23	勤労感謝の日	*kinrookansha no hi*	Labor Thanksgiving Day
December 23	天皇誕生日	*ten-noo tanjoobi*	Emperor's Birthday

MONTHS OF THE YEAR AND DATES

今日は何月何日ですか。

Kyoo wa *nangatsu nannichi* desu ka?

What's today's date?

今日は十二月十一日です。

Kyoo wa juuni*gatsu* juuichi*nichi* desu.

Today is December 11.

一月	*ichigatsu*	January
二月	*nigatsu*	February
三月	*sangatsu*	March
四月	*shigatsu*	April
五月	*gogatsu*	May
六月	*rokugatsu*	June
七月	*shichigatsu*	July
八月	*hachigatsu*	August
九月	*kugatsu*	September
十月	*juugatsu*	October
十一月	*juuichigatsu*	November
十二月	*juunigatsu*	December
一日	*tsuitachi*	the first
二日	*futsuka*	the second
三日	*mikka*	the third
四日	*yokka*	the fourth
五日	*itsuka*	the fifth
六日	*muika*	the sixth
七日	*nanoka*	the seventh
八日	*yooka*	the eighth
九日	*kokonoka*	the ninth
十日	*tooka*	the tenth
十一日	*juuichinichi*	the eleventh
十二日	*juuninichi*	the twelfth
十三日	*juusannichi*	the thirteenth
十四日	*juuyokka*	the fourteenth
十五日	*juugonichi*	the fifteenth
二十日	*hatsuka*	the twentieth
二十四日	*nijuuyokka*	the twenty-fourth

| 三十日 | *sanjuunichi* | the thirtieth |
| 三十一日 | *sanjuuichinichi* | the thirty-first |

TELLING TIME

今、何時ですか。

Ima, nanji desu ka?

What time is it now?

1 時

Ichi*ji* desu.

one **o'clock**

6 時 5 分

roku*ji* go*fun*

6:05

午前 4 時 10 分

gozen yoji juppun

4:10- **a.m.**

午後 5 時 15 分

gogo goji juugofun

5:15 **p.m.**

7 時半

shichiji *han*

seven **thirty (half)**

8 時 5 分前

hachiji gofun *mae*

five to eight

ちょうど 9 時

choodo kuji

exactly nine o'clock

10 時頃

juuji *goro*

about ten o'clock

11 時少し前

juuichiji *sukoshi mae*

a little before eleven

12 時少し過ぎ

juuniji *sukoshi sugi*

a little after twelve

今日は、時間通りに会社に着きました。

Kyoo wa, *jikandoori ni* kaisha ni tsukimashita.

on time

遅く

osoku

late

早く

hayaku

early

朝、新聞を読みました。

Asa, shinbun o yomimashita.

in the morning

昼、買い物に出かけました。

Hiru, kaimono ni dekakemashita.

noon (midday)

夜、食事に行きました。

Yoru, shokuji ni ikimashita.

at night

夕方、友達に会いました。   in the evening
Yuugata, tomodachi ni aimashita.

午前中、家にいました。   during the morning
Gozenchuu, uchi ni imashita.

午後、仕事をしました。   in the afternoon
Gogo, shigoto o shimashita.

DIVISIONS OF TIME

60 秒	rokujuu *byoo*	sixty **seconds**
15 分	juugo *fun*	fifteen **minutes**
一時間	ichi *jikan*	one **hour**
一日	ichi *nichi*	one **day**
二週間	ni *shuukan*	two **weeks**
三か月	san *kagetsu*	three **months**
三年（三年間）	san *nen* (san *nenkan*)	three **years**
二十一世紀	nijuuis*seeki*	twenty-first **century**

OTHER TIME EXPRESSIONS

今日	*kyoo*	today
明日	*ashita*	tomorrow
あさって	*asatte*	the day after tomorrow
きのう	*kinoo*	yesterday
おととい	*ototoi*	the day before yesterday
夕べ	*yuube*	last night
毎日	*mainichi*	everyday
今週	*konshuu*	this week
来週	*raishuu*	next week
先週	*senshuu*	last week
毎週	*maishuu*	every week
今月	*kongetsu*	this month
来月	*raigetsu*	next month
先月	*sengetsu*	last month
毎月	*maitsuki*	every month
今年	*kotoshi*	this year
来年	*rainen*	next year
去年	*kyonen*	last year
毎年	*maitoshi*	every year

一日おきに	ichinichi *okini*	every other day
二週間おきに	nishuukan *okini*	every two weeks
今月の初め	kongetsu no *hajime*	**the beginning of** the month
今年の終わり	kotoshi no *owari*	**the end of** this year
先月の半ば	sengetsu no *nakaba*	**the middle of** last month

Appendix 3: Food
付録3：食べ物と飲み物
Tabemono to nomimono

Vegetables	**野菜**	**yasai**			
artichoke	アーティチョーク	aatichooku	zucchini	ズッキーニ	zukkiini
asparagus	アスパラガス	asuparagasu	**果物**	**fruits**	**kudamono**
bamboo shoot	たけのこ	takenoko	apple	りんご	ringo
been sprouts	もやし	moyashi	apricots	あんず	anzu
beet	赤かぶ	akakabu	avocado	アボガド	abogado
bracken	わらび	warabi	banana	バナナ	banana
broccoli	ブロッコリー	burokkorii	blueberry	ブルーベリー	buruuberii
brussels sprouts	芽キャベツ	mekyabetsu	cherry	さくらんぼ	sakuranbo
burdock	ごぼう	goboo	fig	いちぢく	ichijiku
cabbage	キャベツ	kyabetsu	grape	ぶどう	budoo
carrot	にんじん	ninjin	grapefruit	グレープフルーツ	gureepufuruutsu
cauliflower	カリフラワー	karifurawaa			
celery	セロリー	serorii	kiwifruit	キウイ	kiui
chicory	チコリ	chikori	lemon	レモン	remon
chinese cabbage	白菜	hakusai	lime	ライム	raimu
chinese chive	にら	nira	loquat	びわ	biwa
chinese yam	長いも	nagaimo	lyychee	ライチ	raichi
corn	とうもろこし	toomorokoshi	mango	マンゴー	mangoo
cucumber	きゅうり	kyuuri	melon	メロン	meron
daikon, white radish	大根	daikon	mikan, tangerine	みかん	mikan
eggplant	なす	nasu	navel orange	ネーヴル	neevuru
enokitake	えのきだけ	enokidake	nectarine	ネクタリン	nekutarin
garden peas	さやえんどう	sayaendoo	olive	オリーブ	oriibu
gerlic	にんにく	ninniku	orange	オレンジ	orenji
ginger	しょうが	shooga	papaya	パパイア	papaia
green pepper	ピーマン	piiman	peach	桃	momo
head lettuce	サラダ菜	saradana	pear	なし	nashi
horse radish	ホースラディッシュ	hoosuradisshu	persimmon	柿	kaki
			pineapple	パインアップル	pain-appuru
jew's-ear	きくらげ	kikurage		パイナップル	painappuru
kidney beans	いんげんまめ	ingenmame	pomegranate	ざくろ	zakuro
leaf lettuce	サニーレタス	saniiretasu	prune	プルーン	puruun
leek	西洋ねぎ	seeyoonegi	raspberry	ラズベリー	razuberii
lettuce	レタス	retasu	sour orange	だいだい	daidai
lotus root	れんこん	renkon	strawberry	いちご	ichigo
matsutake	まつたけ	matsutake	watermelon	すいか	suika
mushroom	マッシュルーム	masshuruumu			
okura	オクラ	okura	**Meats and fowl**	**肉と鶏肉**	**niku to toriniku**
onion	玉ねぎ	tamanegi	bacon	ベーコン	beekon
perilla	しそ	shiso	beef	牛肉	gyuuniku
potato	じゃがいも	jagaimo	brisket	胸肉	muneniku
pumpkin	かぼちゃ	kabocha	rib	あばら肉（リブ）	abaraniku (ribu)
radish	二十日大根	hatsukadaikon	shoulder	肩肉	kataniku
red cabbage	紫キャベツ	murasakikyabetsu	tongue	タン	tan
red pepper, chili	とうがらし	toogarashi	veal	子牛の肉	koushi no niku
scallion	ねぎ	negi	chicken	鶏肉	toriniku
shiitake	しいたけ	shiitake	kidney	じん臓	jinzoo
spinach	ほうれん草	hoorensoo	leg	足	ashi
squash	西洋かぼちゃ	seeyookabocha	liver	肝臓	kanzoo
sweet potato, yam	さつまいも	satsumaimo	wing	手羽肉	tebaniku
tomato	トマト	tomato	thigh	もも肉	momoniku
turnip	かぶ	kabu	duck	鴨	kamo
wasabi	わさび	wasabi	ground, minced	ひき肉	hikiniku
watercress	クレソン	kureson	ham	ハム	hamu
			mutton	羊肉	yooniku

183

lamb	子羊の肉（ラム）	*kohitsuji no niku*
pork	豚肉	*butaniku*
sparerib	あばら肉	*abaraniku*
sausage	ソーセージ	*sooseeji*
turkey	七面鳥（ターキー）	*shichimenchoo (taakii)*

Sea Food	**魚介類**	***gyokal rul***
anchovy	アンチョビ	*anchobi*
angler-fish	あんこう	*ankoo*
barracuda	かます	*kamasu*
carp	こい	*koi*
codfish	たら	*tara*
crab	かに	*kani*
crayfish	いせえび	*iseebi*
eel	うなぎ	*unagi*
flatfish	かれい	*karee*
grouper	はた	*hata*
herring	にしん	*nishin*
lobster	ロブスター	*robusutaa*
mackerel	さば	*saba*
mullet	ぼら	*bora*
red mullet	ひめじ	*himeji*
mussel	ムール貝	*muurugai*
octopus	たこ	*tako*
oyster	かき	*kaki*
prawns	車えび	*kurumaebi*
ray	えい	*ei*
red snapper	きんめだい	*kinmedai*
salmon	さけ	*sake*
sardine	いわし	*iwashi*
scallops	ほたて貝	*hotategai*
sea bass	すずき	*suzuki*
sea bream	たい	*tai*
sea urchin	うに	*uni*
shrimp	えび（子えび）	*ebi (koebi)*
snail	たにし	*tanishi*
squid	いか	*ika*
swordfish	かじき	*kajiki*
tongue sole	舌平目	*shitabirame*
trout	ます	*masu*
tuna	まぐろ	*maguro*

Eggs	**卵**	***tamago***
boiled eggs	ゆで卵	*yudetamago*
hard-boiled eggs	堅ゆで	*katayude*
soft-boiled eggs	半熟卵	*hanjukutamago*
fried eggs	卵焼き	*tamagoyaki*
sunny-side up	目玉焼き	*medamayaki*
omelet	オムレツ	*omuretsu*
raw eggs	生卵	*namatamago*
scrambled eggs	炒り卵（スクランブルエッグ）	*iritamago (sukuranburu eggu)*

Sweets and desserts	**お菓子とデザート**	***okashi to dezaato***
cake	ケーキ	*keeki*
candy	キャンディ	*kyandi*
cookie	クッキー	*kukkii*
custard	カスタード	*kasutaado*
doughnut	ドーナツ	*doonatsu*
ice cream	アイスクリーム	*aisukuriimu*

jam	ジャム	*jamu*
jelly	ジェリー	*jerii*
meringue	メレンゲ	*merenge*
pancakes	パンケーキ	*pankeeki*
pie	パイ	*pai*
pudding	プリン	*purin*
sponge cake	スポンジケーキ	*suponjikeeki*
syrup	シロップ	*shiroppu*
tart	タルト	*taruto*
waffle	ワッフル	*waffuru*

Beverage	**飲み物**	***nominomo***
aperitif	食前酒	*shokuzenshu*
beer	ビール	*biiru*
draft beer	生ビール	*namabiiru*
champagne	シャンペン	*shanpen*
cider	サイダー	*saidaa*
cocoa	ココア	*kokoa*
coffee	コーヒー	*koohii*
black coffee	ブラックコーヒー	*burakkukoohii*
cafe au lait	カフェオレ	*kafeore*
iced coffee	アイスコーヒー	*aisukoohii*
espresso	エスプレッソ	*esupuresso*
coke	コーラ	*koora*
ice	氷（アイス）	*koori (aisu)*
juice	ジュース	*juusu*
lemonade	レモネード	*remoneedo*
milk	牛乳（ミルク）	*gyuunyuu (miruku)*
milkshake	ミルクセーキ	*mirukuseeki*
mineral water	ミネラルウォーター	*mineraruwootaa*
sake	日本酒	*nihonshu*
sherry	シェリー酒	*sheriishu*
soda	ソーダ	*sooda*
tea	お茶	*ocha*
green tea	緑茶	*ryokucha*
black tea	紅茶	*koocha*
iced tea	アイスティー	*aisutii*
water	水	*mizu*
wine	ワイン	*wain*
red wine	赤ワイン	*akawain*
rose wine	ロゼ	*roze*
white wine	白ワイン	*shirowain*

Spices	**香辛料**	***kooshinryoo***
basil	バジリコ	*bajiriko*
bay leaf	ローリエ	*roorie*
chervil	チャービル	*chaabiru*
chive	チャイブ	*chaibu*
cinnamon	シナモン	*shinamon*
coriander	コリアンダー	*koriandaa*
fennel	フェンネル	*fen-neru*
garlic	にんにく（ガーリック）	*ninniku (gaarikku)*
ginger	しょうが（ジンジャー）	*shooga (jinjaa)*
ketchup	ケチャップ	*kechappu*
marjoram	マージョラム	*maajoramu*
mayonnaise	マヨネーズ	*mayoneezu*
mint	ミント	*minto*

mustard	からし（マスタード）	karashi (masutaado)	yogurt	ヨーグルト	yooguruto
nutmeg	ナツメグ	natsumegu	**Methods of cooking**	**調理方法**	***choori hoohoo***
oregano	オレガノ	oregano	add	加える	kuwaeru
paprika	パプリカ	papurika	bake	オーブンで焼く	oobun de yaku
parsley	パセリ	paseri	blend	混ぜ合わせる	maze awaseru
pepper	こしょう	koshoo	boil	ゆでる	yuderu
red pepper	とうがらし	toogarashi	braise	蒸し煮にする	mushini ni suru
rosemary	ローズマリー	roozumarii	broil	あぶる	aburu
saffron	サフラン	safuran	chill	冷やす	hiyasu
sage	セージ	seeji	chop	ぶつ切りにする	butsugiri ni suru
salt	塩	shio	chop up	切り刻む	kiri kizamu
sesame	ごま	goma	cook slowly	ゆっくり煮こむ	yukkuri nikomu
syrup	シロップ	shiroppu	core	芯をとる	shin o toru
tarragon	タラゴン	taragon	deep-fry	揚げる	ageru
thyme	タイム	taimu	defrost	解凍する	kaitoo suru
vanilla	バニラ	banira	dissolve	溶かす	tokasu
vinegar	ビネガー	binegaa	drain	水気を切る	mizuke o kiru
rice vinegar	酢、お酢	su, osu	fill	詰める	tsumeru
			grate	すりおろす	suriorosu
Others	**そのほか**		grease	油をぬる	abura o nuru
bread	パン	pan	grill	焼く、あぶる	yaku, aburu
butter	バター	bataa	heat	温める	atatameru
cereal	シリアル	shiriaru	melt	溶かす	tokasu
cheese	チーズ	chiizu	mince	みじん切りにする	mijingiri ni suru
cornstarch	コーンスターチ	koonsutaachi			
cream	クリーム	kuriimu	mix	混ぜる	mazeru
egg white	白身	shiromi	pan-fry	フライパンで炒める	furaipan de itameru
egg yolk	黄身（卵黄）	kimi (ran-oo)			
flour	小麦粉	komugiko	peel	皮をむく	kawa o muku
lard	ラード	raado	pour	注ぐ	sosogu
nut	ナッツ	nattsu	rinse	洗う、すすぐ	arau, susugu
oil	オイル（油）	oiru (abura)	sautee	炒める、ソテーする	itameru. sotee suru
olive oil	オリーブオイル	oriibuoiru			
peanut	ピーナッツ	piinattsu	season	味付けする	ajitsuke suru
pickles	ピクルス	pikurusu	slice	薄切りにする	usugiri ni suru
sandwich	サンドイッチ	sandoicchi	soak	つけておく	tsukete oku
snack	スナック	sunakku	sprinkle	ふりかける	furikakeru
spaghetti	スパゲッティ	supagetti	steam	蒸す	musu
sugar	砂糖	satoo	strain	こす	kosu
toast	トースト	toosuto	whip	泡立てる	awadateru
yeast	イースト	iisuto			

Answers to exercises

練習問題の答え

Chapter 1: At the airport

1. 1. タクシー　2. タクシー　3. バス　4. 電車　5. 市内　6. バスターミナル
   1. takushii　2. takushii　3. basu　4. densha　5. shinai　6. basu taaminaru

2. 1. ターミナル　2. ターミナル　3. 国際　4. 国内
   1. taaminaru　2. taaminaru　3. kokusai　4. kokunai

3. 1. 航空会社　2. カウンター　3. 列　4. 係員　5. チケット(航空券)　6. パスポート
   1. kookuugaisha　2. kauntaa　3. retsu　4. kakariin　5. chiketto (kookuu ken)　6. pasupooto

4. 1. 行き　2. 国際、パスポート　3. 窓、通路、窓　4. 座席番号、列　5. 手荷物
   1. iki　2. kokusai, pasupooto　3. mado, tsuuro, mado　4. zasekibangoo, retsu　5. tenimotsu

   6. 搭乗券、出発、搭乗口（ゲート）　7. おみやげ、免税品店、おみやげ
   6. toojooken, shuppatsu, toojooguchi (geeto)　7. omiyage, menzeehinten, omiyage

5. 1. 航空会社のカウンターにいます。
   1. Kookuugaisha no kauntaa ni imasu.

   2. 係員と話しています。
   2. Kakariin to hanashite imasu.

   3. 航空券(チケット)を見せます。
   3. Kookuuken (chiketto) o misemasu.

   4. 二つあります。
   4. Futatsu arimasu.

   5. 一つあります。
   5. Hitotsu arimasu.

   6. 前の座席の下か、上の棚に入れます。
   6. Mae no zaseki no shita ka, ue no tana ni iremasu.

   7. 荷物引換券と搭乗券を渡します。
   7. Nimotsu hikikaeken to toojooken o watashimasu.

   8. 五番ゲート(搭乗口)に行きます。
   8. Goban geeto (toojooguchi) ni ikimasu.

   9. 22列のＡに座ります。
   9. nijuuni retsu no ee ni suwarimasu.

   10. 窓側です。
   10. Mado gawa desu.

6. 1. (a)　2. (a)　3. (c)　4. (b)　5. (a)

7. 1. 係員、アナウンス　2. 出発　3. 発、便　4. セキュリティーチェック　5. 搭乗口（ゲート）, 乗ります　6. 行き先　7. 降ります
   1. kakariin, anaunsu　2. shuppatsu　3. hatsu, bin　4. sekyuritii chekku　5. toojooguchi (geeto), norimasu　6. ikisaki　7. orimasu

8. 1. 出発　2. 〜着　3. 降ります
   1. shuppatsu　2. – chaku　3. orimasu

9. 1. 乗り遅れた　2. 出発　3. 空席　4. 満席　5. 料金（値段）　6. 料金（値段）
   1. noriokureta　2. shuppatsu　3. kuuseki　4. manseki　5. ryookin (nedan)　6. ryookin (nedan)

   7. 追加料金　8. 直行便　9. 経由
   7. tsuka ryookin　8. chokkoobin　9. keeyu

10. 1. ターミナル、国際、国内　2. 国際線　3. 航空会社のカウンター、チェックイン
    1. taaminaru, kokusai, kokunai　2. kokusaisen　3. kookuugaisha no kauntaa, chekku in

    4. 係員、航空券、パスポート　5. スーツケース　6. 荷物引換券、荷物
    4. kakariin, kookuuken, pasupooto　5. suutsu keesu　6. nimotsu hikikaeken, nimotsu

    7. 座席の下、棚　8. 予約、通路、窓　9. 窓、空席、窓
    7. zaseki no shita, tana　8. yoyaku, tsuuro, mado　9. mado, kuuseki, mado

13847ۿ

20,97 $.19 2
713277

10. 直行、止まります　11. セキュリティーチェック、搭乗口（ゲート）

10. chokkoo, · tomarimasu　　11. sekyuritii chekku, toojooguchi (geeto)

Chapter 2: On the airplane

1. 1. 乗務員　2. 操縦士（パイロット）　3. 客室乗務員　4. エコノミークラス

1. joomuin　2. soojuushi (pairotto)　3. kyakushitsu joomuin　4. ekonomii kurasu

5. 操縦室（コックピット）　6. 離陸　7. 着陸

5. soojuushitsu (kokku pitto)　6. ririku　7. chakuriku

2. 1. 離陸　2. 飛行時間　3. 高度　4. 時速　5. 飛行

1. ririku　2. hikoo jikan　3. koodo　4. jisoku　5. hikoo

3. 1. 座席の下にあります。

1. Zaseki no shita ni arimasu.

2. 酸素マスクが下りてきます。

2. Sanso masuku ga orite kimasu.

3. 乗務員の指示を待たなくてはいけません。

3. Joomuin no shiji o matanakute wa ikemasen.

4. 1. 通路　2. 座席ベルト（シートベルト）　3. 安全　4. 座席ベルト（シートベルト）

1. tsuuro　2. zaseki beruto (shiito beruto)　3. anzen　4. zaseki beruto (shiito beruto)

5. 1. 禁煙、たばこ　2. お手洗い　3. 喫煙所

1. kin-en, tabako　2. otearai　3. kitsuenjo

6. 1. 手荷物　2. 手荷物　3. 上の棚　4. 背もたれ　5. テーブル

1. tenimotsu　2. tenimotsu　3. ue no tana　4. semotare　5. teeburu

7. 1. 食事　2. 新聞　3. 雑誌　4. ヘッドホン　5. 音楽　6. 上映される　7. 毛布　　8. 枕

1. shokuji　2. shinbun　3. zasshi　4. heddohon　5. ongaku　6. jooee sareru　7. moofu　8. makura

8. 1. 食事　2. 毛布　3. 枕　4. 背もたれ　5. 紙袋

1. shokuji　2. moofu　3. makura　4. semotare　5. kamibukuro

9. 1. キャビン、前方キャビン、キャビン　2. 酸素マスク、救命胴衣　3. 手荷物、上の棚

1. kyabin　2. zenpoo kyabin, kyabin　2. sanso masuku, kyuumee dooi　3. tenimotsu, ue no tana

4. 禁煙　5. 背もたれ、元の位置　6. ヘッドホン　7. 毛布、枕

4. kin-en　5. semotare, moto no ichi　6. heddohon　7. moofu, makura

10. 1. (b)　2. (g)　3. (j)　4. (e)　5. (i)　6. (c)　7. (h)　8. (d)　9. (f)　10. (a)

11. 1. 二つあります。

1. Futatsu arimasu.

2. 通路を歩いてはいけません。

2. Tsuuro o aruite wa ikemasen.

3. 酸素マスクや救命胴衣について説明します。

3. Sanso masuku ya kyuumee dooi ni tsuite setsumee shimasu.

4. 喫煙室で吸えます。

4. Kitsuenshitsu de suemasu.

5. 毛布と枕を持ってきてもらえます。

5. Moofu to makura o mottekite moraemasu.

6. 映画を見ることができます。

6. Eega o miru koto ga dekimasu.

Chapter 3: Passport control and customs

1. 1. パスポート（旅券）　2. 滞在　3. 泊まります　4. 泊まります　5. 商用（ビジネス）　6. 観光　7. 観光

1. pasupooto (ryoken)　2. taizai　3. tomarimasu　4. tomarimasu　5. shooyoo (bijinesu)　6. kankoo　7. kankoo

2. 1. 荷物、申告、申告　2. 三本、税金　3. 税関申告書　4. 荷物

1. nimotsu, shinkoku, shinkoku　2. sanbon, zeekin　3. zeekan shinkokusho　4. nimotsu

Chapter 4: At the train station

1. 1. 切符　2. 片道切符　3. 往復切符　4. 片道切符
   1. kippu　2. katamichi kippu　3. oofuku kippu　4. katamichi kippu

2. 1. 切符　2. 片道切符　3. 往復切符　4. 往復切符
   1. kippu　2. katamichi kippu　3. oofuku kippu　4. oofuku kippu

3. 1. 切符　2. 窓口　3. 自動販売機　4. 乗車　5. 特急　6. 出発　7. コインロッカー
   1. kippu　2. madoguchi　3. jidoohanbaiki　4. joosha　5. tokkyuu　6. shuppatsu　7. koin rokkaa

4. 1. 時刻表で見ます。
   1. Jikokuhyoo de mimasu.
   2. 14 時 20 分に出発するはずでした。
   2. Juuyoji nijuppun ni shuppatsu suru hazu deshita.
   3. いいえ、出ません。
   3. Iie, demasen.
   4. 事故があったからです。
   4. Jiko ga atta kara desu.
   5. 15 時 20 分頃出るでしょう。
   5. Juugoji nijuppun goro deru deshoo.
   6. 待合室で待ちます。
   6. Machiaishitsu de machimasu.
   7. キオスクで買えます。
   7. Kiosuku de kaemasu.

5. 1. 時間通り　2. 遅れて　3. 待合室
   1. jikandoori　2. okurete　3. machiaishitsu

6. 1. 切符、改札口　2. 行き、ホーム　3. 指定席　4. 両　5. 号車
   1. kippu, kaisatsuguchi　2. iki, hoomu　3. shiteeseki　4. ryoo　5. goosha

7. 1. 車掌　2. 寝台　3. 食堂　4. 自動販売機　5. 公衆電話
   1. shashoo　2. shindai　3. shokudoo　4. jidoohanbaiki　5. kooshuu denwa

8. 1. T　2. F　3. T　4. F　5. F

9. 1. タクシーで行きました。
   1. Takushii de ikimashita.
   2. コインロッカーに預けました。
   2. Koin rokkaa ni azukemashita.
   3. 窓口で買いました。
   3. Madoguchi de kaimashita.
   4. 新幹線で旅行しました。
   4. Shinkansen de ryokoo shimashita.
   5. 指定席の切符を買いました。
   5. Shiteeseki no kippu o kaimashita.
   6. 5 号車に乗りました。
   6. Go goosha ni norimashita.
   7. 21-A でした。
   7. Nijuuichi ee deshita.
   8. 自動販売機があるかどうか聞きました。
   8. Jidoohanbaiki ga aru ka dooka kikimashita.

10. 1. (b)　2. (d)　3. (e)　4. (f)　5. (a)　6. (c)

Chapter 5: The automobile

1. 1. 借りる　2. 走行距離　3. 越える、につき　4. 運転免許証　5. オートマチック
   1. kariru　2. sookookyori　3. koeru, ni tsuki　4. untenmenkyoshoo　5. ootomachikku

2. 1. レンタカー（車）　2. いくら　3. 走行距離　4. 含まれて　5. 運転免許証　6. クレジットカード　7. 保証金

1. rentakaa (kuruma)   2. ikura   3. sookookyori   4. fukumarete   5. untenmenkyoshoo   6. kurejitto kaado   7. hoshookin

3.   1. (b)   2. (a)   3. (b)   4. (a)   5. (c)   6. (c)   7. (c)

4.   1. エンジン、ギア   2. 地図   3. トランク   4. ワイパー

1. enjin, gia   2. chizu   3. toranku   4. waipaa

5.   (e) (c) (f) (b)

6.   1. タンク、ガソリンスタンド   2. 満タン、リットル   3. ラジエーター   4. タイヤ

1. tanku, gasorin sutando   2. mantan, rittoru   3. rajieetaa   4. taiya

5. フロントガラス   6. オイル、ブレーキオイル

5. furonto garasu   6. oiru, bureeki oiru

7.   1. エンジン   2. もれて、オーバーヒート   3. けん引車   4. 部品   5. パンク

1. enjin   2. morete, oobaa hiito   3. ken-insha   4. buhin   5. panku

Chapter 6: Asking for directions

1.   1. 迷って   2. 近い   3. 反対方向   4. まっすぐ   5. 角   6. 曲がります   7. 次

1. mayotte   2. chikai   3. hantaihookoo   4. massugu   5. kado   6. magarimasu   7. tsugi

2.   1. 遠い   2. 乗って   3. バス停   4. 降りて

1. tooi   2. notte   3. basutee   4. orite

3.   1. どうやって   2. 混んで   3. ラッシュアワー   4. 高速道路   5. 高速料金   6. 料金所

1. dooyatte   2. konde   3. rasshu awaa   4. koosoku dooro   5. koosoku ryookin   6. ryookinjo

7. 出口、車線   8. 一方通行   9. 信号   10. 渋滞

7. deguchi, shasen   8. ippootsuukoo   9. shingoo   10. juutai

4.   1. 信号機   2. 高速道路   3. 車線（レーン）   4. 出口   5. 料金所

1. shingooki   2. koosoku dooro   3. shasen (reen)   4. deguchi   5. ryookinjo

5.   1. (b)   2. (d)   3. (g)   4. (c)   5. (f)   6. (e)   7. (a)

Chapter 7: At the hotel

1.   1. シングル   2. ダブル   3. ツイン、ダブル   4. 道路   5. 海   6. 食事   7. サービス

1. shinguru   2. daburu   3. tsuin, daburu   4. dooro   5. umi   6. shokuji   7. saabisu

8. クレジットカード   9. クーラー（エアコン）、ヒーター（暖房）   10. トイレ   11. 予約した

8. kurejitto kaado   9. kuuraa (eakon), hiitaa (danboo)   10. toire   11. yoyaku shita

12. フロント係   13. 満室   14. ボーイ

12. furontogakari   13. manshitsu   14. booi

2.   1. 部屋   2. 満室   3. ツイン   4. ダブル   5. 側   6. 側   7. 泊   8. 税   9. 泊   10. 泊   11. 宿泊カード

1. heya   2. manshitsu   3. tsuin   4. daburu   5. gawa   6. gawa   7. paku   8. zee   9. paku   10. paku   11. shukuhaku kaado

3.   1. メイド   2. 洗濯   3. アイロン   4. ドライクリーニング   5. コンセント   6. 毛布

1. meedo   2. sentaku   3. airon   4. dorai kuriiningu   5. konsento   6. moofu

7. バスタオル   8. せっけん   9. クローゼット   10. トイレットペーパー

7. basu taoru   8. sekken   9. kuroozetto   10. toiretto peepaa

4.   1. 洗面台   2. 便器   3. 毛布   4. ベッド   5. シャワー   6. タオル   7. コンセント

1. senmendai   2. benki   3. moofu   4. beddo   5. shawaa   6. taoru   7. konsento

8. トイレットペーパー   9. ハンガー   10. クローゼット   11. 浴槽（バスタブ）   12. メイド

8. toiretto peepaa   9. hangaa   10. kuroozetto   11. yokusoo (basutabu)   12. meedo

5.   1. 電球、スイッチ   2. 蛇口   3. 洗面台   4. お湯

1. denkyuu, suicchi   2. jaguchi   3. senmendai   4. oyu

6.   1. 請求   2. 電話   3. 合計   4. ルームサービス   5. クレジットカード

1. seekyuu   2. denwa   3. gookee   4. ruumu saabisu   5. kurejitto kaado

7.   1. フロント、フロント係   2. 宿泊カード   3. シングル、ツイン、ダブル   4. サービス   5. 道路

1. furonto, furontogakari   2. shukuhaku kaado   3. shinguru, tsuin, daburu   4. saabisu   5. dooro

6. 予約   7. 満室   8. 荷物   9. メイド   10. エアコン（クーラー）   11. 毛布   12. クローゼット

6. yoyaku   7. manshitsu   8. nimotsu   9. meedo   10. eakon (kuuraa)   11. moofu   12. kuroozetto

13. 洗って   14. チェックアウト   15. 会計   16. 宿泊

13. aratte   14. chekku auto   15. kaikee   16. shukuhaku

8. 1. いいえ、海側です。

1. Iie, umigawa desu.

2. はい、あります。

2. Hai, arimasu.

3. ダブルベッドがあります。

3. Daburubeddo ga arimasu.

4. ダブルの部屋です。

4. Daburù no heya desu.

5. はい、あります。

5. Hai, arimasu.

9. 1. この人たちはフロントにいます。

1. Kono hito tachi wa furonto ni imasu.

2. 今、ホテルに着きました。

2. Ima, hoteru ni tsukimashita.

3. この人たちはフロント係と話しています。

3. Kono hitotachi wa furontogakari to hanashite imasu.

4. この男の人は宿泊カードに住所と名前を書いています。

4. Kono otoko no hito wa shukuhaku kaado ni juusho to namae o kaite imasu.

5. ボーイはルームキーを持っています。

5. Booi ha ruumu kii o motte imasu.

10. 1. ダブルの部屋です。

1. Daburu no heya desu.

2. はい、あります。

2. Hai, arimasu.

3. メイドが働いています。

3. Meedo ga hataraite imasu.

4. 掃除をしています。

4. Sooji o shite imasu.

5. ハンガーがあります。

5. Hangaa ga arimasu.

6. バスルームにあります。

6. Basu ruumu ni arimasu.

7. はい、あります。

7. Hai, arimasu.

Chapter 8: At the bank

1. 1. お金   2. 円   3. 手数   4. 銀行

1. okane   2. en   3. tesuu   4. ginkoo

2. 1. 替えて   2. レート   3. 現金   4. レート   5. ドル

1. kaete   2. reeto   3. genkin   4. reeto   5. doru

3. 1. 現金   2. 現金   3. 現金にします

1. genkin   2. genkin   3. genkin ni shimasu

4. 1. 小銭(小さいお金)   2. 札   3. くずして

1. kozeni (chiisai okane)   2. satsu   3. kuzushite

5. 1. トラベラーズチェック   2. 為替   3. 円   4. 札   5. 札   6. くずして   7. 千円札   8. 小銭(小さいお金)

1. toraberaazu chekku   2. kawase   3. en   4. satsu   5. satsu   6. kuzushite   7. sen-en satsu   8. kozeni (chiisai okane)

6. 1. 預金   2. 口座   3. 窓口   4. 通帳   5. 印鑑   6. 自動現金預け払い機(ATM)   7. キャッシュカード

1. yokin   2. kooza   3. madoguchi   4. tsuuchoo   5. inkan   6. jidoo genkin azukebaraiki (ee-tii-emu)   7. kyasshu kaado

7. 1. 現金にします　2. 預けます　3. くずします　4. おろします　5. 替えます

1. genkin ni shimasu　2. azukemasu　3. kuzushimasu　4. oroshimasu　5. kaemasu

Chapter 9: At the post office

1. 1. 手紙　2. ポスト　3. 切手　4. かかる　5. 郵便局

1. tegami　2. posuto　3. kitte　4. kakaru　5. yuubinkyoku

2. 1. 手紙　2. 速達　3. 切手

1. tegami　2. sokutatsu　3. kitte

3. 1. 350 円かかります。　2. 速達です。　3. 154-0001 です。

1. Sanbyaku gojuu en kakarimasu.　2. Sokutatsu desu　3. Ichi go yon no zero zero zero ichi desu.

4. 1. 荷物、重さ、量ります　2. 保険　3. こわれもの　4. 航空、船、船、航空

1. nimotsu, omosa, hakarimasu　2. hoken　3. kowaremono　4. kookuu, funa, funa, kookuu

5. 1. 郵便物、郵便配達員　2. 私書箱　3. 為替

1. yuubinbutsu, yuubinhaitatsuin　2. shishobako　3. kawase

Chapter 10: Making a telephone call

1. 1. 電話　2. 電話番号　3. 電話帳　4. 通話　5. 通話　6. 市外局番　7. 受話器

1. denwa　2. denwa bangoo　3. denwachoo　4. tsuuwa　5. tsuuwa　6. shigai kyokuban　7. juwaki

8. 発信音　9. ダイヤル　10. 呼び出し音　11. 出ます

8. hasshin-on　9. daiyaru　10. yobidashi on　11. demasu

2. 1. ボタン　2. コードレス　3. 携帯

1. botan　2. koodoresu　3. keetai

3. 1. 市外　2. 市外局番　3. コレクトコール　4. 指名通話　5. 国際、国

1. shigai　2. shigai kyokuban　3. korekuto kooru　4. shimee tsuuwa　5. kokusai, kuni

4. 1. 案内　2. 公衆　3. ボックス　4. テレホン

1. an-nai　2. kooshuu　3. bokkusu　4. terehon

5. 1. もしもし　2. [make up a name]　3. どなた（どちらさま）　4. [give your name]

1. Moshimoshi　2. [make up a name]　3. Donata (dochira sama)　4. [give your name]

5. お待ちください　6. すみません　7. お願いします

5. omachi kudasai　6. sumimasen　7. onegai shimasu

6. 1. 発信　2. 故障　3. 話し　4. 間違えました　5. かけ直して　6. 雑音　7. 切れて

1. hasshin　2. koshoo　3. hanashi　machigaemashita　5. kakenaoshite　6. zatsuon　7. kirete

7. (d) (a) (e) (c) (f) (g) (b)

Chapter 11: At the hairdresser

1. 1. 髪、髪　2. そろえる　3. シャンプー　4. あご、口　5. そって　6. 短く

1. kami, kami　2. soroeru　3. shanpoo　4. ago, kuchi　5. sotte　6. mijikaku

7. はさみ、かみそり　8. 床屋

7. hasami, kamisori　8. tokoya

2. 1. 前　2. えりあし　3. 横　4. 後ろ

1. mae　2. eriashi　3. yoko　4. ushiro

3. 1. (c)　2. (d)　3. (a)　4. (b)　5. (e)

4. 1. パーマ　2. セット　3. カット　4. 染めます

1. paama　2. setto　3. katto　4. somemasu

5. [Personal answers will vary.]

6. 1. ポニーテール　2. カーリーヘア　3. 三つ編み　4. ウェーブ　5. ボブ

1. ponii teeru　2. kaarii hea　3. mitsuami　4. weebu　5. bobu

Chapter 12: At the dry cleaner

1. 1. 縮む、ドライクリーニング　2. 洗濯、アイロン　3. のり　4. 縫い目、縫って　5. 穴、つくろって　6. ボタン　7. しみ

    1. chijimu, dorai kuriiningu 2. sentaku, airon 3. nori 4. nuime, nutte 5. ana, tsukurotte 6. botan 7. shimi

2. 1. かけて 2. のり 3. 取れる 4. 取れる 5. 縮む 6. ドライクリーニング 7. できます

    1. kakete 2. nori 3. toreru 4. toreru 5. chijimu 6. dorai kuriiningu 7. dekimasu

Chapter 13: At the restaurant

1. 1. 予約 2. 高級 3. 外

    1. yoyaku 2. kookyuu 3. soto

2. 1. 予約 2. 席(テーブル) 3. 席(テーブル)

    1. yoyaku 2. seki (teeburu) 3. seki (teeburu)

3. 1. 居酒屋 2. 窓 3. ウエーター（ウエートレス） 4. メニュー

    1. izakaya 2. mado 3. ueetaa (ueetoresu) 4. menyuu

4. 1. 四人います。

    1. Yonin imasu.

    2. ウエーターです。

    2. Ueetaa desu.

    3. 水があります。

    3. Mizu ga arimasu.

    4. メニューを持っています。

    4. Menyuu o motte imasu.

5. 1. フルコース 2. スープ、みそ汁 3. ワインリスト 4. お勧め

    1. furukoosu 2. suupu, misoshiru 3. wain risuto 4. osusume

6. 1. レア 2. ミディアム 3. 胸肉 4. もも肉 5. 揚げた

    1. rea 3. midiamu 3. muneniku 4. momoniku 5. ageta

7. 1. 蒸した 2. ゆでた 3. 刺身

    1. mushita 2. yudeta 3. sashimi

8. 1. ナイフ、スプーン 2. はし置き 3. 塩 4. 固すぎます

    1. naifu, supuun 2. hashioki 3. shio 4. katasugimasu

9. 1. コップ(グラス) 2. 砂糖 3. 塩 4. こしょう 5. コーヒーカップ 6. 皿、 7. ナプキン 8. フォーク 9. ナイフ

    1. Koppu (Gurasu) 2. satoo 3. shio 4. koshoo 5. koohii kappu 6. sara 7. napukin 8. fooku 9. naifu,

    10. ティースプーン 11. スプーン 12. テーブルクロス 13. はし 14. 茶わん 15. おしぼり 16. 湯のみ

    10. tii supuun 11. supuun 12. teeburu kurosu 13. hashi 14. chawan 15. oshibori 16. yunomi

10. 1. サービス 2. お勘定 3. チップ 4. レジ 5. クレジットカード

    1. saabisu 2. okanjoo 3. chippu 4. reji 5. kurejitto kaado

11. 1. レストラン 2. 予約 3. 奥のいい席 4. 外のテーブル(席) 5. ビール 6. ウエートレス 7. メニュー

    1. resutoran 2. yoyaku 3. oku no ii seki 4. soto no teeburu (seki) 5. biiru 6. ueetoresu 7. menyuu

12. 1. はしがありませんでした。

    1. Hashi ga arimasen deshita.

    2. おいしかったです。

    2. Oishikatta desu.

    3. いいえ、食べませんでした。

    3. Iie, tabemasen deshita.

    4. コーヒーを飲みました。

    4. Koohii o nomimashita.

    5. はい、含まれていました。

    5. Hai, fukumarete imashita.

    6. いいえ、払いませんでした。

    6. Iie, haraimasen deshita.

Chapter 14: Shopping for food

1. 1. ケーキ屋 2. 肉屋 3. 八百屋 4. 魚屋 5. パン屋 6. 豆腐屋 7. 酒屋

1. keekiya   2. nikuya   3. yaoya   4. sakanaya   5. pan-ya   6. toofuya   7. sakaya

2.　1. 八百屋　2. パン屋　3. 肉屋　4. 魚屋　5. 八百屋　6. ケーキ屋　7. 米屋

1. yaoya   2. pan-ya   3. nikuya   4. sakanaya   5. yaoya   6. keekiya   7. komeya

3.　1. スーパー　2. かご　3. カート　4. ビニール袋

1. suupaa   2. kago   3. kaato   4. biniirubukuro

Chapter 15: Buying clothing and shoes

1.　1. 靴です。　2. 低いです。　3. はい、ついています。

1. Kutsu desu.   2. Hikui desu.   3. Hai, tsuite imasu.

2.　1. いらっしゃいませ　2. サイズ　3. センチ　4. かかと(ヒール)　5. ハイヒール（かかとが高いの）　6. サイズ　7. 小さ

1. Irasshaimase   2. saizu   3. senchi   4. kakato (hiiru)   5. haihiiru (kakato ga takai no)   6. saizu   7. chiisa

3.　[Answer can vary.]

4.　1. しわ　2. しわ　3. ウール　4. フランネル　5. サイズ　6. 長袖　7. 無地

1. shiwa   2. shiwa   3. uuru   4. furanneru   5. saizu   6. nagasode   7. muji

5.　1. 合いません　2. ファスナー（チャック、ジッパー）　3. ベルト　4. レーンコート　5. シャツ

1. aimasen   2. fasunaa (chakku, jippaa)   3. beruto   4. reenkooto   5. shatsu

6. サイズ、測って　7. 合繊（合成繊維）　8. 大き

6. saizu, hakatte   7. goosen (gooseesen-i)   8. ooki

6.　[Answer can vary.]

7.　1. ストライプ(縞)　2. チェック　3. 水玉模様

1. sutoraipu (shima)   2. chekku   3. mizutamamoyoo

8.　1. しわ、合繊（合成繊維）　2. 合いません　3. 店員

1. shiwa, goosen (gooseesen-i)   2. aimasen   3. ten-in

9.　1. (b)　2. (a)　3. (a)　4. (a)　5. (a)

Chapter 16: At home

1.　1. 食器　2. 蛇口　3. 洗剤　4. 食器　5. すすぎます　6. 水きりかご　7. ふきます

1. shokki   2. jaguchi   3. senzai   4. shokki   5. susugimasu   6. mizukirikago   7. fukimasu

2.　1. 包丁、まな板　2. 缶きり　3. ざる　4. フライ返し　5. 泡だて器　6. やかん　7. 炊飯器　8. ミキサー

1. hoochoo, manaita   2. kankiri   3. zaru   4. furaigaeshi   5. awadateki   6. yakan   7. suihanki   8. mikisaa

3.　1. 鍋　2. フライパン　3. やかん　4. ふた　5. 缶切り　6. 栓抜き　7. フライ返し　8. ボール　9. ざる

1. nabe   2. furaipan   3. yakan   4. futa   5. kankiri   6. sennuki   7. furai gaeshi   8. booru   9. zaru

10. 包丁 11. まな板 12. 炊飯器 13. ミキサー

10. hoochoo   11. manaita   12. suihanki   143 mikisaa

4.　1. 包丁、皮、まな板　2. 湯、ゆでます　3. 洗って、水気　4. といで、炊飯器

1. hoochoo, kawa, manaita   2. yu, yudemasu   3. aratte, mizuke   4. toide, suihanki

5.　1. 焼く　2. ゆでる　3. 溶かす　4. 泡立てる　5. 炒める　6. 揚げる

1. yaku   2. yuderu   3. tokasu   4. awadateru   5. itameru   6. ageru

6.　1. せっけん　2. お風呂、シャワー　3. 脱衣所　4. ふきます　5. 鏡　6. 歯ブラシ　7. 和、洋

1. sekken   2. ofuro, shawaa   3. datsuijo   4. fukimasu   5. kagami   6. haburashi   7. wa, yoo

7.　1. 蛇口　2. シャワー　3. 洗面器　4. せっけん　5. タオル　6. タオルかけ　7. 洗面台　8. 鏡

1. jaguchi   2. shawaa   3. senmenki   4. sekken   5. taoru   6. taoru kake   7. senmendai   8. kagami

9. トイレットペーパー　10. スリッパ

9. toiretto peepaa   10. surippa

8.　1. カーテン、ブラインド 2. 本棚　3. ソファ、おしゃべり　4. テレビ、ステレオ　5. 客　6. 絵

1. kaaten, buraindo   2. hondana   3. sofa, oshaberi   4. terebi, sutereo   5. kyaku   6. e

9.　1. 寝室（ベッドルーム）、サイドテーブル、目覚し時計、電気スタンド　2. ダブルベッド

1. shinshitsu (beddo ruumu), saidoteeburu, mezamashidokee, denki sutando   2. daburu beddo

3. 枕　4. 引き出し　5. ハンガー　6. 押し入れ、敷きます、たたみます

3. makura   4. hikidashi   5. hangaa   6. oshiire, shikimasu, tatamimasu

10. 枕、枕カバー、シーツ、掛ぶとん、毛布、マットレス

makura, makurakabaa, shiitsu, kakebuton, moofu, mattoresu

11. 1. ＿＿時に寝ます。

1. ＿＿ji ni nemasu.

2. はい、します。／ いいえ、しません。

2. Hai, shimasu. / Iie, shimasen.

3. ＿＿時間ぐらい寝ます。

3. ＿＿ jikan gurai nemasu.

4. いいです。／ 悪いです。

4. Iidesu. / Warui desu.

5. ＿＿時に起きます。

5. ＿＿ ji ni okimasu.

12. 1. 洗濯　2. 洗濯機　3. 乾燥機　4. アイロン台　5. かけます　6. 掃除機　7. ほこり　8. ふきます

1. sentaku　2. sentakuki　3. kansooki　4. airondai　5. kakemasu　6. soojiki　7. hokori　8. fukimasu

13. 1. (b)　2. (d)　3. (e)　4. (a)　5. (c)

14. 1. コンセント　2. コンセント　3. 差しこみます

1. konsento　2. konsento　3. sashikomimasu

15. 1. 消えました　2. ヒューズ　3. チェック　4. 修理

1. kiemashita　2. hyuuzu　3. chekku　4. shuuri

16. 1. 流れません　2. 詰まって

1. nagaremasen　2. tsumatte

Chapter 17: At the hospital

1. 1. 診察　2. 受付　3. 用紙　4. 保険証　5. 診察

1. shinsatsu　2. uketsuke　3. yooshi　4. hokenshoo　5. shinsatsu

2. 1. 具合　2. 痛い　3. 寒気　4. 風邪　5. 医者

1. guai　2. itai　3. samuke　4. kaze　5. isha

3. 1. 具合　2. 症状　3. 寒気　4. 口　5. 胸　6. 開けて　7. 息　8. はいて　9. 苦しい

1. guai　2. shoojoo　3. samuke　4. kuchi　5. mune　6. akete　7. iki　8. haite　9. kurushii

10. 熱　11. アレルギー　12. 注射　13. そで　14. 抗生物質　15. 錠

10. netsu　11. arerugii　12. chuusha　13. sode　14. koosee busshitsu　15. joo

4. 1. 心臓　2. アレルギー　3. はしか、おたふくかぜ、水ぼうそう　4. 肺　5. 血液型

1. shinzoo　2. arerugii　3. hashika, otafukukaze, mizuboosoo　4. hai　5. ketsuekigata

6. 精神　7. おこした　8. 血圧　9. 血液　10. 胃

6. seeshin　7. okoshita　8. ketsuatsu　9. ketsueki　10. i

5. 2. 血圧を測ります。

2. Ketsuatsu o hakarimasu.

4. 肺のレントゲン写真をとります。

4. Hai no rentogen shashin o torimasu.

5. 血液検査をするために採血をします。

5. Ketsueki kensa o suru tame ni saiketsu o shimasu.

6. 脈拍を測ります。

6. Myakuhaku o hakarimasu.

8. 心電図をとります。

8. Shindenzu o torimasu.

10. 聴診をします。

10. Chooshin o shimasu.

11. 尿検査をします。

11. Nyoo kensa o shimasu.

6. 1. 骨折　2. レントゲン　3. 骨　4. ギプス　5. 松葉杖

1. kossetsu   2. rentogen   3. hone   4. gipusu   5. matsubazue

7.　1. 指　2. 腕　3. 手首　4. 足　5. 足首　6. 腰　7. 背中

1. yubi   2. ude   3. tekubi   4. ashi   5. ashikubi   6. koshi   7. senaka

8.　1. 救急車で来ました。

1. Kyuukyuusha de kimashita.

2. 救急病院です。

2. Kyuukyuu byooin desu.

3. いいえ、担架で運ばれてきました。

3. Iie, tanka de hakobarete kimashita.

4. 脈拍と血圧を測りました。

4. Myakuhaku to ketsuatsu o hakarimashita.

5. 当直医が診察しました。

5. Toochokui ga shinsatsu shimashita.

6. おなかが痛いと言っています。

6. Onaka ga itai to itte imasu.

9.　1. 救急　2. 救急車　3. 担架、車いす　4. 看護婦　5. 当直医

1. kyuukyuu   2. kyuukyuusha   3. tanka, kurumaisu   4. kangofu   5. toochokui

10.　1. 看護婦　2. 手術室　3. 手術台　4. 麻酔医　5. 外科医

1. kangofu   2. shujutsushitsu   3. shujutsudai   4. masui-i   5. gekai

11.　1. 回復室　2. 酸素、点滴　3. 経過

1. kaifukushitsu   2. sanso, tenteki   3. keeka

12.　1. 妊娠　2. 分娩室　3. 産婦人科

1. ninshin   2. bunbenshitsu   3. sanfujinka

13.　1. 痛く　2. 救急車　3. 担架　4. 脈拍、血圧　5. 症状　6. レントゲン写真　7. 手術

1. itaku   2. kyuukyuusha   3. tanka   4. myakuhaku, ketsuatsu   5. shoojoo   6. rentogen shashin   7. shujutsu

8. 手術台　9. 麻酔　10. 外科医　11. 回復室　12. 酸素マスク、点滴　13. 経過

8. shujutsudai   9. masui   10. gekai   11. kaifukushitsu   12. sansomasuku, tenteki   13. keeka

Chapter 18: Entertainment

1.　1. 劇場　2. 喜劇　3. 役、役　4. 主役　5. 幕　6. 休憩　7. 舞台(ステージ)、観客

1. gekijoo   2. kigeki   3. yaku, yaku   4. shuyaku   5. maku   6. kyuukee   7. butai (suteeji), kankyaku

2.　1. 悲劇　2. 女優　3. 幕が下りる

1. higeki   2. joyuu   3. maku ga oriru

3.　1. 切符（チケット）　2. 売りきれました　3. 切符（チケット）　4. S　5. A　6. B　7. 開場　8. 開場　9. 開演

1. kippu (chiketto)   2. urikiremashita   3. kippu (chiketto)   4. esu   5. ee   6. bii   7. kaijoo   8. kaijoo   9. kaien

4.　1. 切符売り場へ行きました。

1. Kippu uriba e ikimashita.

2. いいえ、行きません。今晩の切符は売切れだったからです。

2. Iie, ikimasen. Konban no kippu wa urikire datta kara desu.

3. いいえ、売り切れではありませんでした。

3. Iie, urikire dewa arimasen deshita.

4. A席の切符を買いました。

4. Ee seki no kippu o kaimashita.

5. S席は売切れだったからです。

5. Esu seki wa urikire datta kara desu.

6. S席の方が高いです。

6. Esu seki no hoo ga takai desu.

5.　1. 切符は切符売り場で買います。

1. Kippu wa kippu uriba de kaimasu.

2. S席が一番いい席です。

2. Esu seki ga ichiban ii seki desu.

3. 舞台が始まると幕が上がります。／ 舞台が終わると幕が下ります。

3. Butai ga hajimaru to maku ga agarimasu. / Butai ga owaru to maku ga orimasu.

4. コートはクロークに預けます。

4. Kooto wa kurooku ni azukemasu.

5. 開演は舞台が始まる時間のことです。

5. Kaien wa butai ga hajimaru jikan no koto desu.

6. 1. 映画、やっています 2. 字幕 3. スクリーン

1. eega, yatteimasu 2. jimaku 3. sukuriin

Chapter 19: Sports

1. 1. 11人います。

1. Juuichi nin imasu.

2. サッカー場(グラウンド)でします。

2. Sakkaajoo (guraundo) de shimasu.

3. ゴールキーパーが守ります。

3. Goorukiipaa ga mamorimasu.

4. 蹴ってパスします。

4. Kette pasu shimasu.

5. 止めます。

5. Tomemasu.

6. 審判員が取ります。

6. Shinpan-in ga torimasu.

7. 笛(ホイッスル)を吹きます。

7. Fue (hoissuru) o fukimasu.

8. 得点板(スコアボード)に出ます。

8. Tokutenban (sukoa boodo) ni demasu.

2. 1. チーム 2. 22 3. 蹴りました 4. 味方 5. ゴールキーパー 6. 前半 7. 対 8. 同点

1. chiimu 2. nijuuni 3. kerimashita 4. mikata 5. goorukiipaa 6. zen-han 7. tai 8. dooten

3. 1. ゴール 2. ゴールキーパー 3. 得点板(スコアボード) 4. ボール 5. 審判員 6. 笛(ホイッスル)

1. gooru 2. goorukiipaa 3. tokutenban (sukoa boodo) 4. booru 5. shinpan-in 6. fue (hoissuru)

4. 1. 試合 2. 表 3. 裏 4. 同点 5. 投げました 6. 受けて 7. 打ちました 8. 対

1. shiai 2. omote 3. ura 4. dooten 5. nagemashita 6. ukete 7. uchimashita 8. tai

5. 1. シングルス、ダブルス 2. ラケット、ボール 3. テニスコート 4. アウト 5. サーブ、打ち返します

1. shingurusu, daburusu 2. raketto, booru 3. tenisu kooto 4. auto 5. saabu, uchikaeshimasu

6. 1. ゴルフ場（コース） 2. ボール 3. クラブ 4. ホール 5. ラウンド 6. ホール 7. ゴルフ練習場

1. gorufujoo (koosu) 2. booru 3. kurabu 4. hooru 5. raundo 6. hooru 7. gorufu renshuujoo

7. 1. 力士 2. 土俵 3. 行司 4. 土俵 5. 土俵 6. 体 7. 場所

1. rikishi 2. dohyoo 3. gyooji 4. dohyoo 5. dohyoo 6. karada 7. basho

8. 1. 静か（おだやか） 2. 荒れていました 3. 干潮 4. 高潮

1. shizuka (odayaka) 2. arete imashita 3. kanchoo 4. takashio

9. 1. (c) 2. (a) 3. (b)

10. 1. 焼けました、紫外線、皮膚ガン、日焼け止め、ビーチパラソル 2. 散歩 3. 浮き輪 4. 水着 5. サーフィン

1. yakemashita, shigaisen, hifugan, hiyakedome, biichi parasoru 2. sanpo 3. ukiwa 4. mizugi 5. saafin

11. 1. ライフガードがいる時 4. 海がおだやかな時

1. raifugaado ga iru toki 4. umi ga odayakana toki

12. 1. スキー場、スキー 2. 初心者、上級者 3. 滑ります 4. リフト

1. sukiijoo, sukii 2. shoshinsha, jookyuusha 3. suberimasu 4. rifuto

13. スキー、ストック、スキー靴、スキーウエア、手袋、スキー帽

sukii, sutokku, sukiigutsu, sukiiuea, tebukuro, sukiiboo

Chapter 20: The weather

1. 1. 暑い、寒い   2. 雨、雪   3. 晴れて   4. 曇って   5. 涼しい   6. 暖かい   7. 霧   8. 蒸し暑い   9. 吹雪   10. 雷

    1. atsui, samui   2. ame, yuki   3. harete   4. kumotte   5. suzushii   6. atatakai   7. kiri   8. mushiatsui   9. fubuki   10. kaminari

2. [Answer may vary.]

    1. 晴れです。(晴れています。)

    1. Hare desu. (Harete imasu.)

    2. 雨です。(雨が降っています。雪です。雪が降っています。曇りです。曇っています。etc.)

    2. Ame desu. (Ame ga futte imasu. Yuki desu. Yuki ga futte imasu. Kumori desu. Kumotte imasu. etc.)

    3. 雨が降ったり止んだりしています。

    3. Ame ga futtari yandari shite imasu.

3. 1. 風   2. 雨、雪、小雨、ひょう   3. 霧   4. 雷

    1. kaze   2. ame, yuki, kosame, hyoo   3. kiri   4. kaminari

4. 1. 曇り   2. 小雨   3. ひょう   4. にわか雨   5. 台風

    1. kumori   2. kosame   3. hyoo   4. niwakaame   5. taifuu

Glossary: Japanese – English
索引：日本語 – 英語

アーティチョーク	aatichooku	artichoke
あばら肉（リブ）	abaraniku (ribu)	rib, sparerib
浴びる	abiru	take a shower
浴びすぎる	abisugiru	exposed too much
アボガド	abogado	avocado
油をぬる	abura o nuru	grease
あぶる	aburu	broil
上がる	agaru	goes up
揚げる	ageru	deep-fry
揚げた	ageta	deep-fried
あごひげ	agohige	beard
アイロン	airon	iron
アイロン台	airon dai	ironing board
アイロンをかける	airon o kakeru	iron
アイスコーヒー	aisukoohii	iced coffee
アイスクリーム	aisukuriimu	ice cream
アイスティー	aisutii	iced tea
相手	aite	opponent, the other party
相手チーム	aite chiimu	opponent team
空いている	aite iru	vacant
味付けする	ajitsuke suru	season
赤い矢印	akai yajirushi	red arrow
赤かぶ	akakabu	beet
赤ん坊	akanboo	baby
赤ワイン	akawain	red wine
開ける	akeru	open
アクセル	akuseru	accelerator
雨	ame	rain
雨が降る	ame ga furu	rain
雨が降ったり止んだりする	ame ga futtari yandari suru	raining on and off
穴	ana	hole
アナウンス	anaunsu	announcement
アンチョビ	anchobi	anchovy
あんこう	ankoo	angler-fish
案内係	an-naigakari	usher
暗証番号	anshoo bangoo	PIN
安全	anzen	safety
あんず	anzu	apricots
洗う	arau	wash
アレルギー、アレルギー体質	arerugii, arerugii taishitsu	allergic
荒れている	arete iru	rough
歩いて	aruite	on foot
朝	asa	in the morning
あさって	asatte	the day after tomorrow
足	ashi	foot, leg,
足首	ashikubi	ankle
明日	ashita	tomorrow
アスパラガス	asuparagasu	asparagus
頭	atama	head
暖かい	atatakai	warm
温める	atatameru	heat
暑い	atsui	hot
合う	au	fit, match
アウト	auto	out
泡だて器	awadateki	whisk
泡立てる	awadateru	whip
預ける	azukeru	check in, deposit, leave
バジリコ	bajiriko	basil
バック	bakku	reverse
～番	~ ban	number ~
～番ゲート	~ ban geeto	gate number ~
～番ホーム	~ ban hoomu	track number ~
バナナ	banana	banana
番号案内	bangoo an-nai	directory assistance
番号を間違える	bangoo o machigaeru	dial a wrong number
バニラ	banira	vanilla
バンパー	banpaa	bumper
バリカン	barikan	hair clipper
バルコニー	barukonii	balcony
場所	basho	regular sumo tournament
抜糸をする	basshi o suru	take out the stitches
バス	basu	bus
バスルーム	basu ruumu	bathroom
バスターミナル	basu taaminaru	bus terminal
バスタオル	basu taoru	bath towel
バス停	basu tee	bus stop
バストイレ	basu toire	bathroom (lit. bath and toilet)
バスマット	basumatto	bathmat
バター	bataa	butter
バッター	battaa	batter
バッテリー	batterii	battery
バット	batto	bat
ベッド	beddo	bed
ベッドカバー	beddo kabaa	bedspread
ベッドを整える	beddo o totonoeru	make the bed
ベージュ	beeju	beige
ベーコン	beekon	bacon
ビニール袋	beniirubukuro	plastic back
便器	benki	toilet
ベルト	beruto	belt
B席	bii seki	B-seat
ビーチパラソル	biichi parasoru	beach umbrella
ビーチリゾート	biichi rizooto	seaside resort
ビーチサンダル	biichi sandaru	beach sandals
ビール	biiru	beer
便	bin	flight
ビネガー	binegaa	vinegar
びわ	biwa	loquat
美容院	biyooin	beauty salon
ビザ（査証）	biza (sashoo)	visa
ボブ	bobu	bob
～本目	~ bonme(~ponme, ~honme)	~ blocks (lit. ~th street)
ボンネット	bon-netto	hood
ボーイ	booi	porter
ボール	booru	ball, bowl
帽子	booshi	cap, hat
ぼら	bora	mullet
ボタン	botan	buttons
ぶどう	budoo	grape
部品	buhin	parts
分	bun	worth
分娩室	bunbenshitsu	delivery room
文化の日	bunka no hi	Culture Day

198

ブラインド	buraindo	blind	ダブルの部屋	daburu no heya	double
ブラジャー	burajaa	brassieréa, bra	ダブルスの試合	daburusu no shiai	doubles match
ブラックコーヒー	burakkukoohii	black coffee	第〜幕	dai ～ maku	the ～ th act
ブラシ	burashi	brush, hair brush	だいだい	daidai	sour orange
ブラウス	burausu	blouse	大根	daikon	daikon, white radish
ブレーキ	bureeki	brake	ダイヤル	daiyaru	dial
ブレーキオイル	bureeki oiru	brake fluid	ダイヤルする	daiyaru suru	dial
ブリーフ	buriifu	brief	男優	dan-yuu	actor (male)
ブロッコリー	burokkorii	broccoli	出す	dasu	send out, take out
ブルーベリー	buruuberii	blueberry	脱衣所	datsuijo	changing room
舞台	butai	show	出口	deguchi	exit
舞台（ステージ）	butai (suteeji)	stage	できる	dekiru	be ready
豚肉	butaniku	pork	デニム	denimu	denim
ぶつ切りにする	butsugiri ni suru	chop	電気スタンド	denki sutando	desk lamp
ブーツ	buutsu	boots	電球	denkyuu	light bulb
秒	byoo	seconds	電車	densha	train
病院	byooin	hospital (clinic)	電子レンジ	denshi renji	microwave oven
病歴	byooreki	medical history	電話	denwa	telephone
病室	byooshitsu	ward	電話番号	denwa bangoo	phone number
チャービル	chaabiru	chervil	電話ボックス	denwa bokkusu	telephone booth
チャイブ	chaibu	chive	電話をかける（する）	denwa o kakeru (suru)	call
茶色	chairo	brown	電話帳	denwachoo	phone book
〜着	～ chaku	arriving at ～	デパート	depaato	department store
着陸する	chakuriku suru	land	出る	deru	come out, answer (lit. appear)
チャンネル	channeru	channels	出ている	dete iru	playing (acting)
茶わん	chawan	rice bowl	デザート	dezaato	desserts
チェック	chekku	checked, checkered	土俵	dohyoo	dohyoo (ring)
チェックアウト	chekku auto	check out	どなた（どちらさま）	donata (dochira sama)	who
チェックする	chekku suru	check	どのぐらい	donogurai	how much
チェックイン	chekkuin	check in	ドーナツ	doonatsu	doughnut
チーム	chiimu	team	道路	dooro	street
小さすぎる	chiisasugiru	too small	道路工事中	dooro koojichuu	Under construction
チーズ	chiizu	cheese	同点	dooten	tie
縮む	chijimu	shrink	ドライクリーニング	dorai kuriiningu	dry-cleaning
近い	chikai	near	ドライヤー	doraiyaa	dryer
近すぎる	chikasugiru	too close	ドラマ	dorama	drama
航空券（チケット）	chiketto	ticket	ドル	doru	dollars
チケット（切符）	chiketto (kippu)	tickets	土曜日	doyoobi	Saturday
チコリ	chikori	chicory	絵	e	picture
チップ	chippu	tips	エアコン（クーラー）	eakon (kuuraa)	air-conditioner
ちりとり	chiritori	dustpan	えび	ebi	lobster, prawn, shrimp
治療をする	chiryoo o suru	treat	A席	ee seki	A-seat
地図	chizu	map	映画	eega	movie
直行便	chokkoobin	nonstop flight	映画館	eegakan	movie theater
チョコレートケーキ	chokoreeto keeki	chocolate cake	ATM（現金自動預け払い機）	ee-tii-emu (genkin jidoo azukebarai ki)	ATM
直接	chokusetsu	directly	えい	ei	ray
腸	choo	bowels	駅	eki	station
ちょうど	choodo	exactly	駅員	ekiin	station employee
長距離電話	chookyori denwa	long distance call	円	en	yen
聴診する	chooshin suru	auscultation; listen to one's chest	演劇（芝居）	engeki (shibai)	play
朝食付き	chooshoku tsuki	with breakfast	エンジン	enjin	engine
中級レベル	chuukyuu reberu	intermediate level	エンジンがかかる	enjin ga kakaru	engine starts
注射	chuusha	injection	エンジンをかける	enjin o kakeru	start the engine
駐車可	chuusha ka	Parking	エンジンを止める	enjin o tomeru	stop the engine
駐車禁止	chuusha kinshi	No parking			
駐停車禁止	chuuteesha kinshi	No stopping/No parking			
ダブルベッド	daburu beddo	double bed			

えのきだけ	enokidake	enokitake		がん	gan	cancer
エンスト	ensuto	engine failure (stalling of an engine)		元旦	gantan	New Year's Day
エンターテイン メント	entaateinmento	entertainment		ガソリン	gasorin	gas
				ガソリンスタン ド	gasorin sutando	gas station
えりあし	eriashi	on the neck		ガソリンタンク	gasorin tanku	gas tank
Ｓ席	esu seki	S-seat (special seat)		ガスこんろ（ガス レンジ）	gasu konro (gasu renji)	gas cooker
エスプレッソ	esupuresso	espresso				
ファースト（ロ ー）	faasuto (roo)	first (low) gear		～側	~ gawa	the side of ~
				外科医	gekai	surgeon
ファーストクラ ス	faasuto kurasu	first class		劇場	gekijoo	theater
				原因	gen-in	cause
ファミリーレス トラン	famirii resutoran	family restaurant		現金	genkin	cash
				現金にする	genkin ni suru	cash
ファスナー（チャ ック、ジッパー	fasunaa (chakku, jippaa)	zipper		ゲレンデ	gerende	slope
				月曜日	getsuyoobi	Monday
フェンネル	fenneru	fennel		ギア	gia	gear
フォーク	fooku	fork		ギアを変える	gia o kaeru	shift gears
吹雪	fubuki	snowstorm		銀行	ginkoo	bank
笛（ホイッスル）	fue (hoissuru)	whistle		ギブスをはめる	gipusu o hameru	put the leg in a cast
ふきん	fukin	dish towel		ごぼう	goboo	burdock
吹く	fuku	blow		午後	gogo	p.m., in the afternoon
服	fuku	clothes		ご飯	gohan	cooked rice
ふく	fuku	wipe, dry		ごま	goma	sesame
含まれている	fukumarete iru	is included		ごみ	gomi	garbage
複雑骨折	fukuzatsu kossetsu	compound fracture		ごみ箱	gomibako	waste basket
踏切あり	fumikiri ari	Railroad crossing		ゴム底	gomuzoko	rubber soles
踏む	fumu	step on		～号	~ goo	size ~
分	fun (pun)	minute		合計で	gookee de	in total
フライ返し	furaigaeshi	turner		ゴール	gooru	goal
フライパン	furaipan	frying pan		ゴールキーパー	gooru kiipaa	goalie
フライパンで炒 める	furaipan de itameru	pan-fry		ゴールをする（決 める）	gooru o suru (kimeru)	make a goal
フランネル	furanneru	flannel		合織（合成繊維）	goosen (goosee sen-i)	synthetic material
触れる	fureru	touch		～号車	~ goosha	car number ~
ふりかける	furikakeru	sprinkle		ゴルフ	gorufu	golf
風呂の椅子	furo no isu	bathroom chair		ゴルフボール	gorufu booru	golf ball
風呂場	furoba	bathroom		ゴルフクラブ	gorufu kurabu	golf club
フロント	furonto	front desk		ゴルフ練習場	gorufu renshuu joo	driving range
フロント係	furonto gakari	receptionist		ゴルフ場（コー ス）	gorufujoo (koosu)	golf course
フロントガラス	furonto garasu	windshield				
風呂桶	furooke	bathtub		午前	gozen	a.m.
風呂桶のふた	furooke no futa	bathtub cover		午前中	gozenchuu	during the morning
風呂桶の栓	furo-oke no sen	plug				
フルコースのメ ニュー	furu koosu no menyuu	full-course meal		具合が悪い	guai ga warui	not feel well
				グレープフルー ツ	gureepufuruutsu	grapefruit
ふすま	fusuma	fusuma, Japanese sliding door		グローブ	guroobu	glove
ふた	futa	lid		グローブボック ス	guroobu bokkusu	glove compartment
ふとん	futon	futon				
布団	futon	Japanese futon		魚介類	gyokai rui	sea food
普通電車	futsuu densha	local train		行司	gyooji	gyooji (referee)
普通預金	futsuu yokin	ordinary deposit		牛肉	gyuuniku	beef
普通郵便	futsuu yuubin	regular mail		牛乳（ミルク）	gyuunyuu (miruku)	milk
沸騰させる	futtoo saseru	heat to boiling		歯	ha	teeth
封筒	fuutoo	envelope		幅	haba	width
ガードル	gaadoru	girdle		歯ブラシ	haburashi	toothbrush
外国為替	gaikoku kawase	foreign exchange		はがき	hagaki	postcard
外国人入国記録	gaikokujin nyuukoku kiroku	disembarkation card for foreigner		肺	hai	lungs
				はい、どうぞ	Hai, doozo.	Here you are.
額縁	gakubuchi	picture frame		ハイヒール	haihiiru	high heels
学生	gakusee	student		ハイオクガソリ ン	haioku gasorin	high-octane

配達される	haitatsu sareru	be delivered	ひげをそる	hige o soru	shave my beard
俳優	haiyuu	actor (male or female)	悲劇	higeki	tragedy
初め	hajime	the beginning	ヒール（かかと）	hiiru (kakato)	heels
測る、計る	hakaru, hakaru	measure, weigh	ヒーター（暖房）	hiitaa (danboo)	heater
吐き気がする	hakike ga suru	nauseated, nausea	引いている	hiite iru	low
運ばれる	hakobareru	be carried	ひじ	hiji	elbow
運ぶ	hakobu	carry	非常口	hijooguchi	emergency exit
はく	haku	sweep	引き出し	hikidashi	drawer
白菜	hakusai	chinese cabbage	ひき肉	hikiniku	ground, minced meat
拍手をする	hakushu o suru	applaud	引き分け	hikiwake	finish in a tie
歯磨き粉	hamigakiko	toothpaste	ひっくり返す	hikkurikaesu	turn over
ハム	hamu	ham	飛行時間	hikoo jikan	flying time
半	han	half past	飛行する	hikoo suru	fly
鼻	hana	nose	飛行中	hikoochuu	during the flight
鼻水が出る	hanamizu ga deru	have a runny nose	飛行機	hikooki	airplane
話し中	hanashichuu	line is busy	ひめじ	himeji	red mullet
話す（おしゃべり する）	hanasu (oshaberi suru)	talk (chat)	ひねる	hineru	sprain (twist), turn on
ハンドブレーキ	hando bureeki	hand brake	開く	hiraku	open
ハンドバッグ	handobaggu	handbag	広すぎる	hirosugiru	too wide
ハンドル	handoru	steering wheel	昼	hiru	noon (midday)
ハンガー	hangaa	hanger	ひたい	hitai	forehead
半熟卵	hanjukutamago	soft-boiled eggs	羊の肉	hitsuji no niku	mutton, lamb
ハンカチ	hankachi	handkerchief	ヒットを打つ	hitto o utsu	make a hit
半袖	hansode	short sleeves	日焼け止め	hiyakedome	sun block
反則（ファール）	hansoku (faaru)	foul	冷やす	hiyasu	chill
反対方向	hantai hookoo	opposite direction	ひざ	hiza	knee
半ズボン	hanzubon	shorts	ホイールキャップ	hoiiru kyappu	hubcap
はらう	harau	brush off			
払う	harau	pay	保険	hoken	insurance
晴れ	hare	fine, clear	保険をかける	hoken o kakeru	insure
晴れている	harete iru	clear	保険証	hokenshoo	health insurance card
はさみ	hasami	scissors	ほこり	hokori	dust
はし	hashi	chopstick	ほころびる	hokorobiru	torn
はし置き	hashi oki	chopstick rest	本棚	hondana	bookshelf
はしか	hashika	measles	骨	hone	bone, fishbone
走る	hashiru	run	骨をつなぐ	hone o tsunagu	set the bone
発信音	hasshin-on	dial tone	包丁	hoochoo	kitchen knife
はた	hata	grouper	ほうき	hooki	broom
〜発	~ hatsu	leaving from ~	ホーム	hoomu	platform (track)
二十日大根	hatsukadaikon	radish	ホームラン	hoomuran	home run
早く	hayaku	early	ほうれん草	hoorensoo	spinach
はずれている	hazurete iru	is off	ホール	hooru	hole
ヘアカーラー	hea kaaraa	roller	ホースラディッ シュ	hoosuradisshu	horse radish
ヘアクリップ	hea kurippu	hair clip			
ヘアピン	hea pin	bobby pin	包帯	hootai	bandage
ヘアリキッド	hea rikiddo	hair lotion	干したの（干物）	hoshita no (himono)	dried
ヘアスプレー	hea supuree	hair spray	保証金	hoshookin	deposit
ヘッドホン	heddohon	headsets	干す	hosu	hang out to dry
ヘッドライト	heddoraito	headlight	ほたて貝	hotategai	scallops
平日	heejitsu	weekday	船便	hunabin	sea mail
変な	hen na	strange	ひょう	hyoo	hailing
変な音がする	hen na oto ga suru	knocking (lit. making a strange sound)	ヒューズ	hyuuzu	fuse
			ヒューズボック ス	hyuuzu bokkusu	fuse box
扁桃腺	hentoosen	tonsils	胃	i	stomach
部屋	heya	room	いちご	ichigo	strawberry
日に焼ける	hi ni yakeru	sunburned, suntanned	一時停止	ichiji teeshi	Stop
			いちぢく	ichijiku	fig
左	hidari	left	一日で	ichinichi de	by the day
皮膚ガン	hifugan	skin cancer	いい天気（天気が いい）	ii tenki (tenki ga ii)	nice weather
ひげ	hige	beard			

イースト	iisuto	yeast	乗車券	joosha ken	train ticket
～以上	~ ijoo	~ or more	女優	joyuu	actress
いか	ika	squid	順調	junchoo	regular
～行き	~ iki	bound for ~	住所	juusho	address
息をはく	iki o haku	breathe out	ジュース	juusu	juice
息を吸う	iki o suu	breathe in	渋滞	juutai	traffic jam
いくら	ikura	how much	じゅうたん(カー ペット)	juutan (kaapetto)	carpet
居間	ima	living room	受話器	juwaki	receiver
インフルエンザ (流感)	infuruenza (ryuukan)	flu	カーリーヘア	kaarii hea	curl (style)
いんげんまめ	ingenmame	kidney beans	カール	kaaru	curl
印鑑	inkan	name seal (inkan)	カーテン	kaaten	curtain
一泊	ippaku	one night stay	カート	kaato	shopping cart
一方通行	ippoo tsuukoo	One way, one-way street	かばん	kaban	bag
			かぼちゃ	kabocha	pumpkin
いらっしゃいま せ	Irasshaimase	May I help you? (lit. Welcome)	かぶ	kabu	turnip
			角	kado	corner
入口	iriguchi	entrance	替える	kaeru	exchange
炒り卵(スクラン ブルエッグ)	iritamago (sukuranburu eggu)	scrambled eggs	カフェオレ	kafeore	cafe au lait
			鏡	kagami	mirror
いせえび	iseebi	crayfish	～か月	~ kagetsu	~ months
医者	isha	doctor	かご	kago	basket
一週間で	isshuukan de	by the week	家具	kagu	furniture
痛い	itai	hurts, painful	～回	~ kai	~ nnings
炒める	itameru	fry	貝	kai	shellfish
炒める、ソテーす る	itameru. sotee suru	sautee	開演	kaien	performance starts
			回復室	kaifuku shitsu	recovery room
炒めた	itameta	pan-fried	開場	kaijoo	door opens
いわし	iwashi	sardine	改札口	kaisatsuguchi	ticket gate
居酒屋	izakaya	izakaya (Japanese style bar)	～階席	~ kaiseki	~ floor seats
			解凍する	kaitoo suru	defrost
じゃがいも	jagaimo	potato	かじき	kajiki	swordfish
蛇口	jaguchi	faucet	係員	kakariin	agent
ジャケット	jaketto	jacket	かかる	kakaru	cost, get (suffer from)
ジャッキ	jakki	jack	掛けぶとん	kakebuton	comforter quilt
ジャム	jamu	jam	掛け軸	kakejiku	hanging scroll
ジャンル	janru	kind (genre)	かけ直す	kakenaosu	call back
ジャズ	jazu	jazz	かき	kaki	oyster
ジェリー	jerii	jelly	柿	kaki	persimmon
自分の～	jibun no ~	one's own ~	書留	kakitome	registered mail
自動販売機	jidoo hanbaiki	vending machine	かます	kamasu	barracuda
自動改札機	jidookaisatsuki	an automatic ticket gate	髪	kami	hair
			髪をとかす	kami o tokasu	comb one's hair
自動車	jidoosha	automobile	紙袋	kamibukuro	paper bags
自動的に	jidooteki ni	automatically	雷	kaminari	thunder
ジーンズ(ジーパ ン)	jiinzu (jiipan)	jeans	雷が鳴っている	kaminari ga natte iru	thundering
			かみそり	kamisori	razor
時間	jikan	hour	鴨	kamo	duck
時間通りに	jikandoori ni	on time	干潮	kanchoo	low tide
事故	jiko	accident	看護婦	kangofu	nurse
時刻表	jikokuhyoo	train schedule	かに	kani	crab
字幕つき	jimaku tsuki	with subtitles	患者	kanja	patient
陣痛	jintsuu	labor pains	缶切り	kankiri	can opener
腎臓	jinzoo	kidney	観光	kankoo	for pleasure (lit. sightseeing)
時速	jisoku	speed an hour			
自由席	jiyuu seki	unreserved seat	観客	kankyaku	spectators
徐行	jokoo	Go slow	乾燥機	kansooki	dryer
～錠	~ joo	counter for pills	肝臓	kanzoo	liver
上映される	jooee sareru	be shown	缶詰	kanzume	canned food
乗客	jookyaku	passengers	顔	kao	face
上級レベル	jookyuu reberu	advanced level	空	kara	empty
上級者	jookyuusha	expert	体	karada	body
乗務員	joomuin	crew			

体の一部	karada no ichibu	a part of the body	金曜日	kin-yoobi	Friday
からし（マスタード）	karashi (masutaado)	mustard	記入する	kinyuu suru	fill in
からすぎる	karasugiru	too spicy, too salty	キオスク	kiosuku	kiosk (newsstand)
かれい	karee	flatfish	切符	kippu	ticket
カリフラワー	karifurawaa	cauliflower	切符売り場	kippu uriba	ticket window
借りる	kariru	rent	切れる	kireru	burn out, cut off
カスタード	kasutaado	custard	切れている	kirete iru	burned out
肩	kata	shoulder	霧	kiri	fog
片道切符	katamichi kippu	one-way ticket	霧が出ている	kiri ga deteiru	foggy
肩肉	kataniku	shoulder (meat)	切り刻む	kiri kizamu	chop up
固すぎる	katasugiru	too hard	キロ（キロメートル）	kiro (kiromeetoru)	kilometer
堅ゆで	katayude	hard-boiled eggs			
勝つ（勝ち）	katsu (kachi)	win	切る	kiru	cut
カット	katto	cut	喫煙席	kitsuen seki	smoking seat
カウンター	kauntaa	counter	喫煙所	kitsuenjo	smoking areas
皮	kawa	leather, skin	きつい	kitsui	tight
皮をむく	kawa o muku	peel	切手	kitte	stamp
乾かす	kawakasu	dry	キウイ	kiui	kiwifruit
代わりに	kawari ni	instead of	傷口	kizuguchi	cut
為替レート	kawase reeto	exchange rate	子供	kodomo	child
火曜日	kayoobi	Tuesday	子供の日	kodomo no hi	Children's Day
かぜ	kaze	cold	子えび	koebi	shrimp
風が強い	kaze ga tsuyoi	windy	越える	koeru	exceed
かぜをひく	kaze o hiku	have a cold	子羊の肉（ラム）	kohitsuji no niku	lamb
かぜ薬	kazegusuri	cold medicine	こい	koi	carp
家族	kazoku	family	コインロッカー	koin rokkaa	coin-operated locker
ケチャップ	kechappu	ketchup	ココア	kokoa	cocoa
ケーキ	keeki	cake	国道	kokudoo	national highway
ケーキ屋	keekiya	pastry shop	国道〜号線	kokudoo ~ goosen	National highway number ~
敬老の日	keeroo no hi	Respect-for-Aged Day	国道番号	kokudoo bangoo	national road number
携帯電話	keetai denwa	cellular phone	国民の休日	kokumin no kyuujitsu	Public Holiday
〜経由	~ keeyu	via ~	国内線	kokunaisen	domestic flight
結核	kekkaku	tuberculosis	国際電話	kokusai denwa	international call
検便	kenben	analysis of the feces	国際線	kokusaisen	international flight
けん引	ken-in	tow	米	kome	rice
憲法記念日	kenkoku kinen bi	Constitution Day	米をとぐ	kome o togu	rinse rice
建国記念の日	kenkokukinen no hi	National Foundation Day	米屋	komeya	rice shop
			込み	komi	included
研修医（インターン）	kenshuui (intaan)	intern	小麦粉	komugiko	flour
			混んでいる	konde iru	crowded
蹴る	keru	kick	今月	kongetsu	this month
化粧	keshoo	makeup	コンサート	konsaato	concert
消す	kesu	turn off	コンサートホール	konsaato hooru	concert hall
血圧	ketsuatsu	blood pressure			
血液検査	ketsueki kensa	blood test	コンセント	konsento	socket (outlet), wall-outlet
血液型	ketsuekigata	blood type			
気圧	kiatsu	air pressure	今週	konshuu	this week
消える	kieru	go off	紅茶	koocha	black tea
喜劇（コメディ）	kigeki (komedii)	comedy	高度	koodo	altitude
キー（かぎ）	kii	key	コードレス電話	koodoresu denwa	cordless
きくらげ	kikurage	jew's-ear	コーデュロイ	koodyuroi	corduroy
黄身（卵黄）	kimi (ran-oo)	egg yolk	公演	kooen	performance
気持ちが悪い	kimochi ga warui	feel sick (nauseated)	後半	koohan	second half
機内	kinai	inside the airplane	コーヒー	koohii	coffee
禁煙	kin-en	no-smoking	コーヒーカップ	koohii kappu	coffee cup
禁煙席	kin-enseki	non-smoking seat	後方キャビン	koohoo kyabin	rear cabin
緊急の場合	kinkyuu no baai	in case of emergency	交換する	kookan suru	change
きんめだい	kinmedai	red snapper	交換手（オペレーター）	kookanshu (opereetaa)	operator
きのう	kinoo	yesterday			
勤労感謝の日	kinrookansha no hi	Labor Thanksgiving Day	航空便（エアメール）	kookuubin (eameeru)	air mail

航空会社	kookuugaisha	airline company	キャベツ	kyabetsu	cabbage
高級	kookyuu	luxurious	キャッチャー	kyacchaa	catcher
コーンスターチ	koonsutaachi	cornstarch	客	kyaku	guest
コーラ	koora	coke	客室乗務員	kyakushitsu joomuin	flight attendants
氷（アイス）	koori (aisu)	ice	キャンディ	kyandi	candy
抗生物質	koosee busshitsu	antibiotic	キャッシュカード	kyasshu kaado	cash card
香辛料	kooshinryoo	spices			
公衆電話	kooshuu denwa	public telephone	去年	kyonen	last year
高速道路	koosoku dooro	express way	今日	kyoo	today
コース	koosu	course	休日	kyuujitsu	holiday (day off)
コート	kooto	coat	急患	kyuukan	emergency case
口座	kooza	account	休憩	kyuukee	intermission
コップ（グラス）	koppu (gurasu)	glass	救急病院	kyuukyuu byooin	emergency hospital
コレクトコール	korekuto kooru	collect call	救急車	kyuukyuusha	ambulance
コリアンダー	koriandaa	coriander	救命胴衣	kyuumeedooi	life jackets
頃	koro/goro	about	きゅうり	kyuuri	cucumber
小雨	kosame	drizzling	マージョラム	maajoramu	marjoram
腰	koshi	hip	町の地図	machi no chizu	city map
こしょう	koshoo	pepper	待合室	machiaishitsu	waiting room
故障している	koshoo shite iru	out of order	窓	mado	window
故障する	koshoo suru	break down	窓ガラス	madogarasu	windowpane
骨折する	kossetsu suru	have a fracture	窓側	madogawa	window side
こす	kosu	strain	窓際	madogiwa	near the window
今年	kotoshi	this year	窓口	madoguchi	cashier's window, ticket window
子牛の肉	koushi no niku	veal			
こわれもの	kowaremono	fragile article	前	mae	bofore, on the top
こわれている	kowarete iru	broken	前髪	maegami	bang
小銭（小さいお金）	kozeni (chiisai okane)	small change	曲がる	magaru	turn
			まぐろ	maguro	tuna
口	kuchi	mouth	マフラー	mahuraa	muffler, scarf
口ひげ	kuchihige	mustache	～枚ください	~ mai kudasai	One for ~, please.
くだもの（果物）	kudamono	fruit	毎日	mainichi	everyday
クッキー	kukkii	cookie	毎週	maishuu	every week
曇り	kumori	cloudy	毎年	maitoshi	every year
曇っている	kumotte iru	cloudy	毎月	maitsuki	every month
国番号	kuni bangoo	country code	負ける（負け）	makeru (make)	loose
クラッチ	kuracchi	clutch	幕	maku	act
クラクション	kurakushon	the horn	巻く	maku	bind up
クラシック	kurashikku	classical music	幕	maku	curtain
クレジットカード	kurejitto kaado	credit card	枕	makura	pillow
			枕カバー	makura kabaa	pillowcase
クレソン	kureson	watercress	まくる	makuru	roll up
クリーム	kuriimu	cream	守る	mamoru	defend
クリーニング屋	kuriininguya	dry cleaner's	まな板	manaita	cutting board
黒	kuro	black	満潮	manchoo	high tide
クローク	kurooku	cloakroom	マンゴー	mangoo	mango
クローゼット	kuroozetto	closet	満席	manseki	full
車	kuruma	car	満室	manshitsu	no vacancies (full)
車えび	kurumaebi	prawns	満タンにする	mantan ni suru	fill it up
車いす	kurumaisu	wheelchair	マニュアル車	manyuaru sha	manual car
苦しい	kurushii	hurt (feel pressure)	マッシュルーム	masshuruumu	mushroom
くし	kushi	comb	まっすぐ	massugu	straight
薬	kusuri	medicine	ます	masu	trout
靴	kutsu	shoes	麻酔	masui	anesthesia
靴ひも	kutsuhimo	shoelace	麻酔医	masuii	anesthesiologist
くつろぐ	kutsurogu	relax	松葉杖	matsubazue	crutches
靴下	kutsushita	socks	まつたけ	matsutake	matsutake
靴墨	kutsuzumi	shoe polish	マットレス	mattoresu	mattress
空席	kuuseki	vacant seat	まわし	mawashi	mawashi (belt)
空室	kuushitsu	vacant room	マヨネーズ	mayoneezu	mayonnaise
加える	kuwaeru	add	混ぜ合わせる	maze awaseru	blend
くずす	kuzusu	break money bill	混ぜる	mazeru	mix

〜目	~ me	~ th
目玉焼き	medamayaki	sunny-side up
メートル	meetoru	meters
メイド	meido	maid
芽キャベツ	mekyabetsu	brussels sprouts
めまいがする	memai ga suru	dizzy
メニュー	menyuu	menu
免税品店	menzeehinten	duty-free shop
メレンゲ	merenge	meringue
メロン	meron	melon
目覚し時計	mezamashidokee	alarm clock
道	michi	street, road
道に迷う	michi ni mayou	be lost
満ちている	michite iru	full
ミディアム（普通）	midiamu (futsuu)	medium
ミディアムレア	midiamu rea	medium-rare
みどりの日	midori no hi	Greenery Day
緑の矢印	midori no yajirushi	green arrow
磨く	migaku	brush
みがく	migaku	scrub
右	migi	right
みじん切りにする	mijingiri ni suru	mince
みかん	mikan	mikan, tangerine
味方	mikata	teammate
ミキサー	mikisaa	blender
耳	mimi	ears
ミネラルウォーター	mineraruwootaa	mineral water
ミント	minto	mint
見る	miru	check (lit. see)
診る	miru	examine
ミルクセーキ	mirukuseeki	milkshake
みそ汁	misoshiru	miso soup
診てもらう	mite morau	see a doctor (have a doctor examine)
三つ編み	mitsuami	braid
ミット	mitto	mitt
水（お水）	mizu (omizu)	water
水ぼうそう	mizuboosoo	chicken pox
水着	mizugi	bathing suit
水気を切る	mizuke o kiru	drain
水切りかご	mizukiri kago	dish drainer
水玉模様	mizutama moyoo	polka-dotted
持ち込む	mochikomu	bring in
戻る	modoru	return
戻す	modosu	put back
目的地	mokutekichi	destination
木曜日	mokuyoobi	Thursday
木綿（コットン）	momen (kotton)	cotton
もみあげ	momiage	sideburns
桃	momo	peach
もも肉	momoniku	thigh
盲腸（虫垂炎）	moochoo (chuusuien)	appendicitis
毛布	moofu	blanket
モーターボート	mootaa booto	motorboat
モップをかける	moppu o kakeru	mop
漏れる	moreru	leak
もしもし	Moshi moshi.	Hello. [on the phone]
元の位置	moto no ichi	original position
もやし	moyashi	been sprouts
無鉛ガソリン	muen gasorin	unleaded
無地	muji	solid colored
迎える	mukaeru	welcome
むく	muku	peel
胸	mune	chest
胸肉	muneniku	breast, brisket
紫キャベツ	murasakikyabetsu	red cabbage
蒸し暑い	mushiatsui	humid
蒸し煮にする	mushini ni suru	braise
蒸した	mushita	steamed
蒸す	musu	steam
ムール貝	muurugai	mussel
脈拍	myakuhaku	pulse
ミュージカル	myuujikaru	musical
鍋	nabe	stew pan
長いも	nagaimo	chinese yam
流れる	nagareru	drain, flush
流し	nagashi	sink
長袖	nagasode	long sleeves
投げる	nageru	pitch
ナイフ	naifu	knife
ナイロン	nairon	nylon
内臓（臓物）	naizoo (zoomotsu)	giblets
半ば	nakaba	the middle
生（刺身）	nama (sashimi)	raw (sashimi)
生ビール	namabiiru	draft beer
生卵	namatamago	raw eggs
波	nami	wave
ナンバープレート	nanbaa pureeto	registration plate
何番	nanban	what number
何曜日	nan-yoobi	what day (of the week)
ナプキン	napukin	napkin
並ぶ	narabu	stand (in line)
鳴らす	narasu	sound
鳴る	naru	sound, ring
なし	nashi	pear
なす	nasu	eggplant
ナツメグ	natsumegu	nutmeg
ナッツ	nattsu	nut
値段	nedan	price
ネーヴル	neevuru	navel orange
ねぎ	negi	scallion
ネクタイ	nekutai	necktie
ネクタリン	nekutarin	nectarine
〜年（年間）	~ nen (nenkan)	~ years
寝る	neru	sleep, go to bed
熱（体温）	netsu (taion)	temperature
熱がある	netsu ga aru	have a fever
寝つきがいい	netsuki ga ii	get to sleep easily
寝つきが悪い	netsuki ga warui	don't get to sleep easily
ネット（ネットボール）	netto (netto booru)	net ball
〜につき	~ ni tsuki	per ~
〜によって違う	~ ni yotte chigau	depend on ~
日	nichi	day
日曜日	nichiyoobi	Sunday
日本のお金（円）	Nihon no okane (en)	Japanese yen

日本語に吹き替えられている（日本語吹き替え）	*nihongo ni fukikaerarete iru (nihongo fukikae)*	dubbed in Japanese	重さ	*omosa*	weight
			表	*omote*	top
			オムレツ	*omuretsu*	omelet
			おなかが痛い	*onaka ga itai*	have a stomachache
日本酒	*nihonshu*	sake	音楽	*ongaku*	music
日光浴をする	*nikkooyoku o suru*	sunbathe	オーバー	*oobaa*	overcoat
煮込む	*nikomu*	simmer (boil for a long time)	オーバーヒート	*oobaahiito*	overheat
			オーブン	*oobun*	oven
煮込んだ	*nikonda*	slowly cooked, simmered	オーブンで焼く	*oobun de yaku*	bake
			横断歩道	*oodan hodoo*	Crosswalks
肉	*niku*	meat	往復切符	*oofuku kippu*	round trip ticket
肉料理	*niku ryoori*	meat and fowl dish	オーケストラ	*ookesutora*	orchestra
肉屋	*nikuya*	meat shop	オーケストラ席	*ookesutoraseki*	orchestra seat
荷物	*nimotsu*	belongings, luggage, package	大きすぎる	*ookisugiru*	too big
			オートマチック車	*ootomachikku sha*	automatic car
荷物引換券	*nimotsu hikikaeken*	baggage claim stub	オレガノ	*oregano*	oregano
にんじん	*ninjin*	carrot	オレンジ	*orenji*	orange
にんにく（ガーリック）	*ninniku (gaarikku)*	garlic	折れる	*oreru*	break
			オリーブ	*oriibu*	olive
妊娠している	*ninshin shite iru*	pregnant	オリーブオイル	*oriibuoiru*	olive oil
にら	*nira*	chinese chive	降りる	*oriru*	get off, deplane
煮る	*niru*	cook	下りる	*oriru*	go down
にしん	*nishin*	herring	おろす	*orosu*	withdraw
庭	*niwa*	courtyard	お酒	*osake*	alcohol
にわか雨	*niwakaame*	shower	お札	*osatsu*	bill
伸びる	*nobiru*	grow long	おしぼり	*oshibori*	small damp towel
のど	*nodo*	throat	押し入れ	*oshiire*	oshiire, Japanese style built-in closet
飲み物	*nominomo*	beverage			
飲む	*nomu*	eat (lit. drink soup etc.)	遅く	*osoku*	late
のり	*nori*	starch	おたふくかぜ	*otafukukaze*	mumps
乗り換える	*norikaeru*	change planes	おたま	*otama*	ladle
乗り遅れる	*noriokureru*	miss	お手洗い（トイレ）	*otearai (toire)*	toilet
乗る	*noru*	get on			
縫い目	*nuime*	seam	大人	*otona*	adult
ぬるい	*nurui*	cold (not warm enough)	おととい	*ototoi*	the day before yesterday
縫う	*nuu*	stitch			
尿検査	*nyoo kensa*	urine test	おつまみ	*otsumami*	Japanese style hors d'oeuvre
入国審査	*nyuukoku shinsa*	passport control			
ニュートラル	*nyuutoraru*	neutral	おわん	*owan*	wooden soup bowl
〜を除いて	*~ o nozoite*	except ~	終わり	*owari*	the end
〜をお願いします	*~ o onegai shimasu*	~, please.	泳ぐ	*oyogu*	swim
			お湯	*oyu*	hot water
〜をお勧めします	*~ o osusume shimasu*	I suggest (recommend)	パーマ	*paama*	permanent wave
			パイ	*pai*	pie
お盆（トレー）	*obon (toree)*	tray	パインアップル パイナップル	*pain-appuru, painappuru*	pineapple
お茶	*ocha*	tea			
お風呂	*ofuro*	bath	パイプ(水道管)	*paipu (suidookan)*	pipes
お風呂に入る	*ofuro ni hairu*	take a bath	パン	*pan*	bread
追い越し禁止	*oikoshi kinshi*	No passing	パンケーキ	*pankeeki*	pancakes
オイル（油）	*oiru (abura)*	oil	パンクする	*panku suru*	get punctured
お勘定	*okanjoo*	bill, check	パンツ	*pantsu*	underpants
お菓子	*okashi*	sweets	パン屋	*pan-ya*	bakery
お決まりですか。	*Okimari desu ka.*	Have you decided?	パパイア	*papaia*	papaya
〜おきに	*~ okini*	every other ~	パプリカ	*papurika*	paprika
起きる	*okiru*	wake up	パセリ	*paseri*	parsley
奥	*oku*	back	パスする	*pasu suru*	toss (the ball)
オクラ	*okura*	okura	パスポート（旅券）	*pasupooto (ryoken)*	passport
遅れる	*okureru*	late			
送る	*okuru*	send	ペニシリン	*penishirin*	penicillin
お店のお勧め料理	*omise no osusume ryoori*	house specialty	ピッチャー	*picchaa*	pitcher
			ピーマン	*piiman*	green pepper
おみやげ	*omiyage*	souvenir	ピーナッツ	*piinattsu*	peanut

Japanese	Romaji	English
ピクルス	pikurusu	pickles
ポニーテール	ponii teeru	pony tail
ポークソテー	pooku sotee	sauteed pork
ポリオ	porio	polio
ポスト	posuto	mailbox
プラグ	puragu	plug
プリン	purin	pudding
プログラム	puroguramu	program
プルーン	puruun	prune
プッシュホン	pusshuhon	push-button phone (touch-tone phone)
プール	puuru	swimming pool
ラード	raado	lard
ライチ	raichi	lyychee
ライフガード	raifu gaado	lifeguard
来月	raigetsu	next month
ライム	raimu	lime
来年	rainen	next year
来週	raishuu	next week
ライト（電気）	raito (denki)	light
雷雨	raiu	thunderstorm
ラジエーター	rajieetaa	radiator
ラジオ	rajio	radio
ラケット	raketto	racket
ランチ	ranchi	lunch
ラッシュアワー	rasshu awaa	rush hour
ラウンド	raundo	round
ラズベリー	razuberii	raspberry
レア	rea	rare
レバー	rebaa	lever
レーンコート	reen kooto	raincoat
レース	reesu	lace
冷凍庫	reetooko	freezer
冷蔵庫	reezooko	refrigerator
レフトバック	refutobakku	left end
レジ（会計）	reji (kaikee)	cashier
レモン	remon	lemon
レモネード	remoneedo	lemonade
れんこん	renkon	lotus root
練習	renshuu	practice
レンタカー	rentakaa	rent-a-car
レントゲン写真	rentogen shashin	x-ray
レストラン	resutoran	restaurant
レタス	retasu	lettuce
列	retsu	line, row
リフト	rifuto	ski lift
力士	rikishi	sumo wrestler
りんご	ringo	apple
離陸する	ririku suru	take off
リットル	rittoru	litters
ロブスター	robusutaa	lobster
ロック	rokku	rock
ローリエ	roorie	bay leaf
ロールブラシ	rooru burashi	curler
ロールパン	roorupan	dinner role
ローズマリー	roozumarii	rosemary
ロゼ	roze	rose wine
～塁ベース	rui beesu	base
ルームサービス	ruumu saabisu	room service
ルームキー（かぎ）	ruumukii (kagi)	room key
緑茶	ryokucha	green tea
～両の電車	~ ryoo no densha	~ car train
料金	ryookin	fare, charge
料金所	ryookinjo	tollbooth
料理	ryoori	cooking
領収書（レシート）	ryooshuusho (reshiito)	receipt
リューマチ	ryuumachi	rheumatism
サービス	saabisu	service
サービス料	saabisuryoo	service charge
サーブ	saabu	serve
サーフィン	saafin	surfing
サーフボード	saafu boodo	surfboard
さば	saba	mackerel
サフラン	safuran	saffron
探す	sagasu	look for
サイダー	saidaa	cider
サイドテーブル	saido teeburu	side table
採血	saiketsu	collect blood
最高速度	saikoo sokudo	speed limit
サイズ	saizu	size
魚	sakana	fish
魚屋	sakanaya	fish market
酒屋	sakaya	liquor store
さけ	sake	salmon
サッカー	sakkaa	soccer
サッカー場（グラウンド）	sakkaajoo (guraundo)	soccer field (ground)
さくらんぼ	sakuranbo	cherry
寒い	samui	cold
寒気がする	samuke ga suru	have a chill
サングラス	san gurasu	sunglasses
サンダル	sandaru	sandals
サンドイッチ	sandoicchi	sandwich
産婦人科医	sanfujinkai	obstetrician (ob-gyn)
サニーレタス	saniiretasu	leaf lettuce
サンオイル	sanoiru	tanning lotion
散歩する	sanpo suru	take a walk
酸素マスク	sansomasuku	oxygen mask
酸素テント	sansotento	oxygen tent
皿	sara	plate
サラダ	sarada	salad
サラダ菜	saradana	head lettuce
差出人	sashidashinin	sender
差しこむ	sashikomu	plug in
砂糖	satoo	sugar
さつまいも	satsumaimo	sweet potato, yam
さやえんどう	sayaendoo	garden peas
性病	seebyoo	venereal disease
セージ	seeji	sage
成人の日	seejin no hi	Coming-of-Age Day
整形外科医	seekeegekai	orthopedic surgeon
世紀	seeki	century
請求	seekyuu	charge
請求書	seekyuusho	bill
生理	seeri	menstrual periods
精神病	seeshinbyoo	mental illness
セーター	seetaa	sweater
西洋かぼちゃ	seeyookabocha	squash
西洋ねぎ	seeyoonegi	leek
席	seki	seat, table
せきが出る	seki ga deru	cough
せっけん	sekken	soap

セキュリティーチェック	*sekyuritiichekku*	security check
狭すぎる	*semasugiru*	too narrow
背もたれ	*semotare*	seat back
背中	*senaka*	back
センチ	*senchi*	centimeter
先月	*sengetsu*	last month
洗面台	*senmendai*	washbasin
洗面所	*senmenjo*	washroom
洗面器	*senmenki*	washbowl
栓抜き	*sen-nuki*	bottle opener
選手	*senshu*	player
先週	*senshuu*	last week
洗濯	*sentaku*	cleaning (laundry service)
洗濯する	*sentaku suru*	do the laundry, wash
洗濯機	*sentakuki*	washing machine
洗濯物	*sentakumono*	laundry
洗剤	*senzai*	liquid detergent
セロリー	*serorii*	celery
セット	*setto*	set
セットメニュー	*setto menyuu*	set meal
シャンペン	*shanpen*	champagne
シャンプー	*shanpuu*	shampoo
車線（レーン）	*sharyoo (reen)*	traffic lane
車両通行止め	*sharyoo tsuukoo dome*	No thoroughfare for vehicles
車掌	*shashoo*	conductor
シャツ	*shatsu*	shirt, undershirt
シャワー	*shawaa*	shower
シェリー酒	*sheriishu*	sherry
試合	*shiai*	game (match)
七面鳥（ターキー）	*shichimenchoo (taakii)*	turkey
シチュー	*shichuu*	stew
市外電話	*shigai denwa*	out-of-town call
市外局番	*shigai kyokuban*	area code
紫外線	*shigaisen*	ultraviolet rays
支払い	*shiharai*	payment
シーフード	*shiifuudo*	sea food dish
しいたけ	*shiitake*	shiitake
シート	*shiito*	seat
シーツ	*shiitsu*	sheet
指示	*shiji*	instruction
敷く	*shiku*	spread out
指名通話	*shimee tsuuwa*	person-to-person call
しめる	*shimeru*	fasten
しみ	*shimi*	stain
芯をとる	*shin o toru*	core
市内	*shinai*	in the city
市内通話	*shinai tsuuwa*	local call
シナモン	*shinamon*	cinnamon
新聞	*shinbun*	newspapers
寝台車	*shindai sha*	sleeping car
心電図	*shindenzu*	electrocardiogram
信号（信号機）	*shingoo (shingooki)*	traffic signal
信号機あり	*shingooki ari*	Traffic light
シングルの部屋	*shinguru no heya*	single room
シングルスの試合	*shingurusu no shiai*	singles match
シニヨン	*shiniyon*	bun
新幹線	*shinkansen*	Shinkansen (bullet train)
申告する	*shinkoku suru*	declare
進入禁止	*shinnyuu kinshi*	Do not enter
審判員（アンパイヤー）	*shinpan-in (anpaiyaa)*	referee (umpire)
診察	*shinsatsu*	medical examination
診察をする	*shinsatsu o suru*	examine
診察券	*shinsatsuken*	appointment card (patient registration card)
寝室（ベッドルーム）	*shinshitsu (beddo ruumu)*	bedroom
心臓	*shinzoo*	heart
心臓病	*shinzoobyoo*	cardiopathy
塩	*shio*	salt
潮	*shio*	tide
調べる	*shiraberu*	check
シリアル	*shiriaru*	cereal
白	*shiro*	white
白身	*shiromi*	egg white
シロップ	*shiroppu*	syrup
白ワイン	*shirowain*	white wine
シルク（絹）	*shiruku (kinu)*	silk
私書箱	*shishobako*	post office box
しそ	*shiso*	perilla
舌平目	*shitabirame*	tongue sole
下着	*shitagi*	underwear
指定席	*shitee seki*	reserved seat
室内履き	*shitsunaibaki*	slippers
しわになりにくい	*shiwa ni narinikui*	wrinkle-free
静か（おだやか）	*shizuka (odayaka)*	calm
食器	*shokki*	dishes
食堂車	*shokudoosha*	dining car
食後	*shokugo*	after meals
食事	*shokuji*	meal
食事付き	*shokuji tsuki*	with meal
食料（食べ物）	*shokuryoo (tabemono)*	foodstuffs
食前	*shokuzen*	before meals
食前酒	*shokuzenshu*	aperitif
少々お待ちください。	*Shooshoo omachi kudasai.*	Hold on a moment, please.
しょうが（ジンジャー）	*shooga (jinjaa)*	ginger
障子	*shooji*	shoji, Japanese sliding paper screen
症状	*shoojoo*	symptoms
ショーツ	*shootsu*	panties (underpants)
商用（ビジネス）	*shooyoo (bijinesu)*	on business
初心者	*shoshinsha*	beginner
初心者用	*shoshinsha yoo*	for beginner
手術	*shujutsu*	operation
手術台	*shujutsudai*	operating table
手術後の経過	*shujutsugo no keeka*	prognosis (progress after an operation)
手術室	*shujutsushitsu*	operating room
宿泊カード	*shukuhaku kaado*	hotel registration card
宿泊料	*shukuhakuryoo*	hotel bill
祝日（祭日）	*shukujitsu (saijitsu)*	national holiday
春分の日	*shunbun no hi*	Vernal Equinox Day
出発	*shuppatsu*	departure
週	*shuu*	week
秋分の日	*shuubun no hi*	Autumnal Equinox Day

集中治療室(ICU)	shuuchuu chiryoo shitsu (ai-shii-yuu)	ICU
週末	shuumatsu	weekend
修理の人	shuuri no hito	repairman
修理する	shuuri suru	repair
修繕（直し）	shuuzen (naoshi)	mend (repair)
主役	shuyaku	protagonist (lead)
主翼	shuyoku	wings (lit. main wings)
そで	sode	sleeve
ソファ	sofa	sofa
底	soko	soles
速達	sokutatsu	express mail
染める	someru	dye
ソーダ	sooda	soda
掃除する	sooji suru	clean
掃除機をかける	soojiki o kakeru	vacuum
操縦士(パイロット)	soojuushi (pairotto)	pilot
操縦室(コックピット)	soojuushitsu (kokkupitto)	cockpit
走行距離	sookoo kyori	mileage
走行距離計	sookoo kyorikee	odometer
ソーセージ	sooseeji	sausage
そろえる	soroeru	trim
そる	soru	shave
注ぐ	sosogu	pour
ソテーした	sotee shita	sauteed
外	soto	outside
酢、お酢	su, osu	rice vinegar
すべりやすい	suberiyasui	slippery
滑る	suberu	ski down
スエード	sueedo	suede
過ごす	sugosu	spend
スイッチ	suicchi	switch
炊飯器	suihanki	rice cooker
水上スキー	suijoo sukii	water-skiing
すいか	suika	watermelon
水曜日	suiyoobi	Wednesday
スカーフ	sukaafu	scarf
スカート	sukaato	skirt
スキー	sukii	ski
スキー帽	sukii boo	ski cap
スキー靴	sukii gutsu	ski boots
スキーウエア	sukii wea	ski suit
スキー場	sukiijoo	skiing ground
スキーヤー	sukiyaa	skier
少し前	sukoshi mae	a little before
少し過ぎ	sukoshi sugi	a little after
スクリーン	sukuriin	screen
スキューバダイビング	sukyuuba daibingu	scuba-diving
相撲	sumoo	sumo
相撲をとる	sumoo o toru	have a sumo bout
スナック	sunakku	snack
スニーカー	suniikaa	sneakers
スパークプラグ	supaaku puragu	spark plugs
スパゲッティ	supagetti	spaghetti
スペアタイア	supea taiya	spare tire
スピードメーター	supiido meetaa	speedometer
スポンジ	suponji	sponge
スポンジケーキ	suponjikeeki	sponge cake

スポーツ	supootsu	sports
スプーン	supuun	spoon
スラックス	surakkusu	trousers
すりおろす	suriorosu	grate
スリッパ	surippa	slippers
スリップ	surippu	slip
すすぐ(洗う)	susugu (arau)	rinse
ステーキ	suteeki	steak
ステレオ	sutereo	stereo
捨てる	suteru	throw away
ストッキング	sutokkingu	panty hose
ストック	sutokku	pole
ストライク	sutoraiku	strike
ストライプ（縞）	sutoraipu (shima)	striped
ストレートヘア	sutoreeto hea	straight hair
吸う	suu	smoke
スーパー	suupaa	supermarket
スープ	suupu	soup
スーツ	suutsu	suit
スーツケース	suutsukeesu	suitcase
すずき	suzuki	sea bass
涼しい	suzushii	cool
ターミナル	taaminaru	terminal
たばこ	tabako	cigarettes
たい	tai	sea bream
～対～	~ tai ~	score of ~ to ~
台風	taifuu	typhoon
体育の日	taiiku no hi	Health-Sports Day
タイム	taimu	thyme
タイツ	taitsu	tights
タイヤ	taiya	tire
タイヤの空気圧	taiya no kuukiatsu	tire pressure
滞在する	taizai suru	stay
高い	takai	expensive
高潮	takashio	tidal wave
高すぎる	takasugiru	too high
たけのこ	takenoko	bamboo shoot
たこ	tako	octopus
炊く	taku	cook (rice)
タクシー	takushii	taxi
卵	tamago	egg
卵焼き	tamagoyaki	fried eggs
玉ねぎ	tamanegi	onion
タン	tan	tongue
棚	tana	compartment
たにし	tanishi	snail
誕生日	tanjoobi	birthday
担架	tanka	stretcher
たんす	tansu	chest, wardrobe
タオル	taoru	towel
タオルかけ	taorukake	towel bar
倒す	taosu	recline
たら	tara	codfish
タラゴン	taragon	tarragon
タルト	taruto	tart
畳	tatami	tatami mat
たたむ	tatamu	fold up
手羽肉	tebaniku	wing
手袋	tebukuro	gloves
テーブル	teeburu	table
テーブルクロス	teeburu kurosu	tablecloth
手紙	tegami	letter

手首	tekubi	wrist
点（得点）を入れる	ten (tokuten) o ireru	score
手荷物	tenimotsu	carry-on (hand) luggage
テニス	tenisu	tennis
テニスコート	tenisu kooto	tennis court
てんかんをおこす	tenkan o okosu	have an epileptic seizure
天気	tenki	weather
天気が悪い	tenki ga warui	bad
天皇誕生日	ten-noo tanjoobi	Emperor's Birthday
てんぷら	tenpura	tempura
点滴	tenteki	intravenous feeding
テレビ	terebi	television set
テレホンカード	terehon kaado	prepaid telephone card
ティースプーン	tii supuun	teaspoon
Tシャツ	tiishatsu	T-shirt
とぶ	tobu	blow
戸棚	todana	cupboard
トイレ	toire	toilet
トイレットペーパー	toiretto peepaa	toilet paper
溶かす	tokasu	dissolve, melt
特急電車	tokkyuu densha	express train
特急券	tokkyuu ken	ticket for express
床の間	toko no ma	tokonoma, alcove
床屋	tokoya	barbershop
とく	toku	comb out
得点	tokuten	score
得点板（スコアボード）	tokutenban (sukoa boodo)	scoreboard
泊まる	tomaru	stay over
トマト	tomato	tomato
止める	tomeru	stop
とんかつ	tonkatsu	breaded pork cutlet
到着	toochaku	arrival
当直医	toochokui	doctor on duty
灯台	toodai	lighthouse
豆腐屋	toofuya	tofu seller
とうがらし	toogarashi	red pepper, chili
遠い	tooi	far
搭乗口（ゲート）	toojooguchi (geeto)	boarding gate
搭乗券	toojooken	boarding pass
とうもろこし	toomorokoshi	corn
トーナメント	toonamento	tournament
糖尿病	toonyoobyoo	diabetes
通り	toori	street (avenue)
トースト	toosuto	toast
トラベラーズチェック	toraberaazu chekku	traveler's check
トランク	toranku	trunk
トランクス	torankusu	boxer shorts
取れる	toreru	come out (lit. remove)
鳥のもも肉	tori no momoniku	chicken thigh
とりあげる	toriageru	deliver (lit. take out)
鶏肉	toriniku	chicken
取る	toru	remove
とって	totte	handle
ツインの部屋	tsuin no heya	twin
付ける	tsukeru	sew (attach)
つけておく	tsukete oku	soak
つく	tsuku	turn on, go on
つくろう	tsukurou	mend, sew
詰まる	tsumaru	clogged up
つま先	tsumasaki	toes
つまっている	tsumatte iru	clogged, is stuffed
詰める	tsumeru	fill
つながる	tsunagaru	be connected
伝える	tsutaeru	tell a message
通帳	tsuuchoo	bankbook
通行止め	tsuukoo dome	No thoroughfare
通行料金	tsuukoo ryookin	toll
通路	tsuuro	aisles
通路側	tsuurogawa	aisle side
家	uchi	home
打ち返す	uchikaesu	return
腕	ude	arm
ウエーター	ueetaa	waiter
ウエートレス	ueetoresu	waitress
上の棚	ue no tana	overhead compartments
動かす	ugokasu	move
受ける	ukeru	catch. have (lit. receive)
受取人	uketorinin	addressee
受付	uketsuke	reception
浮き輪	ukiwa	float ring (life saver)
生まれる	umareru	be born
海	umi	ocean, sea
海の日	umi no hi	Sea Day
海辺	umibe	beach
産む（出産する）	umu (shussan suru)	give birth
うなぎ	unagi	eel
うに	uni	sea urchin
運転免許証	unten menkyoshoo	driver's license
裏	ura	bottom, lining
売られる	urareru	be sold
売りきれる（売り切れ）	urikireru (urikire)	sold out
後ろ	ushiro	in the back
薄切りにする	usugiri ni suru	slice
打つ	utsu	hit
打つ（する）	utsu (suru)	give (lit. shoot)
ウール	uuru	wool
ワッフル	waffuru	waffle
ワイン	wain	wine
ワインリスト	wain risuto	wine list
ワイパー	waipaa	windshield wipers
ワイシャツ	waishatsu	dress shirt
分け目	wakeme	part
ワンピース	wanpiisu	dress (one-piece dress)
わらび	warabi	bracken
わさび	wasabi	wasabi
和式	washiki	Japanese style
渡す	watasu	give
ウェーブ	weebu	wave
ウェルダン	werudan	well-done
ウィンカー（方向指示器）	winkaa (hookoo shijiki)	blinkers
ウィスキー	wiskii	whisky
焼いた	yaita	broiled, grilled
やかん	yakan	kettle
焼きすぎ	yakisugi	overdone

焼く	yaku	bread, bake, grill	雪が降る	yuki ga furu	snow
役	yaku	part (role)	ゆっくり煮こむ	yukkuri nikomu	cook slowly
役をやって（演じて）いる	yaku o yatte (enjite) iru	play the part, take the role	湯のみ	yunomi	Japanese tea cup
焼く、あぶる	yaku, aburu	grill	夕べ	yuube	last night
野球	yakyuu	baseball	郵便番号	yuubin bangoo	zip code
野球場（グラウンド）	yakyuujoo (guraundo)	baseball field	郵便配達員	yuubin haitatsuin	mail carrier
			郵便為替	yuubin kawase	postal money order
山	yama	mountain	郵便物	yuubinbutsu	mail
八百屋	yaoya	green grocer	郵便局	yuubinkyoku	post office
野菜	yasai	vegetable	夕方	yuugata	in the evening
安い	yasui	inexpensive	Ｕターン禁止	yuutaan kinshi	No U turn
やっている	yatte iru	showing	座布団	zabuton	floor cushion
４番バッター	yoban battaa	cleanup (the fourth batter)	ざくろ	zakuro	pomegranate
			ざる	zaru	colander
呼び出し音	yobidashi-on	ringing tone	座席	zaseki	seat
汚れている	yogorete iru	dirty	座席番号	zaseki bangoo	seat number
預金をする	yokin o suru	make a deposit	座席の前のポケット	zaseki no mae no poketto	seat pocket
預金残高	yokin zandaka	balance	座席の前のテーブル	zaseki no mae no teeburu	tray table
横	yoko	on the side			
よく焼けていない	yoku yakete inai	underdone	座席の下	zaseki no shita	under the seats
			座席ベルト（シートベルト）	zasekiberuto (shiitoberuto)	seat belt
浴槽（バスタブ）	yokusoo (basu tabu)	bathtab			
洋服	yoofuku	clothing	雑誌	zasshi	magazine
ヨーグルト	yooguruto	yogurt	座卓	zataku	low table
用紙	yooshi	form	雑音	zatsuon	noise
洋式	yooshiki	Western style	税	zee	tax
夜	yoru	at night	税関	zeekan	customs
予定	yotee	plan	税関の係員	zeekan no kakariin	customs agent
ヨット	yotto	yacht	税関申告書	zeekan shinkokusho	customs declaration
予約	yoyaku	reservation	税金	zeekin	tax
予約する	yoyaku suru	reserve	前半	zenhan	first half
湯をわかす	yu o wakasu	boil the water	前方キャビン	zenpoo kyabin	forward cabin
指	yubi	finger	前菜	zensai	hors d'oeuvres
ゆでる	yuderu	boil	ぜんそく	zensoku	asthma
ゆでた	yudeta	boiled	ぞうきん	zookin	cleaning rag
ゆで卵	yudetamago	boiled eggs	ズボン（パンツ）	zubon (pantsu)	pants
床	yuka	floor	ズッキーニ	zukkiini	zucchini
雪	yuki	snow			

Glossary: English – Japanese
索引：英語 – 日本語

English	Japanese	Romaji
a little after	少し過ぎ	*sukoshi sugi*
a little before	少し前	*sukoshi mae*
a part of the body	体の一部	*karada no ichibu*
a.m.	午前	*gozen*
about	頃	*koro/goro*
accelerator	アクセル	*akuseru*
accident	事故	*jiko*
account	口座	*kooza*
act	幕	*maku*
actor (male)	男優	*dan-yuu*
actor (male or female)	俳優	*haiyuu*
actress	女優	*joyuu*
add	加える	*kuwaeru*
address	住所	*juusho*
addressee	受取人	*uketorinin*
adult	大人	*otona*
advanced level	上級レベル	*jookyuu reberu*
after meals	食後	*shokugo*
agent	係員	*kakariin*
air mail	航空便（エアメール）	*kookuubin (eameeru)*
air pressure	気圧	*kiatsu*
air-conditioner	エアコン（クーラー）	*eakon (kuuraa)*
airline company	航空会社	*kookuugaisha*
airplane	飛行機	*hikooki*
aisle side	通路側	*tsuurogawa*
aisles	通路	*tsuuro*
alarm clock	目覚し時計	*mezamashidokee*
alcohol	お酒	*osake*
allergic	アレルギー、アレルギー体質	*arerugii, arerugii taishitsu*
altitude	高度	*koodo*
ambulance	救急車	*kyuukyuusha*
an automatic ticket gate	自動改札機	*jidookaisatsuki*
analysis of the feces	検便	*kenben*
anchovy	アンチョビ	*anchobi*
anesthesia	麻酔	*masui*
anesthesiologist	麻酔医	*masuii*
angler-fish	あんこう	*ankoo*
ankle	足首	*ashikubi*
announcement	アナウンス	*anaunsu*
answer (lit. appear)	出る	*deru*
antibiotic	抗生物質	*koosee busshitsu*
aperitif	食前酒	*shokuzenshu*
appendicitis	盲腸（虫垂炎）	*moochoo (chuusuien)*
applaud	拍手をする	*hakushu o suru*
apple	りんご	*ringo*
appointment card (patient registration card)	診察券	*shinsatsuken*
apricots	あんず	*anzu*
area code	市外局番	*shigai kyokuban*
arm	腕	*ude*
arrival	到着	*toochaku*
arriving at ~	～着	*~ chaku*
artichoke	アーティチョーク	*aatichooku*
A-seat	A席	*ee seki*
asparagus	アスパラガス	*asuparagasu*
asthma	ぜんそく	*zensoku*
at night	夜	*yoru*
ATM	ATM（現金自動預け払い機）	*ee-tii-emu (genkin jidoo azukebarai ki)*
auscultation; listen to one's chest	聴診する	*chooshin suru*
automatic car	オートマチック車	*ootomachikku sha*
automatically	自動的に	*jidooteki ni*
automobile	自動車	*jidoosha*
Autumnal Equinox Day	秋分の日	*shuubun no hi*
avocado	アボガド	*abogado*
baby	赤ん坊	*akanboo*
back	背中	*senaka*
back	奥	*oku*
bacon	ベーコン	*beekon*
bad	天気が悪い	*tenki ga warui*
bag	かばん	*kaban*
baggage claim stub	荷物引換券	*nimotsu hikikaeken*
bake	オーブンで焼く	*oobun de yaku*
bakery	パン屋	*pan-ya*
balance	預金残高	*yokin zandaka*
balcony	バルコニー	*barukonii*
ball	ボール	*booru*
bamboo shoot	たけのこ	*takenoko*
banana	バナナ	*banana*
bandage	包帯	*hootai*
bang	前髪	*maegami*
bank	銀行	*ginkoo*
bankbook	通帳	*tsuuchoo*
barbershop	床屋	*tokoya*
barracuda	かます	*kamasu*
~ base	～塁ベース	*~ rui beesu*
baseball	野球	*yakyuu*
baseball field	野球場（グラウンド）	*yakyuujoo (guraundo)*
basil	バジリコ	*bajiriko*
basket	かご	*kago*
bat	バット	*batto*
bath	お風呂	*ofuro*
bathtab	浴槽（バスタブ）	*yokusoo (basu tabu)*
bath towel	バスタオル	*basu taoru*
bathing suit	水着	*mizugi*
bathmat	バスマット	*basumatto*
bathroom	バスルーム	*basu ruumu*
bathroom	風呂場	*furoba*
bathroom (lit. bath and toilet)	バストイレ	*basu toire*
bathroom chair	風呂の椅子	*furo no isu*
bathtub	風呂桶	*furooke*
bathtub cover	風呂桶のふた	*furooke no futa*
batter	バッター	*battaa*

battery	バッテリー	batterii
bay leaf	ローリエ	roorie
be born	生まれる	umareru
be carried	運ばれる	hakobareru
be connected	つながる	tsunagaru
be delivered	配達される	haitatsu sareru
be lost	道に迷う	michi ni mayou
be ready	できる	dekiru
be shown	上映される	jooee sareru
be sold	売られる	urareru
beach	海辺	umibe
beach sandals	ビーチサンダル	biichi sandaru
beach umbrella	ビーチパラソル	biichi parasoru
beard	ひげ、あごひげ	hige, agohige
beauty salon	美容院	biyooin
bed	ベッド	beddo
bedroom	寝室(ベッドルーム)	shinshitsu (beddo ruumu)
bedspread	ベッドカバー	beddo kabaa
beef	牛肉	gyuuniku
been sprouts	もやし	moyashi
beer	ビール	biiru
beet	赤かぶ	akakabu
before meals	食前	shokuzen
beginner	初心者	shoshinsha
beige	ベージュ	beeju
belongings	荷物	nimotsu
belt	ベルト	beruto
beverage	飲み物	nominomo
bill (claim)	請求書	seekyuusho
bill	お札	osatsu
bill, check	お勘定	okanjoo
bind up	巻く	maku
birthday	誕生日	tanjoobi
black	黒	kuro
black coffee	ブラックコーヒー	burakkukoohii
black tea	紅茶	koocha
blanket	毛布	moofu
blend	混ぜ合わせる	maze awaseru
blender	ミキサー	mikisaa
blind	ブラインド	buraindo
blinkers	ウィンカー(方向指示器)	winkaa (hookoo shijiki)
~ blocks (lit. ~th street)	~本目	~ bonme(~ponme, ~honma)
blood pressure	血圧	ketsuatsu
blood test	血液検査	ketsueki kensa
blood type	血液型	ketsuekigata
blouse	ブラウス	burausu
blow	とぶ	tobu
blow	吹く	fuku
blueberry	ブルーベリー	buruuberii
boarding gate	搭乗口（ゲート）	toojooguchi (geeto)
boarding pass	搭乗券	toojooken
bob	ボブ	bobu
bobby pin	ヘアピン	hea pin
body	体	karada
bofore	前	mae
boil	ゆでる	yuderu
boil the water	湯をわかす	yu o wakasu
boiled	ゆでた	yudeta

boiled eggs	ゆで卵	yudetamago
bone	骨	hone
bookshelf	本棚	hondana
boots	ブーツ	buutsu
bottle opener	栓抜き	sen-nuki
bottom	裏	ura
bound for ~	~行き	~ iki
bowels	腸	choo
bowl	ボール	booru
boxer shorts	トランクス	torankusu
bracken	わらび	warabi
braid	三つ編み	mitsuami
braise	蒸し煮にする	mushini ni suru
brake	ブレーキ	bureeki
brake fluid	ブレーキオイル	bureeki oiru
brassiere	ブラジャー	burajaa
bread	パン	pan
bread, bake, grill	焼く	yaku
breaded pork cutlet	とんかつ	tonkatsu
break	折れる	oreru
break down	故障する	koshoo suru
break money bill	くずす	kuzusu
breast	胸肉	muneniku
breathe in	息を吸う	iki o suu
breathe out	息をはく	iki o haku
brief	ブリーフ	buriifu
bring in	持ち込む	mochikomu
brisket	胸肉	muneniku
broccoli	ブロッコリー	burokkorii
broil	あぶる	aburu
broiled, grilled	焼いた	yaita
broken	こわれている	kowarete iru
broom	ほうき	hooki
brown	茶色	chairo
brush	磨く	migaku
brush off	はらう	harau
brush, hair brush	ブラシ	burashi
brussels sprouts	芽キャベツ	mekyabetsu
B-seat	B席	bii seki
bumper	バンパー	banpaa
bun	シニヨン	shiniyon
burdock	ごぼう	goboo
burn out	切れる	kireru
burned out	切れている	kirete iru
bus	バス	basu
bus stop	バス停	basu tee
bus terminal	バスターミナル	basu taaminaru
butter	バター	bataa
buttons	ボタン	botan
by the day	一日で	ichinichi de
by the week	一週間で	isshuukan de
cabbage	キャベツ	kyabetsu
cafe au lait	カフェオレ	kafeore
cake	ケーキ	keeki
call	電話をかける(する)	denwa o kakeru (suru)
call back	かけ直す	kakenaosu
calm	静か（おだやか）	shizuka (odayaka)
can opener	缶切り	kankiri
cancer	がん	gan
candy	キャンディ	kyandi

English	Japanese	Romaji
canned food	缶詰	kanzume
cap, hat	帽子	booshi
car	車	kuruma
car number ~	~号車	~ goosha
~ car train	~両の電車	~ ryoo no densha
cardiopathy	心臓病	shinzoobyoo
carp	こい	koi
carpet	じゅうたん（カーペット）	juutan (kaapetto)
carrot	にんじん	ninjin
carry	運ぶ	hakobu
carry-on (hand) luggage	手荷物	tenimotsu
cash	現金にする	genkin ni suru
cash	現金	genkin
cash card	キャッシュカード	kyasshu kaado
cashier	レジ（会計）	reji (kaikee)
cashier's window	窓口	madoguchi
catch	受ける	ukeru
catcher	キャッチャー	kyacchaa
cauliflower	カリフラワー	karifurawaa
cause	原因	gen-in
celery	セロリー	serorii
cellular phone	携帯電話	keetai denwa
centimeter	センチ	senchi
century	世紀	seeki
cereal	シリアル	shiriaru
champagne	シャンペン	shanpen
change	交換する	kookan suru
change planes	乗り換える	norikaeru
changing room	脱衣所	datsuijo
channels	チャンネル	channeru
charge	料金、請求	ryookin, seekyuu
check	チェックする、調べる	chekku suru, shiraberu
check (lit. see)	見る	miru
check in	預ける、チェックイン	azukeru, chekkuin
check out	チェックアウト	chekku auto
checked, checkered	チェック	chekku
cheese	チーズ	chiizu
cherry	さくらんぼ	sakuranbo
chervil	チャービル	chaabiru
chest	胸	mune
chest, wardrobe	たんす	tansu
chicken	鶏肉	toriniku
chicken pox	水ぼうそう	mizuboosoo
chicken thigh	鳥のもも肉	tori no momoniku
chicory	チコリ	chikori
child	子供	kodomo
Children's Day	子供の日	kodomo no hi
chill	冷やす	hiyasu
chinese cabbage	白菜	hakusai
chinese chive	にら	nira
chinese yam	長いも	nagaimo
chive	チャイブ	chaibu
chocolate cake	チョコレートケーキ	chokoreeto keeki
chop	ぶつ切りにする	butsugiri ni suru
chop up	切り刻む	kiri kizamu
chopstick	はし	hashi
chopstick rest	はし置き	hashi oki
cider	サイダー	saidaa
cigarettes	たばこ	tabako
cinnamon	シナモン	shinamon
city map	町の地図	machi no chizu
classical music	クラシック	kurashikku
clean	掃除する	sooji suru
cleaning (laundry service)	洗濯	sentaku
cleaning rag	ぞうきん	zookin
cleanup (the fourth batter)	４番バッター	yoban battaa
clear	晴れている	harete iru
cloakroom	クローク	kurooku
clogged	つまっている	tsumatte iru
clogged up	詰まる	tsumaru
closet	クローゼット	kuroozetto
clothes	服	fuku
clothing	洋服	yoofuku
cloudy	曇っている	kumótte iru
cloudy	曇り	kumori
clutch	クラッチ	kuracchi
coat	コート	kooto
cockpit	操縦室（コックピット）	soojuushitsu (kokkupitto)
cocoa	ココア	kokoa
codfish	たら	tara
coffee	コーヒー	koohii
coffee cup	コーヒーカップ	koohii kappu
coin-operated locker	コインロッカー	koin rokkaa
coke	コーラ	koora
colander	ざる	zaru
cold	かぜ	kaze
cold	寒い	samui
cold (not warm enough)	ぬるい	nurui
cold medicine	かぜ薬	kazegusuri
collect blood	採血	saiketsu
collect call	コレクトコール	korekuto kooru
comb	くし	kushi
comb one's hair	髪をとかす	kami o tokasu
comb out	とく	toku
come out	出る	deru
come out (lit. remove)	取れる	toreru
comedy	喜劇（コメディ）	kigeki (komedii)
comforter quilt	掛けぶとん	kakebuton
Coming-of-Age Day	成人の日	seejin no hi
compartment	棚	tana
compound fracture	複雑骨折	fukuzatsu kossetsu
concert	コンサート	konsaato
concert hall	コンサートホール	konsaato hooru
conductor	車掌	shashoo
Constitution Day	憲法記念日	kenkoku kinen bi
cook	煮る	niru
cook (rice)	炊く	taku
cook slowly	ゆっくり煮こむ	yukkuri nikomu
cooked rice	ご飯	gohan

cookie	クッキー	kukkii
cooking	料理	ryoori
cool	涼しい	suzushii
cordless	コードレス電話	koodoresu denwa
corduroy	コーデュロイ	koodyuroi
core	芯をとる	shin o toru
coriander	コリアンダー	koriandaa
corn	とうもろこし	toomorokoshi
corner	角	kado
cornstarch	コーンスターチ	koonsutaachi
cost	かかる	kakaru
cotton	木綿（コットン）	momen (kotton)
cough	せきが出る	seki ga deru
counter	カウンター	kauntaa
counter for pills	～錠	~joo
country code	国番号	kuni bangoo
course	コース	koosu
courtyard	庭	niwa
crab	かに	kani
crayfish	いせえび	iseebi
cream	クリーム	kuriimu
credit card	クレジットカード	kurejitto kaado
crew	乗務員	joomuin
Crosswalks	横断歩道	oodan hodoo
crowded	混んでいる	konde iru
crutches	松葉杖	matsubazue
cucumber	きゅうり	kyuuri
Culture Day	文化の日	bunka no hi
cupboard	戸棚	todana
curl	カール	kaaru
curl (style)	カーリーヘア	kaarii hea
curler	ロールブラシ	rooru burashi
curtain	カーテン	kaaten
curtain	幕	maku
custard	カスタード	kasutaado
customs	税関	zeekan
customs agent	税関の係員	zeekan no kakariin
customs declaration	税関申告書	zeekan shinkokusho
cut	切る	kiru
cut	傷口	kizuguchi
cut	カット	katto
cut off	切れる	kireru
cutting board	まな板	manaita
daikon, white radish	大根	daikon
day	日	nichi
declare	申告する	shinkoku suru
deep-fried	揚げた	ageta
deep-fry	揚げる	ageru
defend	守る	mamoru
defrost	解凍する	kaitoo suru
deliver (lit. take out)	とりあげる	toriageru
delivery room	分娩室	bunbenshitsu
denim	デニム	denimu
department store	デパート	depaato
departure	出発	shuppatsu
depend on ~	～によって違う	~ ni yotte chigau
deplane	降りる	oriru
deposit	保証金	hoshookin
deposit	預ける	azukeru
desk lamp	電気スタンド	denki sutando
desserts	デザート	dezaato
destination	目的地	mokutekichi
diabetes	糖尿病	toonyoobyoo
dial	ダイヤル	daiyaru
dial	ダイヤルする	daiyaru suru
dial a wrong number	番号を間違える	bangoo o machigaeru
dial tone	発信音	hasshin-on
dining car	食堂車	shokudoosha
dinner role	ロールパン	roorupan
directly	直接	chokusetsu
directory assistance	番号案内	bangoo an-nai
dirty	汚れている	yogorete iru
disembarkation card for foreigner	外国人入国記録	gaikokujin nyuukoku kiroku
dish drainer	水切りかご	mizukiri kago
dish towel	ふきん	fukin
dishes	食器	shokki
dissolve	溶かす	tokasu
dizzy	めまいがする	memai ga suru
Do not enter	進入禁止	shinnyuu kinshi
do the laundry	洗濯をする	sentaku o suru
doctor	医者	isha
doctor on duty	当直医	toochokui
dohyoo (ring)	土俵	dohyoo
dollars	ドル	doru
domestic flight	国内線	kokunaisen
don't get to sleep easily	寝つきが悪い	netsuki ga warui
door opens	開場	kaijoo
double	ダブルの部屋	daburu no heya
double bed	ダブルベッド	daburu beddo
doubles match	ダブルスの試合	daburusu no shiai
doughnut	ドーナツ	doonatsu
draft beer	生ビール	namabiiru
drain	水気を切る	mizuke o kiru
drain	流れる	nagareru
drama	ドラマ	dorama
drawer	引き出し	hikidashi
dress (one-piece dress)	ワンピース	wanpiisu
dress shirt	ワイシャツ	waishatsu
dried	干したの（干物）	hoshita no (himono)
driver's license	運転免許証	unten menkyoshoo
driving range	ゴルフ練習場	gorufu renshuu joo
drizzling	小雨	kosame
dry	乾かす	kawakasu
dry (lit. wipe)	ふく	fuku
dry cleaner's	クリーニング屋	kuriininguya
dry-cleaning	ドライクリーニング	dorai kuriiningu
dryer	ドライヤー	doraiyaa
dryer	乾燥機	kansooki
dubbed in Japanese	日本語に吹き替えられている（日本語吹き替え）	nihongo ni fukikaerarete iru (nihongo fukikae)
duck	鴨	kamo
during the morning	午前中	gozenchuu
during the flight	飛行中	hikoochuu

English	Japanese	Romaji
dust	ほこり	hokori
dustpan	ちりとり	chiritori
duty-free shop	免税品店	menzeehinten
dye	染める	someru
early	早く	hayaku
ears	耳	mimi
eat (lit. drink soup etc.)	飲む	nomu
eel	うなぎ	unagi
egg	卵	tamago
egg white	白身	shiromi
egg yolk	黄身（卵黄）	kimi (ran-oo)
eggplant	なす	nasu
elbow	ひじ	hiji
electrocardio-gram	心電図	shindenzu
emergency case	急患	kyuukan
emergency exit	非常口	hijooguchi
emergency hospital	救急病院	kyuukyuu byooin
Emperor's Birthday	天皇誕生日	ten-noo tanjoobi
empty	空	kara
engine	エンジン	enjin
engine failure (stalling of an engine)	エンスト	ensuto
engine starts	エンジンがかかる	enjin ga kakaru
enokitake	えのきだけ	enokidake
entertainment	エンターテインメント	entaateinmento
entrance	入口	iriguchi
envelope	封筒	fuutoo
espresso	エスプレッソ	esupuresso
every month	毎月	maitsuki
every other ~	～おきに	~ okini
every week	毎週	maishuu
every year	毎年	maitoshi
everyday	毎日	mainichi
exactly	ちょうど	choodo
examine	診る	miru
examine	診察をする	shinsatsu o suru
exceed	越える	koeru
except ~	～を除いて	~ o nozoite
exchange	替える	kaeru
exchange rate	為替レート	kawase reeto
exit	出口	deguchi
expensive	高い	takai
expert	上級者	jookyuusha
exposed too much	浴びすぎる	abisugiru
express mail	速達	sokutatsu
express train	特急電車	tokkyuu densha
express way	高速道路	koosoku dooro
face	顔	kao
family	家族	kazoku
family restaurant	ファミリーレストラン	famirii resutoran
far	遠い	tooi
fare	料金	ryookin
fasten	しめる	shimeru
faucet	蛇口	jaguchi
feel sick (nauseated)	気持ちが悪い	kimochi ga warui
fennel	フェンネル	fenneru
fig	いちぢく	ichijiku
fill	詰める	tsumeru
fill in	記入する	kinyuu suru
fill it up	満タンにする	mantan ni suru
fine, clear	晴れ	hare
finger	指	yubi
finish in a tie	引き分け	hikiwake
first (low) gear	ファースト（ロー）	faasuto (roo)
first class	ファーストクラス	faasuto kurasu
first half	前半	zenhan
fish	魚	sakana
fish market	魚屋	sakanaya
fishbone	骨	hone
fit	合う	au
flannel	フランネル	furanneru
flatfish	かれい	karee
flight	便	bin
flight attendants	客室乗務員	kyakushitsu joomuin
float ring (life saver)	浮き輪	ukiwa
floor	床	yuka
floor cushion	座布団	zabuton
~ floor seats	～階席	~ kaiseki
flour	小麦粉	komugiko
flu	インフルエンザ（流感）	infuruenza (ryuukan)
flush	流れる	nagareru
fly	飛行する	hikoo suru
flying time	飛行時間	hikoo jikan
fog	霧	kiri
foggy	霧が出ている	kiri ga deteiru
fold up	たたむ	tatamu
foodstuffs	食料（食べ物）	shokuryoo (tabemono)
foot	足	ashi
for beginner	初心者用	shoshinsha yoo
for pleasure (lit. sightseeing)	観光	kankoo
forehead	ひたい	hitai
foreign exchange	外国為替	gaikoku kawase
fork	フォーク	fooku
form	用紙	yooshi
forward cabin	前方キャビン	zenpoo kyabin
foul	反則（ファール）	hansoku (faaru)
fragile article	こわれもの	kowaremono
freezer	冷凍庫	reetooko
Friday	金曜日	kin-yoobi
fried eggs	卵焼き	tamagoyaki
front desk	フロント	furonto
fruit	くだもの（果物）	kudamono
fry	炒める	itameru
frying pan	フライパン	furaipan
full	満席	manseki
full	満ちている	michite iru
full-course meal	フルコースのメニュー	furu koosu no menyuu
furniture	家具	kagu
fuse	ヒューズ	hyuuzu

fuse box	ヒューズボックス	*hyuuzu bokkusu*		guest	客	*kyaku*
fusuma, Japanese sliding door	ふすま	*fusuma*		gyooji (referee)	行司	*gyooji*
				hailing	ひょう	*hyoo*
futon	ふとん	*futon*		hair	髪	*kami*
game (match)	試合	*shiai*		hair clip	ヘアクリップ	*hea kurippu*
garbage	ごみ	*gomi*		hair clipper	バリカン	*barikan*
garden peas	さやえんどう	*sayaendoo*		hair lotion	ヘアリキッド	*hea rikiddo*
garlic	にんにく（ガーリック）	*ninniku (gaarikku)*		hair spray	ヘアスプレー	*hea supuree*
				half past	半	*han*
gas	ガソリン	*gasorin*		ham	ハム	*hamu*
gas cooker	ガスこんろ（ガスレンジ）	*gasu konro (gasu renji)*		hand brake	ハンドブレーキ	*hando bureeki*
				handbag	ハンドバッグ	*handobaggu*
gas station	ガソリンスタンド	*gasorin sutando*		handkerchief	ハンカチ	*hankachi*
				handle	とって	*totte*
gas tank	ガソリンタンク	*gasorin tanku*		hang out to dry	干す	*hosu*
gate number ~	～番ゲート	*~ ban geeto*		hanger	ハンガー	*hangaa*
gear	ギア	*gia*		hanging scroll	掛け軸	*kakejiku*
gerlic	にんにく	*ninniku*		hard-boiled eggs	堅ゆで	*katayude*
get (suffer from)	かかる	*kakaru*		have (lit. receive)	受ける	*ukeru*
get off	降りる	*oriru*				
get on	乗る	*noru*		have a chill	寒気がする	*samuke ga suru*
get punctured	パンクする	*panku suru*		have a cold	かぜをひく	*kaze o hiku*
get to sleep easily	寝つきがいい	*netsuki ga ii*		have a fever	熱がある	*netsu ga aru*
				have a fracture	骨折する	*kossetsu suru*
giblets	内臓（臓物）	*naizoo (zoomotsu)*		have a runny nose	鼻水が出る	*hanamizu ga deru*
ginger	しょうが（ジンジャー）	*shooga (jinjaa)*		have a stomachache	おなかが痛い	*onaka ga itai*
				have a sumo bout	相撲をとる	*sumoo o toru*
girdle	ガードル	*gaadoru*				
give	渡す	*watasu*		have an epileptic seizure	てんかんをおこす	*tenkan o okosu*
give (lit. shoot)	打つ（する）	*utsu (suru)*				
give birth	産む（出産する）	*umu (shussan suru)*		Have you decided?	お決まりですか。	*Okimari desu ka.*
glass	コップ（グラス）	*koppu (gurasu)*		head	頭	*atama*
glove	グローブ	*guroobu*		head lettuce	サラダ菜	*saradana*
glove compartment	グローブボックス	*guroobu bokkusu*		headlight	ヘッドライト	*heddoraito*
				headsets	ヘッドホン	*heddohon*
gloves	手袋	*tebukuro*		health insurance card	保険証	*hokenshoo*
go down	下りる	*oriru*				
go off	消える	*kieru*		Health-Sports Day	体育の日	*taiiku no hi*
Go slow	徐行	*jokoo*				
goal	ゴール	*gooru*		heart	心臓	*shinzoo*
goalie	ゴールキーパー	*gooru kiipaa*		heat	温める	*atatameru*
goes up	上がる	*agaru*		heat to boiling	沸騰させる	*futtoo saseru*
golf	ゴルフ	*gorufu*		heater	ヒーター（暖房）	*hiitaa (danboo)*
golf ball	ゴルフボール	*gorufu booru*		heels	ヒール（かかと）	*hiiru (kakato)*
golf club	ゴルフクラブ	*gorufu kurabu*		Hello. [on the phone]	もしもし	*Moshi moshi.*
golf course	ゴルフ場（コース）	*gorufujoo (koosu)*				
				Here you are.	はい、どうぞ	*Hai, doozo.*
grape	ぶどう	*budoo*		herring	にしん	*nishin*
grapefruit	グレープフルーツ	*gureepufuruutsu*		high heels	ハイヒール	*haihiiru*
				high-octane	ハイオクガソリン	*haioku gasorin*
grate	すりおろす	*suriorosu*				
grease	油をぬる	*abura o nuru*		high tide	満潮	*manchoo*
green arrow	緑の矢印	*midori no yajirushi*		hip	腰	*koshi*
green grocer	八百屋	*yaoya*		hit	打つ	*utsu*
green pepper	ピーマン	*piiman*		Hold on a moment, please.	少々お待ちください。	*Shoo shoo omachi kudasai.*
green tea	緑茶	*ryokucha*				
Greenery Day	みどりの日	*midori no hi*		hole	ホール	*hooru*
grill	焼く、あぶる	*yaku, aburu*		hole	穴	*ana*
ground, minced	ひき肉	*hikiniku*		holiday (day off)	休日	*kyuujitsu*
grouper	はた	*hata*		home	家	*uchi*
grow long	伸びる	*nobiru*				

English	Japanese	Romaji
home run	ホームラン	hoomuran
hood	ボンネット	bon-netto
hors d'oeuvres	前菜	zensai
horse radish	ホースラディッシュ	hoosuradisshu
hospital (clinic)	病院	byooin
hot	暑い	atsui
hot water	お湯	oyu
hotel bill	宿泊料	shukuhakuryoo
hotel registration card	宿泊カード	shukuhaku kaado
hour	時間	ikan
house specialty	お店のお勧め料理	omise no osusume ryoori
how much	いくら	ikura
how much	どのぐらい	donogurai
hubcap	ホイールキャップ	hoiiru kyappu
humid	蒸し暑い	mushiatsui
hurt (feel pressure)	苦しい	kurushii
hurts	痛い	itai
I suggest ~ (recommend)	～をお勧めします	~ o osusume shimasu
ice	氷（アイス）	koori (aisu)
ice cream	アイスクリーム	aisukuriimu
iced coffee	アイスコーヒー	aisukoohii
iced tea	アイスティー	aisutii
ICU	集中治療室(ICU)	shuuchuu chiryoo shitsu (ai-shii-yuu)
in case of emergency	緊急の場合	kinkyuu no baai
in the afternoon	午後	gogo
in the back	後ろ	ushiro
in the city	市内	shinai
in the evening	夕方	yuugata
in the morning	朝	asa
in total	合計で	gookee de
included	込み	komi
inexpensive	安い	yasui
injection	注射	chuusha
~ innings	～回	~ kai
inside the airplane	機内	kinai
instead of	代わりに	kawari ni
instruction	指示	shiji
insurance	保険	hoken
insure	保険をかける	hoken o kakeru
intermediate level	中級レベル	chuukyuu reberu
intermission	休憩	kyuukee
intern	研修医（インターン）	kenshuui (intaan)
international call	国際電話	kokusai denwa
international flight	国際線	kokusaisen
intravenous feeding	点滴	tenteki
iron	アイロン	airon
iron	アイロンをかける	airon o kakeru
ironing board	アイロン台	airon dai
is included	含まれている	fukumarete iru
is off	はずれている	hazurete iru
is stuffed	つまっている	tsumatte iru
izakaya (Japanese style bar)	居酒屋	izakaya
jack	ジャッキ	jakki
jacket	ジャケット	jaketto
jam	ジャム	jamu
Japanese futon	布団	futon
Japanese style	和式	washiki
Japanese style hors d'oeuvre	おつまみ	otsumami
Japanese tea cup	湯のみ	yunomi
Japanese yen	日本のお金（円）	Nihon no okane (en)
jazz	ジャズ	jazu
jeans	ジーンズ（ジーパン）	jiinzu (jiipan)
jelly	ジェリー	jerii
jew's-ear	きくらげ	kikurage
juice	ジュース	juusu
ketchup	ケチャップ	kechappu
kettle	やかん	yakan
key	キー（かぎ）	kii
kick	蹴る	keru
kidney	腎臓	jinzoo
kidney beans	いんげんまめ	ingenmame
kilometer	キロ(キロメートル)	kiro (kiromeetoru)
kind (genre)	ジャンル	janru
kiosk (newsstand)	キオスク	kiosuku
kitchen knife	包丁	hoochoo
kiwifruit	キウイ	kiui
knee	ひざ	hiza
knife	ナイフ	naifu
knocking (lit. making a strange sound)	変な音がする	hen na oto ga suru
labor pains	陣痛	jintsuu
Labor Thanksgiving Day	勤労感謝の日	kinrookansha no hi
lace	レース	reesu
ladle	おたま	otama
lamb	子羊の肉（ラム）	kohitsuji no niku
land	着陸する	chakuriku suru
lard	ラード	raado
last month	先月	sengetsu
last night	夕べ	yuube
last week	先週	senshuu
last year	去年	kyonen
late	遅れる、遅く	okureru, osoku
laundry	洗濯物	sentakumono
leaf lettuce	サニーレタス	saniiretasu
leak	漏れる	moreru
leather	皮	kawa
leave	預ける	azukeru
leaving from	発	hatsu
leek	西洋ねぎ	seeyoonegi
left	左	hidari
left end	レフトバック	refutobakku
leg, foot	足	ashi
lemon	レモン	remon
lemonade	レモネード	remoneedo
letter	手紙	tegami

lettuce	レタス	*retasu*
lever	レバー	*rebaa*
lid	ふた	*futa*
life jackets	救命胴衣	*kyuumeedooi*
lifeguard	ライフガード	*raifu gaado*
light	ライト（電気）	*raito (denki)*
light bulb	電球	*denkyuu*
lighthouse	灯台	*toodai*
lime	ライム	*raimu*
line is busy	話し中	*hanashichuu*
line, row	列	*retsu*
lining	裏	*ura*
liquid detergent	洗剤	*senzai*
liquor store	酒屋	*sakaya*
litters	リットル	*rittoru*
liver	肝臓	*kanzoo*
living room	居間	*ima*
lobster	ロブスター	*robusutaa*
lobster, prawn, shrimp	えび	*ebi*
local call	市内通話	*shinai tsuuwa*
local train	普通電車	*futsuu densha*
long distance call	長距離電話	*chookyori denwa*
long sleeves	長袖	*nagasode*
look for	探す	*sagasu*
loose	負ける（負け）	*makeru (make)*
loquat	びわ	*biwa*
lotus root	れんこん	*renkon*
low	引いている	*hiite iru*
low table	座卓	*zataku*
low tide	干潮	*kanchoo*
luggage	荷物	*nimotsu*
lunch	ランチ	*ranchi*
lungs	肺	*hai*
luxurious	高級	*kookyuu*
lyychee	ライチ	*raichi*
mackerel	さば	*saba*
magazine	雑誌	*zasshi*
maid	メイド	*meido*
mail	郵便物	*yuubinbutsu*
mail carrier	郵便配達員	*yuubin haitatsuin*
mailbox	ポスト	*posuto*
make a deposit	預金をする	*yokin o suru*
make a goal	ゴールをする（決める）	*gooru o suru (kimeru)*
make a hit	ヒットを打つ	*hitto o utsu*
make the bed	ベッドを整える	*beddo o totonoeru*
makeup	化粧	*keshoo*
mango	マンゴー	*mangoo*
manual car	マニュアル車	*manyuarusha*
map	地図	*chizu*
marjoram	マージョラム	*maajoramu*
match	合う	*au*
matsutake	まつたけ	*matsutake*
mattress	マットレス	*mattoresu*
mawashi (belt)	まわし	*mawashi*
May I help you? (lit. Welcome)	いらっしゃいませ	*Irasshaimase*
mayonnaise	マヨネーズ	*mayoneezu*
meal	食事	*shokuji*
measles	はしか	*hashika*
measure	測る(計る)	*hakaru*
meat	肉	*niku*
meat and fowl dish	肉料理	*niku ryoori*
meat shop	肉屋	*nikuya*
medical examination	診察	*shinsatsu*
medical history	病歴	*byooreki*
medicine	薬	*kusuri*
medium	ミディアム（普通）	*midiamu (futsuu)*
medium-rare	ミディアムレア	*midiamu rea*
melon	メロン	*meron*
melt	溶かす	*tokasu*
mend (repair)	修繕（直し）	*shuuzen (naoshi)*
mend, sew	つくろう	*tsukurou*
menstrual periods	生理	*seeri*
mental illness	精神病	*seeshinbyoo*
menu	メニュー	*menyuu*
meringue	メレンゲ	*merenge*
meters	メートル	*meetoru*
microwave oven	電子レンジ	*denshi renji*
mikan, tangerine	みかん	*mikan*
mileage	走行距離	*sookoo kyori*
milk	牛乳（ミルク）	*gyuunyuu (miruku)*
milkshake	ミルクセーキ	*mirukuseeki*
mince	みじん切りにする	*mijingiri ni suru*
minced meat	ひき肉	*hikiniku*
mineral water	ミネラルウォーター	*mineraruwootaa*
mint	ミント	*minto*
minute	分	*fun (pun)*
mirror	鏡	*kagami*
miso soup	みそ汁	*misoshiru*
miss	乗り遅れる	*noriokureru*
mitt	ミッド	*mitto*
mix	混ぜる	*mazeru*
Monday	月曜日	*getsuyoobi*
~ months	～か月	*~ kagetsu*
mop	モップをかける	*moppu o kakeru*
motorboat	モーターボート	*mootaa booto*
mountain	山	*yama*
mouth	口	*kuchi*
move	動かす	*ugokasu*
movie	映画	*eega*
movie theater	映画館	*eegakan*
muffler, scarf	マフラー	*mahuraa*
mullet	ぼら	*bora*
mumps	おたふくかぜ	*otafukukaze*
mushroom	マッシュルーム	*masshuruumu*
music	音楽	*ongaku*
musical	ミュージカル	*myuujikaru*
mussel	ムール貝	*muurugai*
mustache	口ひげ	*kuchihige*
mustard	からし（マスタード）	*karashi (masutaado)*
mutton, lamb	羊の肉	*hitsuji no niku*
name seal (inkan)	印鑑	*inkan*
napkin	ナプキン	*napukin*

National Foundation Day	建国記念の日	kenkokukinen no hi	on the side	横	yoko
			on the top	前	mae
national highway	国道	kokudoo	on time	時間通りに	jikandoori ni
			One for ~, please.	～枚ください	~ mai kudasai
National highway number ~	国道～号線	kokudoo ~ goosen	one night stay	一泊	ippaku
			One way	一方通行	ippoo tsuukoo
national holiday	祝日（祭日）	shukujitsu (saijitsu)	one's own ~	自分の～	jibun no ~
national road number	国道番号	kokudoo bangoo	one-way street	一方通行	ippoo tsuukoo
			one-way ticket	片道切符	katamichi kippu
nauseated, nausea	吐き気がする	hakike ga suru	onion	玉ねぎ	tamanegi
			open	開く	hiraku
navel orange	ネーヴル	neevuru	open	開ける	akeru
near	近い	chikai	operating room	手術室	shujutsushitsu
near the window	窓際	madogiwa	operating table	手術台	shujutsudai
necktie	ネクタイ	nekutai	operation	手術	shujutsu
nectarine	ネクタリン	nekutarin	operator	交換手（オペレーター）	kookanshu (opereetaa)
net ball	ネット（ネットボール）	netto (netto booru)			
			opponent	相手	aite
neutral	ニュートラル	nyuutoraru	opponent team	相手チーム	aite chiimu
New Year's Day	元旦	gantan	opposite direction	反対方向	hantai hookoo
newspapers	新聞	shinbun			
next month	来月	raigetsu	~ or more	～以上	~ ijoo
next week	来週	raishuu	orange	オレンジ	orenji
next year	来年	rainen	orchestra	オーケストラ	ookesutora
nice weather	いい天気（天気がいい）	ii tenki (tenki ga ii)	orchestra seat	オーケストラ席	ookesutoraseki
			ordinary deposit	普通預金	futsuu yokin
No passing	追い越し禁止	oikoshi kinshi	oregano	オレガノ	oregano
No parking	駐車禁止	chuusha kinshi	original position	元の位置	moto no ichi
No stopping/No parking	駐停車禁止	chuuteesha kinshi	orthopedic surgeon	整形外科医	seekeegekai
No thoroughfare	通行止め	tsuukoo dome	oshiire, Japanese style built-in closet	押し入れ	oshiire
No thoroughfare for vehicles	車両通行止め	sharyoo tsuukoo dome			
			out	アウト	auto
No U turn	Uターン禁止	yuutaan kinshi	out of order	故障している	koshoo shite iru
no vacancies (full)	満室	manshitsu	out-of-town call	市外電話	shigai denwa
			outside	外	soto
noise	雑音	zatsuon	oven	オーブン	oobun
non-smoking seat	禁煙席	kin-enseki	overcoat	オーバー	oobaa
			overdone	焼きすぎ	yakisugi
nonstop flight	直行便	chokkoobin	overhead compartments	上の棚	ue no tana
noon (midday)	昼	hiru			
nose	鼻	hana	overheat	オーバーヒート	oobaahiito
no-smoking	禁煙	kin-en	oxygen mask	酸素マスク	sansomasuku
not feel well	具合が悪い	guai ga warui	oxygen tent	酸素テント	sansotento
~ number	～番	~ ban	oyster	かき	kaki
nurse	看護婦	kangofu	p.m.	午後	gogo
nut	ナッツ	nattsu	package	荷物	nimotsu
nutmeg	ナツメグ	natsumegu	painful	痛い	itai
nylon	ナイロン	nairon	pancakes	パンケーキ	pankeeki
obstetrician (ob-gyn)	産婦人科医	sanfujinkai	pan-fried	炒めた	itameta
			pan-fry	フライパンで炒める	furaipan de itameru
ocean	海	umi			
octopus	たこ	tako			
odometer	走行距離計	sookoo kyorikee	panties (underpants)	ショーツ	shootsu
oil	オイル	oiru			
oil	オイル（油）	oiru (abura)	pants	ズボン（パンツ）	zubon (pantsu)
okura	オクラ	okura	panty hose	ストッキング	sutokkingu
olive	オリーブ	oriibu	papaya	パパイア	papaia
olive oil	オリーブオイル	oriibuoiru	paper bags	紙袋	kamibukuro
omelet	オムレツ	omuretsu	paprika	パプリカ	papurika
on business	商用（ビジネス）	shooyoo (bijinesu)	Parking	駐車可	chuusha ka
on foot	歩いて	aruite	parsley	パセリ	paseri
on the neck	えりあし	eriashi	part	分け目	wakeme

part (role)	役	yaku
parts	部品	buhin
passengers	乗客	jookyaku
passport	パスポート（旅券）	pasupooto (ryoken)
passport control	入国審査	nyuukoku shinsa
pastry shop	ケーキ屋	keekiya
patient	患者	kanja
pay	払う	harau
payment	支払い	shiharai
peach	桃	momo
peanut	ピーナッツ	piinattsu
pear	なし	nashi
peel	むく	muku
peel	皮をむく	kawa o muku
penicillin	ペニシリン	penishirin
pepper	こしょう	koshoo
per ~	～につき	~ ni tsuki
performance	公演	kooen
performance starts	開演	kaien
perilla	しそ	shiso
permanent wave	パーマ	paama
persimmon	柿	kaki
person-to-person call	指名通話	shimee tsuuwa
phone book	電話帳	denwachoo
phone number	電話番号	denwa bangoo
pickles	ピクルス	pikurusu
picture	絵	e
picture frame	額縁	gakubuchi
pie	パイ	pai
pillow	枕	makura
pillowcase	枕カバー	makura kabaa
pilot	操縦士（パイロット）	soojuushi (pairotto)
PIN	暗証番号	anshoo bangoo
pineapple	パインアップル パイナップル	pain-appuru, painappuru
pipes	パイプ(水道管)	paipu (suidookan)
pitch	投げる	nageru
pitcher	ピッチャー	picchaa
plan	予定	yotee
plastic back	ビニール袋	beniirubukuro
plate	皿	sara
platform (track)	ホーム	hoomu
play	演劇（芝居）	engeki (shibai)
play the part, take the role	役をやって（演じて）いる	yaku o yatte (enjite) iru
player	選手	senshu
playing (acting)	出ている	dete iru
~, please.	～をお願いします	~ o onegai shimasu
plug	プラグ	puragu
plug	風呂桶の栓	furo-oke no sen
plug in	差しこむ	sashikomu
pole	ストック	sutokku
polio	ポリオ	porio
polka-dotted	水玉模様	mizutama moyoo
pomegranate	ざくろ	zakuro
pony tail	ポニーテール	ponii teeru
pork	豚肉	butaniku

porter	ボーイ	booi
post office	郵便局	yuubinkyoku
post office box	私書箱	shishobako
postal money order	郵便為替	yuubin kawase
postcard	はがき	hagaki
potato	じゃがいも	jagaimo
pour	注ぐ	sosogu
practice	練習	renshuu
prawns	車えび	kurumaebi
pregnant	妊娠している	ninshin shite iru
prepaid telephone card	テレホンカード	terehon kaado
price	値段	nedan
prognosis (progress after an operation)	手術後の経過	shujutsugo no keeka
program	プログラム	puroguramu
protagonist (lead)	主役	shuyaku
prune	プルーン	puruun
Public Holiday	国民の休日	kokumin no kyuujitsu
public telephone	公衆電話	kooshuu denwa
pudding	プリン	purin
pulse	脈拍	myakuhaku
pumpkin	かぼちゃ	kabocha
push-button phone (touch-tone phone)	プッシュホン	pusshuhon
put back	戻す	modosu
put the leg in a cast	ギプスをはめる	gipusu o hameru
racket	ラケット	raketto
radiator	ラジエーター	rajieetaa
radio	ラジオ	rajio
radish	二十日大根	hatsukadaikon
Railroad crossing	踏切あり	fumikiri ari
rain	雨	ame
rain	雨が降る	ame ga furu
raincoat	レーンコート	reen kooto
raining on and off	雨が降ったり止んだりする	ame ga futtari yandari suru
rare	レア	rea
raspberry	ラズベリー	razuberii
raw (sashimi)	生（刺身）	nama (sashimi)
raw eggs	生卵	namatamago
ray	えい	ei
razor	かみそり	kamisori
rear cabin	後方キャビン	koohoo kyabin
receipt	領収書（レシート）	ryooshuusho (reshiito)
receiver	受話器	juwaki
reception	受付	uketsuke
receptionist	フロント係	furonto gakari
recline	倒す	taosu
recovery room	回復室	kaifuku shitsu
red arrow	赤い矢印	akai yajirushi
red cabbage	紫キャベツ	murasakikyabetsu
red mullet	ひめじ	himeji
red pepper, chili	とうがらし	toogarashi
red snapper	きんめだい	kinmedai
red wine	赤ワイン	akawain

referee (umpire)	審判員（アンパイヤー）	*shinpan-in (anpaiyaa)*
refrigerator	冷蔵庫	*reezooko*
registered mail	書留	*kakitome*
registration plate	ナンバープレート	*nanbaa pureeto*
regular	順調	*junchoo*
regular mail	普通郵便	*futsuu yuubin*
regular sumo tournament	場所	*basho*
relax	くつろぐ	*kutsurogu*
remove	取る	*toru*
rent	借りる	*kariru*
rent-a-car	レンタカー	*rentakaa*
repair	修理する	*shuuri suru*
repairman	修理の人	*shuuri no hito*
reservation	予約	*yoyaku*
reserve	予約する	*yoyaku suru*
reserved seat	指定席	*shitee seki*
Respect-for-Aged Day	敬老の日	*keeroo no hi*
restaurant	レストラン	*resutoran*
return	戻る	*modoru*
return	打ち返す	*uchikaesu*
reverse	バック	*bakku*
rheumatism	リューマチ	*ryuumachi*
rib	あばら肉（リブ）	*abaraniku (ribu)*
rice	米	*kome*
rice bowl	茶わん	*chawan*
rice cooker	炊飯器	*suihanki*
rice shop	米屋	*komeya*
rice vinegar	酢、お酢	*su, osu*
right	右	*migi*
ringing tone	呼び出し音	*yobidashi-on*
rinse	洗う、すすぐ	*arau, susugu*
rinse rice	米をとぐ	*kome o togu*
rock	ロック	*rokku*
roll up	まくる	*makuru*
roller	ヘアカーラー	*hea kaaraa*
room	部屋	*heya*
room key	ルームキー（かぎ）	*ruumukii (kagi)*
room service	ルームサービス	*ruumu saabisu*
rose wine	ロゼ	*roze*
rosemary	ローズマリー	*roozumarii*
rough	荒れている	*arete iru*
round	ラウンド	*raundo*
round trip ticket	往復切符	*oofuku kippu*
row	列	*retsu*
rubber soles	ゴム底	*gomuzoko*
run	走る	*hashiru*
rush hour	ラッシュアワー	*rasshu awaa*
safety	安全	*anzen*
saffron	サフラン	*safuran*
sage	セージ	*seeji*
sake	日本酒	*nihonshu*
salad	サラダ	*sarada*
salmon	さけ	*sake*
salt	塩	*shio*
sandals	サンダル	*sandaru*
sandwich	サンドイッチ	*sandoicchi*
sardine	いわし	*iwashi*
Saturday	土曜日	*doyoobi*
sausage	ソーセージ	*sooseeji*
sautee	炒める、ソテーする	*itameru. sotee suru*
sauteed	ソテーした	*sotee shita*
sauteed pork	ポークツテー	*pooku sotee*
scallion	ねぎ	*negi*
scallops	ほたて貝	*hotategai*
scarf	スカーフ	*sukaafu*
scissors	はさみ	*hasami*
score	点（得点）を入れる	*ten (tokuten) o ireru*
score	得点	*tokuten*
score of ~ to ~	～対～	*~ tai ~*
scoreboard	得点板（スコアボード）	*tokutenban (sukoa boodo)*
scrambled eggs	炒り卵（スクランブルエッグ）	*iritamago (sukuranburu eggu)*
screen	スクリーン	*sukuriin*
scrub	みがく	*migaku*
scuba-diving	スキューバダイビング	*sukyuuba daibingu*
sea	海	*umi*
sea bass	すずき	*suzuki*
sea bream	たい	*tai*
Sea Day	海の日	*umi no hi*
sea food	魚介類	*gyokai rui*
sea food dish	シーフード	*shiifuudo*
sea mail	船便	*hunabin*
sea urchin	うに	*uni*
seam	縫い目	*nuime*
seaside resort	ビーチリゾート	*biichi rizooto*
season	味付けする	*ajitsuke suru*
seat	座席、シート、席	*zaseki, shiito, seki*
seat back	背もたれ	*semotare*
seat belt	座席ベルト（シートベルト）	*zasekiberuto (shiitoberuto)*
seat number	座席番号	*zaseki bangoo*
seat pocket	座席の前のポケット	*zaseki no mae no poketto*
second half	後半	*koohan*
seconds	秒	*byoo*
security check	セキュリティーチェック	*sekyuritiichekku*
see a doctor (have a doctor examine)	診てもらう	*mite morau*
send	送る	*okuru*
send out	出す	*dasu*
sender	差出人	*sashidashinin*
serve	サーブ	*saabu*
service	サービス	*saabisu*
service charge	サービス料	*saabisuryoo*
sesame	ごま	*goma*
set	セット	*setto*
set meal	セットメニュー	*setto menyuu*
set the bone	骨をつなぐ	*hone o tsunagu*
sew (attach)	付ける	*tsukeru*
shampoo	シャンプー	*shanpuu*
shave	そる	*soru*
shave my beard	ひげをそる	*hige o soru*

sheet	シーツ	shiitsu
shellfish	貝	kai
sherry	シェリー酒	sheriishu
shift gears	ギアを変える	gia o kaeru
shiitake	しいたけ	shiitake
Shinkansen (bullet train)	新幹線	shinkansen
shirt, undershirt	シャツ	shatsu
shoe polish	靴墨	kutsuzumi
shoelace	靴ひも	kutsuhimo
shoes	靴	kutsu
shoji, Japanese sliding paper screen	障子	shooji
shopping cart	カート	kaato
short sleeves	半袖	hansode
shorts	半ズボン	hanzubon
shoulder	肩	kata
shoulder (meat)	肩肉	kataniku
show	舞台	butai
shower	シャワー	shawaa
shower (rain)	にわか雨	niwakaame
showing	やっている	yatte iru
shrimp	えび（子えび）	ebi (koebi)
shrink	縮む	chijimu
side table	サイドテーブル	saido teeburu
sideburns	もみあげ	momiage
silk	シルク（絹）	shiruku (kinu)
simmer (boil for a long time)	煮込む	nikomu
single room	シングルの部屋	shinguru no heya
singles match	シングルスの試合	shingurusu no shiai
sink	流し	nagashi
size	サイズ	saizu
size ~	～号	~ goo
ski	スキー	sukii
ski boots	スキー靴	sukii gutsu
ski cap	スキー帽	sukii boo
ski down	滑る	suberu
ski lift	リフト	rifuto
ski suit	スキーウエア	sukii wea
skier	スキーヤー	sukiiyaa
skiing ground	スキー場	sukiijoo
skin	皮	kawa
skin cancer	皮膚ガン	hifugan
skirt	スカート	sukaato
sleep, go to bed	寝る	neru
sleeping car	寝台車	shindai sha
sleeve	そで	sode
slice	薄切りにする	usugiri ni suru
slip	スリップ	surippu
slippers	スリッパ	surippa
slippers	室内履き	shitsunaibaki
slippery	すべりやすい	suberiyasui
slope	ゲレンデ	gerende
slowly cooked, simmered	煮込んだ	nikonda
small change	小銭（小さいお金）	kozeni (chiisai okane)
small damp towel	おしぼり	oshibori
smoke	吸う	suu
smoking areas	喫煙所	kitsuenjo
smoking seat	喫煙席	kitsuen seki
snack	スナック	sunakku
snail	たにし	tanishi
sneakers	スニーカー	suniikaa
snow	雪	yuki
snow	雪が降る	yuki ga furu
snowstorm	吹雪	fubuki
soak	つけておく	tsukete oku
soap	せっけん	sekken
soccer	サッカー	sakkaa
soccer field (ground)	サッカー場（グラウンド）	sakkaajoo (guraundo)
socket (outlet)	コンセント	konsento
socks	靴下	kutsushita
soda	ソーダ	sooda
sofa	ソファ	sofa
soft-boiled eggs	半熟卵	hanjukutamago
sold out	売りきれる（売り切れ）	urikireru (urikire)
soles	底	soko
solid colored	無地	muji
sound	鳴らす	narasu
sound, ring	鳴る	naru
soup	スープ	suupu
sour orange	だいだい	daidai
souvenir	おみやげ	omiyage
spaghetti	スパゲッティ	supagetti
spare tire	スペアタイア	supea taiya
sparerib	あばら肉	abaraniku
spark plugs	スパークプラグ	supaaku puragu
spectators	観客	kankyaku
speed an hour	時速	jisoku
speed limit	最高速度	saikoo sokudo
speedometer	スピードメーター	supiido meetaa
spend	過ごす	sugosu
spices	香辛料	kooshinryoo
spinach	ほうれん草	hoorensoo
sponge	スポンジ	suponji
sponge cake	スポンジケーキ	suponjikeeki
spoon	スプーン	supuun
sports	スポーツ	supootsu
sprain, twist	ひねる	hineru
spread out	敷く	shiku
sprinkle	ふりかける	furikakeru
squash	西洋かぼちゃ	seeyookabocha
squid	いか	ika
S-seat (special seat)	S席	esu seki
stage	舞台（ステージ）	butai (suteeji)
stain	しみ	shimi
stamp	切手	kitte
stand (in line)	並ぶ	narabu
starch	のり	nori
start the engine	エンジンをかける	enjin o kakeru
station	駅	eki
station employee	駅員	ekiin
stay	滞在する	taizai suru
stay over	泊まる	tomaru
steak	ステーキ	suteeki

steam	蒸す	*musu*
steamed	蒸した	*mushita*
steering wheel	ハンドル	*handoru*
step on	踏む	*fumu*
stereo	ステレオ	*sutereo*
stew	シチュー	*shichuu*
stew pan	鍋	*nabe*
stitch	縫う	*nuu*
stomach	胃	*i*
Stop	一時停止	*ichiji teeshi*
stop	止める	*tomeru*
stop the engine	エンジンを止める	*enjin o tomeru*
straight	まっすぐ	*massugu*
straight hair	ストレートヘア	*sutoreeto hea*
strain	こす	*kosu*
strange	変な	*hen na*
strawberry	いちご	*ichigo*
street, road	道路、道	*dooro, michi*
street (avenue)	通り	*toori*
stretcher	担架	*tanka*
strike	ストライク	*sutoraiku*
striped	ストライプ（縞）	*sutoraipu (shima)*
student	学生	*gakusee*
suede	スエード	*sueedo*
sugar	砂糖	*satoo*
suit	スーツ	*suutsu*
suitcase	スーツケース	*suutsukeesu*
sumo	相撲	*sumoo*
sumo wrestler	力士	*rikishi*
sun block	日焼け止め	*hiyakedome*
sunbathe	日光浴をする	*nikkooyoku o suru*
sunburned, suntanned	日に焼ける	*hi ni yakeru*
Sunday	日曜日	*nichiyoobi*
sunglasses	サングラス	*san gurasu*
sunny-side up	目玉焼き	*medamayaki*
supermarket	スーパー	*suupaa*
surfboard	サーフボード	*saafu boodo*
surfing	サーフィン	*saafin*
surgeon	外科医	*gekai*
sweater	セーター	*seetaa*
sweep	はく	*haku*
sweet potato, yam	さつまいも	*satsumaimo*
sweets	お菓子	*okashi*
swim	泳ぐ	*oyogu*
swimming pool	プール	*puuru*
switch	スイッチ	*suicchi*
swordfish	かじき	*kajiki*
symptoms	症状	*shoojoo*
synthetic material	合繊（合成繊維）	*goosen (goosee sen-i)*
syrup	シロップ	*shiroppu*
table	テーブル	*teeburu*
table	席	*seki*
tablecloth	テーブルクロス	*teeburu kurosu*
take a bath	お風呂に入る	*ofuro ni hairu*
take a shower	浴びる	*abiru*
take a walk	散歩する	*sanpo suru*
take off	離陸する	*ririku suru*
take out	出す	*dasu*

take out the stitches	抜糸をする	*basshi o suru*
talk (chat)	話す（おしゃべりする）	*hanasu (oshaberi suru)*
tanning lotion	サンオイル	*sanoiru*
tarragon	タラゴン	*taragon*
tart	タルト	*taruto*
tatami mat	畳	*tatami*
tax	税金、税	*zeekin, zee*
taxi	タクシー	*takushii*
tea	お茶	*ocha*
team	チーム	*chiimu*
teammate	味方	*mikata*
teaspoon	ティースプーン	*tii supuun*
teeth	歯	*ha*
telephone	電話	*denwa*
telephone booth	電話ボックス	*denwa bokkusu*
television set	テレビ	*terebi*
tell a message	伝える	*tsutaeru*
temperature	熱（体温）	*netsu (taion)*
tempura	てんぷら	*tenpura*
tennis	テニス	*tenisu*
tennis court	テニスコート	*tenisu kooto*
terminal	ターミナル	*taaminaru*
~ th	～目	*~ me*
the ~ th act	第～幕	*dai ~ maku*
the beginning	初め	*hajime*
the day after tomorrow	あさって	*asatte*
the day before yesterday	おととい	*ototoi*
the end	終わり	*owari*
the horn	クラクション	*kurakushon*
the middle	半ば	*nakaba*
the other party	相手	*aite*
the side of ~	～側	*~ gawa*
theater	劇場	*gekijoo*
thigh	もも肉	*momoniku*
this month	今月	*kongetsu*
this week	今週	*konshuu*
this year	今年	*kotoshi*
throat	のど	*nodo*
throw away	捨てる	*suteru*
thunder	雷	*kaminari*
thundering	雷が鳴っている	*kaminari ga natte iru*
thunderstorm	雷雨	*raiu*
Thursday	木曜日	*mokuyoobi*
thyme	タイム	*taimu*
ticket	航空券（チケット）	*chiketto*
ticket	切符	*kippu*
ticket for express	特急券	*tokkyuu ken*
ticket gate	改札口	*kaisatsuguchi*
ticket window	窓口	*madoguchi*
ticket window	切符売り場	*kippu uriba*
tickets	チケット（切符）	*chiketto (kippu)*
tidal wave	高潮	*takashio*
tide	潮	*shio*
tie	同点	*dooten*
tight	きつい	*kitsui*
tights	タイツ	*taitsu*
tips	チップ	*chippu*
tire	タイヤ	*taiya*

tire pressure	タイヤの空気圧	taiya no kuukiatsu
toast	トースト	toosuto
today	今日	kyoo
toes	つま先	tsumasaki
tofu seller	豆腐屋	toofuya
toilet	トイレ、お手洗い 便器	toire, otearai, benki
toilet paper	トイレットペーパー	toiretto peepaa
tokonoma, alcove	床の間	toko no ma
toll	通行料金	tsuukoo ryookin
tollbooth	料金所	ryookinjo
tomato	トマト	tomato
tomorrow	明日	ashita
tongue	タン	tan
tongue sole	舌平目	shitabirame
tonsils	扁桃腺	hentoosen
too big	大きすぎる	ookisugiru
too close	近すぎる	chikasugiru
too hard	固すぎる	katasugiru
too high	高すぎる	takasugiru
too narrow	狭すぎる	semasugiru
too small	小さすぎる	chiisasugiru
too spicy, too salty	からすぎる	karasugiru
too wide	広すぎる	hirosugiru
toothbrush	歯ブラシ	haburashi
toothpaste	歯磨き粉	hamigakiko
top	表	omote
torn	ほころびる	hokorobiru
toss (the ball)	パスする	pasu suru
touch	触れる	fureru
tournament	トーナメント	toonamento
tow	けん引	ken-in
towel	タオル	taoru
towel bar	タオルかけ	taorukake
track number ~	~番ホーム	~ ban hoomu
traffic jam	渋滞	juutai
traffic lane	車線（レーン）	sharyoo (reen)
Traffic light	信号機あり	shingooki ari
traffic signal	信号（信号機）	shingoo (shingooki)
tragedy	悲劇	higeki
train	電車	densha
train schedule	時刻表	jikokuhyoo
train ticket	乗車券	joosha ken
traveler's check	トラベラーズチェック	toraberaazu chekku
tray	お盆（トレー）	obon (toree)
tray table	座席の前のテーブル	zaseki no mae no teeburu
treat	治療をする	chiryoo o suru
trim	そろえる	soroeru
trousers	スラックス	surakkusu
trout	ます	masu
trunk	トランク	toranku
T-shirt	Tシャツ	tiishatsu
tuberculosis	結核	kekkaku
Tuesday	火曜日	kayoobi
tuna	まぐろ	maguro
turkey	七面鳥（ターキー）	shichimenchoo (taakii)

turn	曲がる	magaru
turn off	消す	kesu
turn on	ひねる	hineru
turn on, go on	つく	tsuku
turn over	ひっくり返す	hikkurikaesu
turner	フライ返し	furaigaeshi
turnip	かぶ	kabu
twin	ツインの部屋	tsuin no heya
typhoon	台風	taifuu
ultraviolet rays	紫外線	shigaisen
Under construction	道路工事中	dooro koojichuu
under the seats	座席の下	zaseki no shita
underdone	よく焼けていない	yoku yakete inai
underpants	パンツ	pantsu
underwear	下着	shitagi
unleaded	無鉛ガソリン	muen gasorin
unreserved seat	自由席	jiyuu seki
urine test	尿検査	nyoo kensa
usher	案内係	an-naigakari
vacant	空いている	aite iru
vacant room	空室	kuushitsu
vacant seat	空席	kuuseki
vacuum	掃除機をかける	soojiki o kakeru
vanilla	バニラ	banira
veal	子牛の肉	koushi no niku
vegetable	野菜	yasai
vending machine	自動販売機	jidoo hanbaiki
venereal disease	性病	seebyoo
Vernal Equinox Day	春分の日	shunbun no hi
via ~	~経由	~ keeyu
vinegar	ビネガー	binegaa
visa	ビザ（査証）	biza (sashoo)
waffle	ワッフル	waffuru
waiter	ウェーター	ueetaa
waiting room	待合室	machiaishitsu
waitress	ウエートレス	ueetoresu
wake up	起きる	okiru
wall-outlet	コンセント	konsento
ward	病室	byooshitsu
warm	暖かい	atatakai
wasabi	わさび	wasabi
wash	洗う、洗濯する	arau, sentaku suru
washbasin	洗面台	senmendai
washbowl	洗面器	senmenki
washing machine	洗濯機	sentakuki
washroom	洗面所	senmenjo
waste basket	ごみ箱	gomibako
water	水（お水）	mizu (omizu)
watercress	クレソン	kureson
watermelon	すいか	suika
water-skiing	水上スキー	suijoo sukii
wave	波	nami
wave	ウェーブ	weebu
weather	天気	tenki
Wednesday	水曜日	suiyoobi
week	週	shuu
weekday	平日	heejitsu
weekend	週末	shuumatsu
weigh	計る	hakaru

weight	重さ	*omosa*	wing	手羽肉	*tebaniku*
welcome	迎える	*mukaeru*	wings (lit. main wings)	主翼	*shuyoku*
well-done	ウェルダン	*werudan*			
Western style	洋式	*yooshiki*	wipe	ふく	*fuku*
what day (of the week)	何曜日	*nan-yoobi*	with breakfast	朝食付き	*chooshoku tsuki*
			with meal	食事付き	*shokuji tsuki*
what number	何番	*nanban*	with subtitles	字幕つき	*jimaku tsuki*
wheelchair	車いす	*kurumaisu*	withdraw	おろす	*orosu*
whip	泡立てる	*awadateru*	wooden soup bowl	おわん	*owan*
whisk	泡だて器	*awadateki*			
whisky	ウィスキー	*wisukii*	wool	ウール	*uuru*
whistle	笛（ホイッスル）	*fue (hoissuru)*	worth	分	*bun*
white	白	*shiro*	wrinkle-free	しわになりにくい	*shiwa ni narinikui*
white wine	白ワイン	*shirowain*			
who	どなた（どちらさま）	*donata (dochira sama)*	wrist	手首	*tekubi*
			x-ray	レントゲン写真	*rentogen shashin*
width	幅	*haba*	yacht	ヨット	*yotto*
win	勝つ（勝ち）	*katsu (kachi)*	~ years	～年（年間）	*~ nen (nenkan)*
window	窓	*mado*	yeast	イースト	*iisuto*
window side	窓側	*madogawa*	yen	円	*en*
windowpane	窓ガラス	*madogarasu*	yesterday	きのう	*kinoo*
windshield	フロントガラス	*furonto garasu*	yogurt	ヨーグルト	*yooguruto*
windshield wipers	ワイパー	*waipaa*	zip code	郵便番号	*yuubin bangoo*
			zipper	ファスナー（チャック、ジッパー）	*fasunaa (chakku, jippaa)*
windy	風が強い	*kaze ga tsuyoi*			
wine	ワイン	*wain*			
wine list	ワインリスト	*wain risuto*	zucchini	ズッキーニ	*zukkiini*